THE BUTTERFLY HUNTER

ALSO BY CHRIS BALLARD

Hoops Nation

THE BUTTERFLY HUNTER

ADVENTURES OF PEOPLE WHO

FOUND THEIR **TRUE CALLING**

WAY OFF THE **BEATEN PATH**

Chris Ballard

Broadway Books
New York

BROADWAY

PRINTED IN THE UNITED STATES OF AMERICA

BROADWAY BOOKS and its logo, a letter B bisected on the
diagonal, are trademarks of Random House, Inc.

Visit our Web site at www.broadwaybooks.com

Book design by Richard Oriolo

LIBRARY OF CONGRESS CATALOGING-IN-PUBLICATION DATA

Ballard, Chris.
The butterfly hunter : adventures of people who found
their true calling way off the beaten path / Chris Ballard.
 p. cm.
Includes bibliographical references.
1. Vocational interests—United States—Case studies.
2. Successful people—United States—Case studies. 3. Job
satisfaction—United States—Case studies. I. Title.

HF5381.5.B23 2005
650.92'2—dc22
[B]
                                                     2005053169

ISBN 0-7679-1868-1

10 9 8 7 6 5 4 3 2 1

First Edition

To Alexandra

Contents

INTRODUCTION   1

ONE: The Skywalker   21

TWO: The Eyeball Artisan   51

THREE: The Lady Lumberjack   71

FOUR: The Rail-aholic   93

FIVE: The Time-Clock Philosopher Amid an
        Industry of Answers   119

SIX: The Sixty-Second Salesman   137

SEVEN: The Fungus Prospector   163

EIGHT: The Notebook Detective   185

NINE: The Pigskin Preacher   205

TEN: The Butterfly Hunter   229

        EPILOGUE   261

        NOTES   265

Acknowledgments

A heartfelt thanks to the following people:

To John Ware, for being instrumental in shaping the book's premise and for providing frequent support and unending advocacy. John, you're the Charles Oakley of agents, something I say only because I know you'll take it as a compliment.

To Kris Puopolo at Broadway Books, who believed in the concept from the get-go and pushed me to make it better. Somehow, she was able to be enthusiastic even when providing constructive criticism, much to my benefit. Also, to Bill Thomas for signing off on this peculiar book concept, and to Beth Haymaker for keeping me in line.

To the stars of this show, the eleven people who let me shuffle around their lives for inordinate amounts of time and were, to a man and woman, gracious and forthcoming: Spiderman Mulholland, Willie Danz, Penny Halvorson, John Nehrich, Amy Wrzesniewski, Don LaFontaine, Rex Swartzendruber, Sarah and Ruth Holmes, Doug Blevins, and Phil DeVries. Additionally, to all the friends, colleagues, and families of the above eleven, too numerous to name here, who took the time to talk with me. Special thanks go to Amy Wrzesniewski, both for becoming an unwitting subject for the book and explaining much of organizational psychology to me. May your plants always flourish.

To Terry McDonell and the editors at *Sports Illustrated*, in particular Hank Hersch, for indulging me in taking on this project. It is wonderful to work at a place that encourages writers' voices.

To my parents, who were, as ever, the ultimate support team and provided invaluable feedback and inspiration. Likewise, to Duffy and

Angela Ballard for providing their editorial insight on everything from the manuscript to the book title. I expect to read Hayley's first bestseller in twenty years or so.

To all those who took the time to read parts of the manuscript and/or provide writing counsel, including Walter Blass, Beth and Mel Keiser, Pete Demarco, Dan Zehr, Mark "Team W" Stroh, Corey Rich, Danny Habib, Trini Perera, Pete McEntegart, and Max Cann. Also, big hugs to Pat Cottrell, for brainstorming, horseshoes, and a place to stay in Madison; and to Eric Kneedler for the carpet-cleaning tips, not to mention the friendship. The celebration is indeed in progress.

To Jessie Graham, for her brief but valuable assistance in researching potential book characters, and to the inimitable Owen Good, for helping out a friend by looking up weird facts and finding Spiderman. Duct tape never goes out of fashion, big guy.

To Heinz Kluetmeier for the photo, Sandy Padwe for being such an idealist, and Steve Fratello, who didn't make it into the final manuscript but was generous with his time.

To all that made Manhattan simultaneously the best and worst place to try to write a book: the New York Public Library, New Kam Lai, Riley, the Dive Bar, the West Side Tavern, Basketball City (you're missed, Ira), and afternoons in Riverside Park.

Finally, but most important, to my wife, Alexandra, for being an editor, cheerleader, critic, inspiration, and all-around superstar. Your students are lucky to have you, and so am I.

INTRODUCTION

We control our own destiny. . . . So, when the Kirby
Opportunity was presented, I began to dream
again—not just to dream the dream, but to live the
dream.

—TESTIMONIAL FROM A SALESMAN ON THE KIRBY WEB SITE

WHY DO WE WORK? SOMETIMES it's to pay the rent. Other
times, it's because we find it rewarding. Then, still other times,
it's because a friend from Vermont calls and persuades us to sell
vacuum cleaners.

Or at least that's what happened to me six months after college,
when my friend Eric contacted me.

"You think I should sell what?" I asked, incredulous.

"Vacuums," he said, as if this were the most natural idea in the
world. "But not just any vacuums. These are *Kirbys.*"

My first reaction was to laugh. But Eric, who'd been peddling the
machines for a few months, was resolute. Not only was there a big pay-

check involved, he assured me, but the work was *ridiculously* easy. Just show up, smile real big, and the machine practically sold itself. I pointed out that I hadn't spent four years at a liberal arts college so that I could sell vacuums. He countered that I hadn't spent four years preparing to be a bartender either, but it hadn't stopped me from doing that. He had a point.

So I headed to a local Kirby dealership in Philadelphia, confident that I would be an instant success. After all, how hard could it be? I'd always fancied myself something of a natural salesman, primarily because I'd made a killing selling raffle tickets in my younger days. More important, I assumed anything Eric could do, I could do at least as well, if not better. I figured I'd match or overtake his sales figures within two months—three, tops.

Calling this a misconception does not do justice to the word. Not only was I not a "natural salesman," it is debatable whether I could have even been considered a salesman, as by definition salesmen make sales. In the five weeks I worked for Kirby, I moved a total of two vacuums, and if it weren't for my exceptionally supportive parents, it would have been only one. In hindsight, I think my downfall was that I didn't believe that the people I was pitching the vacuums to really needed them. When they would frown at me and say, "We can't afford a vacuum that costs $1,400," I felt like responding, "Who can?"

But of course I couldn't say that. What I was supposed to say was, "The question is, can you afford *not* to buy a Kirby today?" I wasn't ever to refer to the Kirby as anything as pedestrian as a vacuum either. Rather, the Kirby was a "cleaning system," one that, if you believed my sales pitch, was possibly the most technologically advanced household product ever created, if not the pinnacle of humankind's evolution from a preindustrial society. It featured something billed as a "TechDrive Variable Power Assist" and an internal fan redesigned with the help of NASA. Yeah, I would tell potential customers, *that* NASA.

There is no doubt that the Kirby—heavy, metallic, and tanklike, with a headlight in the front—is an impressive machine. To convince customers of this, the company sells the machines solely through in-home sales calls camouflaged as "free carpet cleanings," each of which lasts at least ninety minutes. The key to these demos was to make the customers feel worthless. So we would attack their carpets and remove gobs and gobs of dirt, all of it collected on small, round paper demonstration filters we pulled from the guts of the Kirby. (I say "we" because all Kirby acolytes used the same approach, drilled into us in a two-day training session.) Then we would brandish these filters in the face of the customers to show them how despicably, dangerously, disgustingly filthy their home was. I felt like a detective yanking out the crucial piece of evidence. *Recognize this, Mrs. Walker?*

Next came the infamous Kirby video, which showed horrifically enlarged armies of dust mites marching in formation across the pillows and sofas of America, accompanied by an ominous voice-over detailing the health dangers these microscopic monsters pose for children. More specifically, *your* children. And where were these mites lurking? Ah, that led to the final touch, the purposeful climb up the stairs to the bedroom, where we would despoil any sense of security that remained: we vacuumed the bed. Oh the horror when filter after filter—fifteen, twenty of them, each stained brown with thousands of little dust mite carcasses—was lifted from the mattress—the very mattress, it needed no underscoring, where their children slept every night.

And just when our potential customers felt the absolute worst, when every shred of self-respect was banished, we would salve their battered psyche with the following redemptive phrase: *It's not your fault.* No, the blame lay with that archaic contraption, the one that hid in the back of their closet, curled up in an apathetic ball, wasting electricity, and running over their carpet like a toothless comb. And we would condemn it from on high, their cowering vacuum, and hurl epithets at it. "Electrolux?" we would say mockingly. "More like Electrosux." And they were supposed to laugh along with us, reassured and now educated about the error of their ways. Then they would hand over the check for $1,400.

Or at least that was how I envisioned things going for other sales-men, the ones who actually sold Kirbys instead of just cleaning people's houses for free, which is essentially what I did.

Eric was one of those salesmen. He started working for Kirby after graduation, when he answered a newspaper ad on a whim. In his first month he sold twenty-two of the machines, or twenty more than I did during my entire "career." Tall and sturdy—though being from Penn-sylvania, he always brought to mind the description "corn-fed"—he has a habit of putting his right hand on your left shoulder when he wants to convey that, yes, he understands what you are saying. In the world of vacuum sales, this bond is very important, for often what people are say-ing is "I haven't the slightest interest in buying that thing." To be able to empathize with and simultaneously disagree with someone is not easy, but Eric was able to pull it off.

Within a month and a half, he was the top new salesman in the Eastern States Division and his photo was on the cover of *Positive Action*, which billed itself as "The Magazine for the Serious Kirby Professional!" ("Serious" was set off in red type against the surrounding blue print and, when framed against the white background, was presumably meant to suggest that peddling Kirbys was an exercise in patriotism.) Two months later, he was honored at a New Orleans awards banquet as the new sales-man of the year, a title bestowed on whoever sold the most machines in one month. In a packed ballroom humming with the fervor of a politi-cal convention and decorated with enormous photos of legends of the industry, Eric entered to the strains of "Pump Up the Volume," then stood up before a crowd of more than three hundred. To prolonged ap-plause, he spoke of his surefire strategies and added some self-deprecation for good measure. "The biggest cheer," he told me later, "was when, in a cheap attempt to win over the crowd, I said that I'd just graduated from college, and wasn't that a waste of four years of my life." He was a star; that night over beers, Kirby dealers from all over the Southeast tried to recruit him to their operations.

Just because guys like Eric could sell Kirbys, however, that didn't mean I could. When, four months after he began, Eric left the business to attend graduate school, he confided to me that had he continued with the job he could have been making six figures within a year, and that he had already been offered his own franchise in New Hampshire. Had all stayed on course, he would have become a very wealthy man. All because he could sell vacuum cleaners.

Though putting it like that may be oversimplifying things. He wasn't really selling a machine so much as a domestic ideal, a dirt-siphoning totem of the good life that was affordable to anyone who could make the low, low, always negotiable monthly payments. His ability to pull this off was remarkable, and I say that not just to make myself feel better (though it does). He could arrive unannounced on someone's doorstep and within two hours convince them not only that he knew what was best for them but that what was best for them was to invest $1,400 in a product they'd never seen before. To be fair, the Kirby is a good investment for some people—the kind who own expensive carpets and have the means to care for them. Still, to sell anyone such a contrivance cold requires charisma, persuasiveness, empathy, resilience, and a healthy dose of ruthlessness, all of which have to be employed strategically.

These are not skills taught in any classroom. There are no graduate courses in Advanced Living Room Commerce. Practice helps, but either you enjoy the process—of winning over people, of surmounting objections, of bartering, of closing a deal—or you don't. Emphatically, I didn't.

Still, I came away from my Kirby experience having learned an important lesson: Just as certain clothes will never fit, regardless of how much one inhales one's gut, certain jobs don't fit, no matter how much we may try to squeeze ourselves into them.

For this reason, I've always found it comical when a certain profession is described across the board as a "dream job," as if we could all agree upon what constitutes such an ideal. Professional athletes are often said to have dream jobs, but, as someone who covers them on a regular basis as a staff writer at *Sports Illustrated,* I can attest to the fact that some of them are among the most jaded individuals I've ever met. Somewhere along the way from passion to profession, they lost touch with the nine-year-old they once were, the one who put on mittens to go shoot baskets in the winter, retrieving the ball each time from its snow dimple. So we impugn them when they complain, because *they're being paid millions to play a child's game, for God's sake.* They should be the happiest people on the planet, or so the equation goes: something you love to do plus gobs of money to do it equals happiness.

This math is part of a larger, and, as it turns out, thoroughly modern, belief that we are *supposed* to find happiness through our work. We speak of finding meaningful work, or, more grandly, a "true calling." Originally, this was a religious concept, that man is called by God to his profession; the Bible says, "Seest thou a man active in his calling, he shall stand before Kings." Today, however, the meaning has been thoroughly secularized. In the course of researching this book, I saw the term used in a full-page ad for a Chevrolet Cobalt sedan ("IT'S NOT A SIGNAL. IT'S A CALLING"), in the admissions materials for St. Olaf College (defined as, "when your day's work and your life's work meet"), and in a job posting for a cell phone company ("Find your calling; Find your future with T-Mobile").

The concept of a "dream job" is bandied about just as casually. During a one-month period in 2004, one could have purchased the following magazines at a newsstand: an issue of *Men's Journal* trumpeting "the 50 Best Jobs in America" and offering up fishing guide, general manager of a pro baseball team, and NFL quarterback as examples (apparently, the jobs didn't necessarily need to be attainable); a copy of *Business 2.0* magazine with a cover story entitled "How to Land Your Dream Job," in which the first two sentences read, "Wouldn't you really rather be doing something else for a living? Be honest," before elevating professions such as the stay-at-home blogger, an MD-turned-mutual fund manager, and the same baseball GM (Paul DePodesta of the Dodgers); and, finally, *Worthwhile,* a magazine bearing the credo "Work with Purpose, Passion and Profit" that cited a Gallup poll finding that only 29 percent of workers in America are "actively engaged" in their work, and touted nine people who loved their jobs (including the chef Alice Waters).

The upshot is that people feel as though they're expected to find this elusive calling but—as with the notion of true love—no one's quite sure exactly what it is. So just as the luckless romantic turns to speed dating or Match.com hoping for a quick-fix solution, the job seeker turns to self-help books (the search phrase "How to Find a Job" on Amazon.com returns 262,082 results), career counselors (many of whom churn out the books), and personality tests (a $400-million-a-year industry that features 2,500 different types of tests). All in the name of better understanding what we should be doing with our lives.

So what, I wanted to know, makes some people so sure? What is it about the fit between a job and a person that makes someone consider his work a calling? That's what I set out to investigate two years ago, when I went in search of people who truly loved their work. Not just any people, though. I wanted to see what I could learn from men and women who are very good at very unusual jobs, those people who are, to borrow a phrase from the author Ted Conover, "conscientious objectors to the nine-to-five work world." I'd always been drawn to such people, as they seemed to possess a certitude about their work.

Certainly, I could have interviewed doctors and lawyers, or line cooks and postal workers, and I'm sure it would have been interesting, but it's easy to understand how people enter such careers. With most jobs, there are pre-worn paths to follow—this is not to say they are easy paths, but at least they are marked. Why is it, I wanted to know, that some people ignore the trail and start bushwhacking through the occupational landscape, oblivious to the obstacles? Do they know something the rest of us don't?

It seemed to be rich, unmined territory. To quote Richard Florida from his book *The Rise of the Creative Class,* "Everything interesting happens at the margins." I had some research to go on as well. In 1986, a pair of Harvard Business School professors, Gene Dalton and Paul Thompson, studied the career stages of professionals and found that "most of the instances that we heard about concerning a deep interest in work involve unusual circumstances." Furthermore, they noted that while a certain level of interest was considered normal among professionals, a "deep and absorbing" interest—which they found in those "unusual circumstances" and with people "performing individual tasks"—was not. They didn't tackle why this was. I would.

First, however, it's important to provide some context. For to understand how we became a nation obsessed with finding meaning through our work, one that fetishizes dream jobs and has gone from "working to live" to, in many cases, "living to work," one must look to the past.

A BRIEF HISTORY OF HATING OUR JOBS

CONSIDERING ITS ELEVATED STATUS IN the modern world, it is interesting to note that for the majority of history "work" has been considered a burdensome, demeaning necessity. As such, it has been alternately mandated, adjudicated, and, more often than not, outsourced to the less fortunate. Early Christians believed that men were condemned to toil for their sins. The Greeks and Romans thought labor was best left to slaves, and that the pursuit of education and enlightenment was how man found fulfillment and achieved greatness (an idea espoused by men like Plato and Aristotle who, it just so happened, spent their time in pursuit of education and enlightenment). The closest word the Greeks had to "work" was *ponos,* which also meant "pain," and the Latin *poena* means "sorrow." Manual labor was frowned upon unless, of course, that labor involved killing other Romans or Greeks in vast numbers; this was held in high esteem. (Some things, it seems, never change.)

Attitudes began to shift when the first craft guilds sprang up in Europe around A.D. 1100 and, with them, the concept that there is honor in being a craftsman. People began to take on the surname of their trade. Many of these names persevere to this day: Cook, Baker, Thatcher, and Smith. It wasn't until the Protestant Reformation, however, that the concept of work as inherently honorable became popular, or, as the early-twentieth-century author Adriano Tilgher put it, "[Martin] Luther placed a crown on the sweaty forehead of labor." Luther, a German monk, believed that one's vocation was one's calling, a sacred duty to God and a moral obligation. In a departure from the prevailing mind-set, he also believed it was honorable for a man to pursue an occupation other than that of his father if he was so "called." Around the same time, the French theologian John Calvin espoused a similar idea about work as God's will, while stressing that any work could be meaningful. Thus, one could find one's "calling" in a humble trade just as easily as in the clergy, a precept that later functioned as a virtual advertising slogan for the Industrial Revolution. *You may be working on an assembly line for twelve hours a day, but God loves you for every widget.*

Early Americans, adventurous colonists that we were, latched on to this Protestant work ethic, as Max Weber later labeled it, and attempted to till and toil our way to salvation. Such was the fervor for work in the colonies that, in 1648, Massachusetts passed legislation making idleness a crime. The difference between the emerging American view on work and that of the Calvinists and the Lutherans—who saw virtue in an ascetic lifestyle—was that, to those early colonists, it wasn't just labor that honored God, but also the creation of great wealth. In this respect, the country's most passionate preacher was Benjamin Franklin, who coined the phrase "time is money" and whose philosophy could be summed up as, in his words, "Money can beget money, and its offspring can beget more, and so on and so on." Franklin, no dummy, followed his own advice by printing up his aphorisms in a tome, titled *The Way to Wealth,* that sold a quarter million copies and became the second most popular book in the colonies (behind the Bible, of course), thus paving the way for that most American of phenomenons: the self-help guru. (A mantle swiftly grasped by the Reverend Thomas P. Hunt, who got right to the point in his 1836 bestseller entitled *The Book of Wealth: In Which It Is Proved From the Bible That It Is the Duty of Every Man to Become Rich.*)

Not everyone agreed with Franklin's view. The Austrian writer Ferdinand Kürnberger derided it as "a philosophy of avarice." Weber feared that capitalism was creating "specialists without spirit, hedonists without a heart." Marx indicted the pursuit of happiness through lucre in his own inimitable style. "Political economy knows the worker only as a working animal—as a beast reduced to strictest bodily needs," he wrote, adding, "The true purpose of work is no longer man, but money."[1]

Grim assessments, but in the United States, the rise of capitalism within a democratic society meant that people at least had the freedom to question what they got from their work. By the twentieth century, the idea of a "calling" had lost much of its religious connotation; we began to work for the rewards of work itself, not for some promised payoff in the afterlife. There was no shame in manual labor if it furthered one's life; we glorified those who went from "rags to riches" or came from the "school of hard knocks" or pulled themselves "up by the bootstraps." The promise of a better life through work, the great allure of America to the immigrant, began to evolve into the promise of better work, period.

Give a man too many choices, however, and he will be unable to make one. With the freedom of occupational options came the shackles of self-doubt. Enter the first career counselor, a Boston social worker named Frank Parsons, who in 1908 founded the imposingly titled Vocation Bureau at Civic Service House in Boston, the first career counseling institution in the United States (five years later, the U.S. Department of Labor was formed, and on its heels the National

1. It should be stressed, however, that Marx was not antiwork, just anticapitalism. He saw work as providing inherent creative and social rewards, among them the gratification of producing one's own goods. He felt that factory work, the lynchpin of capitalism at the time, alienated workers and disassociated them from the product of their work.

Vocational Guidance Association). Parsons believed there were three factors that affected the choice of vocation: "1) a clear understanding of yourself; 2) a knowledge of the requirements and conditions for success . . . in different lines of work; and 3) true reasoning on the relation of these two groups of facts."

Vocational psychology got its next boost during World War I, when the army hired teams of psychologists in an effort to classify huge numbers of new entrants. According to Richard Donkin's chronology of work, *Blood, Sweat & Tears,* by the end of the war, 1,750,000 men had taken the original Stanford-Binet personality assessment test, either in its Alpha form (for those who could read) or its Beta (for those who couldn't). Perhaps launching the practice of looking to the military for management solutions—something taken to rather ludicrous extremes in today's age of *Leadership Secrets of Attila the Hun*—Western Electric followed the army's lead and used the questionnaire on its employees and potential hires, becoming one of the first companies to screen its workers with a personality test. The process was further streamlined during World War II, which saw the development of the Army General Classification Test, a predecessor of the test that high school counselors give students to this day. More and more, it was believed that there was a right answer to what any man should be doing; it just needed to be scored and analyzed.

After the war, Americans, flush with prosperity, began to look inward. As the GNP rose, work satisfaction, tellingly, did not follow suit. The richer people got, the more, it seemed, they wanted out of their lives. Look at a U.S. chart of real income per capita versus the percentage of people who say they are "very happy" from 1945 to 2000 and it looks like the maw of a crocodile, real income rising at a nearly forty-five-degree angle while the bottom level of happiness stays constant at 25 percent or so.

As the decades passed, increasing automation and industrialization gave us the easy work life, but not a satisfying one. In 1973, the Work in America Report, an overarching and quite depressing study prepared by the U.S. Department of Health, Education and Welfare, determined to get to the root of what were popularly known as the "white collar woes" and "blue collar blues." The report found that significant numbers of employees felt they were mired in jobs that consisted of "dull, repetitive [and] seemingly meaningless tasks, offering little challenge or autonomy." The disaffected American worker was symbolized by television characters like Archie Bunker, while musicians tapped in to our collective desire to simultaneously detest our boss and listen to some kick-ass tunes by penning songs like "9 to 5" (Dolly Parton), "Working for the Weekend" (Loverboy), "Take This Job and Shove It" (David Allen Coe), "Working for a Living" (Huey Lewis and the News), and "Feel Like a Number," Bob Seger's lament about facelessness as "just another drone." Hating one's work became something of a national hobby; offices were papered with posters of kittens clinging to brick walls above the motto "Hang in there; Friday's coming!" while a common sentiment, "Thank God it's Friday," became so popular it inspired a huge chain of restaurants that are virtually unavoidable today (sort of like work itself).

Ironically, just as many Americans were busy hating their jobs, others were becoming addicted to them. By the early eighties, the term "workaholic" had entered the vernacular. In her 1978 look at the phenomenon, *Workaholics: Living with Them, Working with Them*, Marilyn Machlowitz argued in defense of the trend. "As a group," she wrote, "workaholics are surprisingly happy. They are doing exactly what they love—work—and they can't seem to get enough of it." She included a quiz entitled "Are You a Workaholic?" and lionized anecdotes such as the one about two associates at a prestigious Manhattan law firm who "were said to have a bet about who could bill the most hours in a day. One worked around the clock, billed twenty-four, and felt assured of victory. His competitor, however, having flown to California in the course of the day and worked on the plane, was able to bill twenty-seven."

This trend continued, buoyed by the roaring eighties and the dot-com nineties, and a strange new math emerged regarding one's well-being, namely that the fewer hours one slept, the more important one was perceived to be. Work, once seen as a signifier of low social status, had become an emblem of importance; in the 1890s, the poorest 10 percent of men worked two hours more per day than the richest 10 percent, while by 1991, the richest 10 percent were working a half hour *more* per day than the poorest 10 percent. Dot-com offices had pool tables and leisurely dress codes, the trappings of a relaxed environment, but still expected employees to sleep at their ergonomically correct desks. Today, as Donkin nicely puts it in *Blood, Sweat & Tears*, we're at the point where instead of knocking off for the day, we take "leisure snacks" of a few hours and head back to work; during our free time, we are apt to take "work snacks," checking e-mail, reading memos, or making a phone call during the halftime of the game. (Workmania has even infected the most stoically languorous of populations, the French, who under the slogan "Work more to earn more," in March of 2005 voted to rescind the mandatory thirty-five-hour workweek limit, allowing people to work up to forty-eight hours—which proves, if nothing else, that slogan writing is not the French's strong suit.)

We hate our jobs; we're addicted to our jobs. These sentiments are two sides of the same coin, and the coin is our national obsession with finding our place in the world of work. Faced with so many potential careers, and with companies seeing workers not as lifelong employees but as replaceable parts, it is harder to make a commitment. In 1951, the Columbia economist Eli Ginzberg delineated three periods of occupational choice, which he termed *fantasy, tentative,* and *realistic.* The fantasy period applied to children ten to twelve years old, the tentative period to those twelve to seventeen, and the realistic period ran through later adolescence and into early adulthood. How things have changed; now, one could argue that the tentative period lasts well into people's late twenties, if not early thirties (and, in some cases, perhaps their entire lives).

It is the most common complaint of young people today: I don't know what to do with my life (which could be subtitled: So I Will Sit Here and Play Xbox in the Meantime). My generation, and the one that followed it, is waiting longer, and testing out more avenues, as evidenced by the recent trend of a "boomerang generation" of children living with their parents for a longer period of time (which inspired a BBC documentary titled *Honey, We Can't Get Rid of the Kids*), postponing marriage, and, according to 2001 data from the Bureau of Labor Statistics, changing jobs an average of every 1.1 years while in their twenties, sometimes by choice and sometimes due to a rattled economy. Still, we have more resources within our reach, more options, and more latitude, not to mention a longer incubation period, than any population in human history. When we do finally choose a career, we should be happy, right?

Only we aren't. A 2004 Gallup poll found that only 50 percent of American workers say they are more than "somewhat satisfied" with their jobs, and that number doesn't appear poised to rise anytime soon. This has engendered a backlash of sorts, embodied by people who want to shift the dialogue from *how* to find a calling to *whether* such a thing reasonably exists. As the argument goes, it is foolish, if not downright self-indulgent and self-destructive, for us to see our work as anything more than a means to an end. As the author and scholar Alain de Botton wrote in a *New York Times* editorial in 2004: "Today, claims are made on behalf of almost all kinds of work that are patently out of sync with what reality can provide. Yes, a few jobs are certainly fulfilling, but the majority are not and never can be. We would therefore be wise to listen to some of the pessimistic voices of the pre-modern period, if only to stop torturing ourselves for not being as happy in our work as we were told we could be."

In a twisted way, this line of reasoning seems meant to reassure people, but it's also awfully fatalistic. If only certain jobs can be fulfilling, are we supposed to accept that if we don't hit the job lotto, then we're condemned to a life of meaningless drudgery, and that furthermore we should get used to it? Something tells me that the position of door-to-door salesman wouldn't make Botton's cut for "fulfilling jobs," but try telling that to one of Kirby's National Salesman of the Year winners.

So why are so many of us unhappy at work? Perhaps it's not because of the nature of the jobs but because of the nature of us. As a number of researchers, including Daniel Gilbert, a psychology professor at Harvard, have concluded, happiness is both relative and hard to predict. We are content when we are as happy or more happy than others; in other words, as long as my job is better than your job, I'm psyched about it (and so long as my car is bigger than your car, and so on). The result: We're left with an uneasy uncertainty and want to know once and for all what happiness at work means—What is the pinnacle?—so we can compare ourselves to that standard.

The answer, I learned, is that there is no one pinnacle, nor even half a dozen. Rather, imagine a mountain range that stretches for thousands and thousands of miles, each peak fashioned by different geographic factors, each one unique. Climb someone else's mountain and you may not like the view, but reach your own summit and you can see for miles.

HUNTING BUTTERFLIES

I EMBARKED UPON THIS PROJECT because I was interested in what it was like at the top of that metaphorical peak. Maybe it was wonderful. Then again, maybe the view was great but it was cold as hell and the mountain goats pee on your tent.

So I went in search of people who, when faced with the high school guidance counselor's multiple choice test, chose none of the above—the dreamers, schemers, and iconoclasts who either found their own niche or, better yet, carved it out themselves. The anti-Babbits of the world. Movie stars, CEOs, and rock gods may be the subjects of biographies, but who's to say they're the only ones we can learn from?

Everybody I talked to had suggestions about whom to profile. One woman suggested a gynecologist for racehorses; one of my friends (who shall remain nameless) thought I should seek out the World Fellating Champion. A number of people suggested themselves. In the end, however, I followed a rather simple test: was the person passionate about unusual work, was he or she very good at it, and was his or her life story interesting.

I traveled from the woods of Oregon to the heart of San Francisco, from a skyscraper in Florida to a home office in Michigan, from a professor's office in Greenwich Village to the "Super Bowl of Career Counseling" in Sacramento. In the process, I learned how to cut through sixteen inches of white pine in under ten seconds, why one must never park one's car near a prime mushroom patch, how a model train set can engulf a man's life, the usefulness of the Pledge of Allegiance in a movie career, and that, when it comes to finding rare butterflies—in the case of the man who inspired this book's title—it's best to put on one's headlamp.

I was continually surprised by what I found, and not just because I was venturing into some pretty strange subcultures. I uncovered passion in the unlikeliest of places and wisdom where I never would have expected it. I was astonished at the candor and compassion of many of my subjects. They let me into their lives, and I took the opportunity— metaphorical visitor tag attached to my chest—to see what drove them, what inspired them, and what they hoped to achieve. Not all the stories were inspirational; some were cautionary, others complex. In the end, despite their diverse careers and at times peculiar worldviews, there were a handful of common themes that tied them together. Consider the following field notes from an exploration into unusual lives.

First and foremost, *there aren't ten steps, or seven steps, or any steps for that matter.* The people I talked to didn't have it any easier than the rest of us; they didn't follow any magic formula, or, with a couple of exceptions, feel born into their work. Some stumbled into it, others lucked into it, one even married into it. If anything, most hadn't even given the matter a lot of thought, at least not consciously; they were just doing *what they do.*

A calling is the single most interesting thing in the world. Nothing is as fascinating or important. At least to the person who has that calling. Almost to the man and woman, the people I interviewed saw their work affecting other lives in ways I would have been hard-pressed to notice. Where others might not see meaning, they created it. Conversely, and tellingly, many of them laughed at the "weirdness" of the other jobs I was profiling.

Just because someone loves their work, it does not mean he or she is happy. All people can ask for is that their job enhances their life. Expecting it to solve unrelated problems is like expecting a new lawn mower to repair your marriage. The author Thomas Carlyle wrote in the nineteenth century, "Work is the grand cure of all the maladies and miseries that ever beset mankind." Carlyle was full of shit.

Perceived autonomy trumps actual autonomy. The ideal of being "one's own boss" isn't really so much about freedom; it's about one's perception of freedom, an important distinction. In other words, working fourteen hours at something one loves is more liberating than spending nine hours at something one doesn't, even if the first situation actually provides less tangible freedom.

In the details of work, one finds a voice. This was a unifying theme among the people I met. Just as Tom Wolfe's writing style is instantly recognizable, or a music buff can hear a two-second snippet of a song and—bam!—identify the guitarist, people who are passionate about their work develop a voice. It may be evident in unusual ways—the signature stylings of a woodworker, for example—but it stamps their work product as deeply personal.

There is no proper balance for everyone's life, only a proper balance for each individual's life. Read a profile of a CEO and it's likely that he (or she) will boast about sleeping four hours a night and multitasking by taking conference calls from the restroom. This does not make his or her life a blueprint for success. Some of us can dedicate 70 percent of our lives to our work and be happy; for others doing so can be disastrous.

Work can make us superstars. By that I mean a job can summon the best version of us—the person you were on your prom night or, if your prom night happened to be a debacle, the analogous day of your life when all your jokes were funny and you couldn't help but admire yourself in the mirror because, damn if you didn't look sharp. Some people prefer themselves when drunk, or when seen in profile, or while singing "Total Eclipse of the Heart" at a karaoke bar. People who love their work, like the ones I met, love themselves at work.

Everyone has bee people. In the video for "No Rain," by the band Blind Melon, a little girl in a bee costume spends the majority of the song walking through the world forlorn until, at the end, she comes upon a field of children in similar bee suits. Exultation follows. The same applies to work; somewhere, there is a community of people who are passionate about the same (potentially weird) things as each of us. Find them and find home. Conversely, find someone else's and it can be a surreal experience. Vacuum cleaner salesmen, for example, were clearly not my bee people.

Anxiety fuels passion. In the area between challenge and boredom, there is a nexus of excitement and apprehension that drives people. Even if the people I spent time with professed to love their work, they also loved—like all of us—to bitch about it. This is not necessarily a bad thing (except, maybe, for the person who has to listen to the bitching). Complaining can be a measure of engagement, and far preferable to boredom and indifference.

And, finally, *idiosyncrasies are an asset.* Instead of hiding them, or burying them under layers of social niceties, the people I met embraced them. They took their unique skills (or obsessions) and made them assets. Weird is, after all, as weird does. There's a reason Aldous Huxley envisioned a world where the Epsilons, his factory workers born into predestined roles, represented the epitome of work's evils. Strange and eccentric are just one bus stop away from creative and innovative.

· · ·

The poet W. H. Auden once wrote, "A tremendous number of people in America work very hard at something that bores them. Even a rich man thinks he has to go down to the office every day. Not because he likes it but because he can't think of anything else to do." The characters I met had a different story: they couldn't think of anything else they'd *want* to do. What I wanted to know was, in so many words, how did they pull that off?

ONE

THE SKYWALKER

SOMETIMES A WONDERFUL CONFLUENCE OCCURS and what a person does for a living not only makes him happy but also makes the rest of us happy. By that I don't mean that this person is providing some service that makes our lives better. Rather, I mean that this person being content, and, more important, occupied, is preferable for the rest of us, because God knows what he'd be doing otherwise. In the case of Spiderman Mulholland, he followed his own unusual interests and found not only a calling, but, in many ways, peace.

I heard about Mulholland when my friend Owen, who was then working at the *Rocky Mountain News,* in Denver, forwarded me a story from his paper, dated April 27, 2004, titled, "The Amazing Spiderman Saves the Day with Flag Fix." Here's how the story began:

BROWN PALACE HIRES HERO'S
NAMESAKE FOR AERIAL REPAIR

A real-life version of classic Marvel comics hero
Spider-Man created a spectacle for passers-by when he
scaled one of the Denver landmark's rooftop flagpoles
to make an otherwise routine repair before rappelling
headfirst to safety.

The hotel flew in Spiderman Scott Mulholland
from his home base in Pensacola, Fla., to fix a pulley
that got stuck about six weeks ago at the top of a
40-foot flagpole at the edge of the 10-story building's
roof.

The 42-year-old former Marine, who has built a
multimillion-dollar business doing repairs and cleaning
on what he calls "suicidal buildings," said he paid
Marvel to use the Spiderman name for his business.
He flashed his driver's license to prove he legally
changed his own first name as well.

It seemed too good, or perhaps too weird, to be true. A former
Marine who calls himself Spiderman and scales buildings. Unusual:
check. Enthusiastic: check. Potentially unstable: also a check. But if so,
he was certainly a functional delusional, and that is the most interesting
kind (Howard Hughes being a prime example).

I pulled up some more newspaper stories on Mulholland, including
an account of how he taught a Florida SWAT team to enter buildings by
rappelling the exterior and then busting through the windows boot-first,
like they do in action movies. Next, I checked out his Web site, which included what appeared to be an ad detailing Mulholland's work on the
First National Bank of Mobile using a Dow Corning sealant. The ad read:

He's a wall climber. He is a curtainwall consultant, past
president of the Exterior Design Institute, a forensic

expert on waterproofing failures, and a certified
waterproofing contractor in his own right. But at
heart, Spiderman Mulholland is a wall climber. A life of
foster homes, drugs and detention took a turn when
Scott Mulholland joined the Marines and received
specialized training in advanced rappelling, helicopter
extractions, and skyrigging. His experience in the
Marines led to his career choice—climbing walls.

This, I thought, was the kind of guy I was looking for. I called him
one morning in the fall and reached him on his cell phone as he drove
to a construction site. "Very, very, very few people do what I do," he said,
his voice coming loud and fast. "Most people do not have this kind of
passion for it, VERY FEW are willing to go up the side of a building for
it, and very few understand forensic investigations."

He was extremely busy at the moment, he told me. His office was
in Pensacola, Florida, so he was right in the midst of the devastation
from Hurricane Ivan, the last in a series of four hurricanes that ravaged
the Florida coast during a nine-week period in the summer of 2004, leaving 107 people dead and causing approximately $40 billion in damage.
The hurricane had been disastrous for the general populace but a boon
for someone who repairs buildings. As long as I didn't mind tagging
along, Mulholland said he'd be happy to show me the ropes, in this case
literally. "You and me, we'll go jump off some buildings," he said. "You
ain't gonna believe it when you see it!"

THERE HAS BEEN A FAIR amount of research done on why people are
drawn to dangerous activities and occupations. In 1973, Bruce Ogilvie,
who is considered by many to be the father of sports psychology, performed a study on 293 "high-risk" competitors, including skydivers, race
car drivers, fencers, and aerobatic pilots. In contrast to the conventional
wisdom of the time, which equated such pastimes with a death wish,
Ogilvie found these people to be success-oriented, strongly extroverted,

and, compared to the general population, above average in abstract thinking ability and intelligence. Rather than being reckless, he found their risk taking was calculated; he estimated that only 6 percent of the athletes he studied competed out of anger, because of an inferiority complex, or because they were trying to prove something.

Two decades later, *Psychology Today* did a story on risk taking in which the magazine culled the opinions of top researchers and psychologists and came to similar, if less ebullient, conclusions. The consensus among the scientists was that, among other things, an inclination to take risks may be "hard-wired into the brain . . . and may offer such a thrill that it functions like an addiction." Extroverts are more likely to be risk takers, the experts concluded, a finding that seems logical. But the researchers were divided on what propels the impulse; some argued that it is an internal drive, an urge hardwired into one's personality, while others argued that environmental factors play a large role. Marvin Zuckerman, a pioneering psychologist in the field, labels some people "high sensation seeking," or HSS individuals, whereas other researchers break people down into Type A, Type B, and Type T, for thrill.

For all but a few Americans, a job is not an outlet for sensation seeking. Unless you're a firefighter or a logger, the most dangerous part of most people's workday comes during the commute to work (though in Manhattan, it's probably a tie between taking a taxi and ordering a "salad," whether it be tuna, chicken, or egg, at one of the city's smaller delis or bodegas). So the HSS individuals among us take "expedition vacations" and summit mountains in faraway lands and spend our weekends eating cardboard-flavored carbohydrate bars and hanging off cliffs in neoprene outfits, all in search of an adrenal rush.

But not all can handle the heights. It takes a certain type of man, or woman, to seek out the sky. In 1999, 23 percent of Americans described themselves as "very afraid" of heights (technically, it's acrophobia). The only thing we are more afraid of as a country, at least statistically speaking, is snakes.

Mulholland claimed to be scared of nothing.

• • •

NOT LONG AFTER MY INITIAL phone conversation with Mulholland, I booked a trip to Pensacola. Even though it had been weeks since the hurricane hit, all the hotels within a 120-mile radius were full of storm refugees, an indication of how much work remained for people like Spiderman, so I stayed a ways down the coast.

The morning of my meeting with Mulholland, I awoke before dawn and drove to Pensacola. As the sky brightened into a pale orange, I began to see the aftermath of Ivan. The road ran parallel to the water; to my left a thirty-foot boat had been thrown up on the roadside like a child's toy, its hull pocked with puncture marks. Towering piles of debris, thick with garbage, uprooted trees, sheets of bent aluminum and wood, lay at regular intervals like so many unkindled bonfires. Everywhere there were reminders of the storm—the "Goodbye Ivan Clearance Sale" at the mattress store, the woman in the State Farm Catastrophe team T-shirt at the coffee stand, the bulldozers rumbling down the highway, the plaintive graffiti scrawled on one house that read, simply, IVAN SUCKS.

Mulholland lived inland but his house had still taken a beating. A tree branch had fallen through his carport, just missing his Escalade, and almost all the vegetation in his yard had been either flattened or uprooted. Defiantly, Mulholland, his wife, their seventeen-year-old daughter, and their thirteen-year-old son John (Mulholland's two older sons no longer live at home) had hunkered down during the ten-hour storm as winds battered the modest two-story brick home. This might seem rather foolhardy, but once I got to know Mulholland, it didn't surprise me at all.

When I pulled into his long dirt driveway, Mulholland fairly bounded out of his house to meet me. His handshake was akin to meeting an oncoming linebacker, fast and firm and delivered with no small amount of elbow-pumping force. Though a relatively squat man, about five nine and broad, he possessed a coiled energy, like a crouched cat stalking its prey. He was wearing his work "uniform," which consisted of a tucked-in polo shirt, jeans, black Rockport sneakers, and an ID badge clipped to his shirt that read SPIDERMAN MULHOLLAND, BENNET SHUMAN ARCHITECTS, the name of the architect he partnered with much of the time. He was exquisitely clean-shaven, and his full black hair was gelled into a politician's helmet. He looked less like a daredevil and more like someone who might sell me kitchen appliances.

We headed to his office, a one-story, three-room building separate from the main house, to talk about his work. Or, more specifically, for Mulholland to talk about his work. Best described as a one-way conversationalist, Mulholland doesn't interact so much as preach; it is as if he's speaking in ALL CAPS. He also likes to make an enthusiastic hooting noise before and after sentences, a sort of hybrid of "Hooo boy" and "Whoopee," and often follows particularly exciting declarations with a high-pitched, wheezing laugh that causes his face to scrunch up in a manner reminiscent of Jeff Daniels in the movie *Dumb and Dumber*. So, for instance, were Mulholland eating a sandwich, he wouldn't describe it so much as champion it. "WOOOOOO! NOW THAT'S THE BEST SANDWICH IN FLORIDA RIGHT THERE," he would say in his loud, raspy voice. "I MIGHT JUST GET A COOLER AND FILL IT WITH THOSE SANDWICHES, HEH, HEH, HEEEAH-HHHHH."

Not that Mulholland ate any sandwiches while I was with him, or, for that matter, any solid food. At the time, he was on day three of one of his semi-regular fasts (he alternates between three-day, seven-day, and ten-day liquid fasts, and his wife and kids often join him). Over the course of two days, all I saw him consume was water, V-8, Gatorade, and coffee. "I'm stronger when I'm fasting than when I'm not," he explained to me. "Your body and your mind become sharp, son. It's like a RAZOR," he said, snapping his fingers. "You think by not eating you'd get weak"—and here he shook his head emphatically—"I came off a twenty-one-day fast about ten years ago and it was in the heat of summer and 111 degrees and I was just out there flying down the sides of buildings, JUST FLYING."

So, in observance of his fast, he drank his "breakfast" of black coffee while giving me a tour. His office was large, exceptionally clean, and lined with bookshelves, which included a mixture of building mainte- nance tomes such as *Sick Buildings,* and motivational books such as *Do It Now!"* and *Break the Procrastination Habit.* The walls were pasted with various trade school diplomas (the Exterior Design Institute), thank-you notes (from the SWAT team I'd read about, on behalf of the sheriff), framed news clips ("Spiderman Coaxes Jumper Off of a Water Tower"), and motivational reminders ("Take a look at your appearance. Do you look like a polished professional?"). An assortment of photo collages from his Marine Corps days graced the walls.

I pointed to a picture of him standing in a jungle, wearing fatigues and camouflage paint and cradling an enormous black gun. "That's my rifle there, that's my puppy," he said in the manner of someone identi- fying a nephew or a niece in a family snapshot. "That's an M-40 A1 sniper rifle, ten by magnification, fires around 2,550 feet per second with a bolt tail projectile. I could hit a helium balloon on the wind at *three and a half football fields away.* I have a 20/17 shooting eye. I outshot every- body in the Marine Corps except one man."

And the next photo, of a bunch of soldiers suspended from lines be- low a helicopter in jungle terrain. Rappelling?

"Nope, that's spy rigging," he said. "They hooked us up, chained us in, and took us up. Four guys go out north, south, east, and west. The helicopter comes in and you lock yourself in, with each line shorter than the other. When the helicopter starts going you start walking and it just picks you up. [So the soldiers are hooked, one above the other, to the same line.] On that day, we lost four guys. They got killed. They hit the power lines. It was just a miscalculation."

He shook his head in a brief moment of remembrance, then headed toward his computer. "Hey, you gotta see my DVD!"

He popped in a disc and the hard-charging chords of Steppenwolf's

"Born to Be Wild" blared from his computer speakers. Mulholland nodded along. "OH YEAH, HERE WE GO!"

The screen came to life and there he was, hanging upside down about a hundred feet below the top of a skyscraper, attached at the waist by a long rope, looking something like an unspooled yo-yo. As I watched, he inverted himself and began walking along the side of the building, then running, using the tautness of the rope to remain perpendicular. With a strong push of his leg, he launched himself into the air and did one, two, now three spins before landing against the glass with arms out, cushioning the impact like a cat falling from a height. Then he tore off the other way across the building, soaring out thirty feet—"THIRTY-SEVEN FEET, SON," to be exact—performing twelve turns in the air and finally wrapping himself around the edge, briefly disappearing from sight. "After twenty-two years on buildings, you name it and I can do it," he said as we watched. "If you open your legs, it slows your speed, if you close your legs you spin. I can see the building and after a while you can get pretty good at it, so I never hit my back. Probably been six years since I hit my back."

The video was impressive—I felt like I was watching a segment on *That's Incredible!* or some new extreme sports competition on late-night ESPN2—but I wasn't clear how these stunts helped him with his job. He explained that he used his rappelling and wall-climbing skills to make high-risk repairs—whether it be fixing a flagpole as he had done in Denver or doing mechanical repairs on top of a water tower or ascending a cracked atrium—that would otherwise require cranes or helicopters or a team of specialists. At this point in his career, however, the bulk of his job involved assessing buildings damaged by water intrusion for insurance purposes, often focusing on toxic mold danger. As part of this process, he often rappelled down the sides of these buildings to examine their exteriors and take samples, using wall-walking systems to go from side to side, thus eliminating the need for multiple rappels. Doing so allowed him to save his clients time and money, reach areas that would be nearly impossible to reach by other means, work alone when need be, and do repair work on the spot. A one-day building inspection, he told me, can pay up to $5,000. Considering that he has inspected over four thousand buildings and cleaned the windows of or repaired an additional eight thousand in his twenty-plus years on the job, that adds up. In the past year, working with Shuman, he estimated he'd taken in $400,000.

He showed me an example of a recent job. "Here's a building I just did in July," he said, pulling out a green plastic binder the size of the Manhattan phone book. "This is a twenty- to thirty-MILLION-dollar building. We look at all the problems, the coating system, a lot of hydrostatic dynamic testing, a lot of scanners, we'll hit it with infrared. Once we find out everything that's wrong with the building, then we put together this color-coded binder for the insurance companies and building owners."

He flipped through the binder to convey just how much detail and wisdom lay within. It was indeed impressive, full of graphs and diagrams and blueprints and digital photos marked with superimposed arrows to indicate damage, making the building look as if it were the site of a multistory gun battle that had been roped off and tagged as a crime scene. Then he snapped the binder shut to regain my full attention.

"I started this July 24 and I finished August 9. I burned 218 hours to produce these documents. That's sixteen, nineteen, eighteen, seventeen, twenty, twenty-three hours A DAY. They told me there was physically no way I could have done this. I said, 'YES THERE IS.' Have you heard of sniper school, U.S. Marines? That's three months, twenty hours a day, nonstop. Start with fifty Marines, six graduate. I graduated the top of my class. I said, 'Listen, don't tell me I don't have a PASSION for what I do. JUST BACK IT UP, PUT UP OR SHUT UP. I'll have your report in two weeks.' It just floored them."

Then he paused and pointed to the binder. "They paid me about FORTY THOUSAND DOLLARS for that." He rubbed his thumb and forefinger together gleefully and laughed. Then he grabbed my shoulder firmly, anchoring me to the ground. "Now, let's get out there and DO SOME WORK!"

MULHOLLAND GOT HIS START IN the business cleaning windows. At sixteen, he cleaned the front of Smith Tower in Seattle, scaling the forty-two-story structure using the window ledges and a belt system. He had been an inveterate climber since he was a child, when he'd roost in trees on his family's block and his mother nicknamed him "Monkey." Window washing came easy to him and, after his stint in the Marines—two years of which were inactive—he came back to the job. He found that, using his own homemade pulley and wall-walking systems, which he designed and tested himself with the help of a welder, he could clean windows faster and provide a nice PR boost, for both the company and himself. He called his business Spiderman's Professional Services[1] and branched out into restoration, waterproofing, and concrete repairs. He started out cleaning windows at $2 a window, then realized he could also caulk them at $36 per window, then, later, inspect them at $100 a window.

His high-tech approach is a far cry from the window cleaners of yore. Until the last few decades, the predominant cleaning technique involved hanging in a wooden chair or clipping into the side of the building with a cotton belt. Neither was very safe. Early scaffolds were rudimentary wood planks attached by ropes; when they tipped due to frayed belts or strong winds, the cleaners, their hands lifted to the glass, tumbled off like keepsakes sliding off a tilted mantelpiece.

Today, washers bolt into window frames for security and use nylon instead of cotton, but many buildings—including most skyscrapers—are designed with automated systems. The 1,454-foot Sears Tower, for

---

1. For a while, he wore a Spider-Man shirt and tights as he cleaned, though never a mask. He says Marvel contacted him, threatening to sue, and the parties came to an agreement: He could keep the Spiderman name (no hyphen, unlike the comic-book character) but wouldn't wear the costume. So he says he now holds the service mark—that is, business name—for the Spiderman name in Florida. Marvel retains the national registered trademark.

example, uses six window-washing machines that run on tracks, spraying the building with water and detergent, scrubbing the windows, and then sucking up the water, which is filtered and reused.

Still, according to the International Window Cleaning Association, an organization of six hundred businesses, twelve to fifteen window cleaners have been killed each year over the past decade while working on high-rises.

Mulholland told me that he has come close to dying only twice. Once he was about to rappel when he heard a voice from on top of the building. He retreated to see who it was but found no one there. He did find, however, that his rope was untied; had he stepped off, he would have plummeted to his death (the warning voice, he believed, was God's). Another time, while doing structural repairs on a 225-foot water tower at an air force base, he mistimed a ten-foot jump from a helicopter onto the roof and almost fell off. "It was a dumb stunt," he admitted, then grinned like a carnival huckster. "Risky, yes, but somebody had to do it. Sounded like a job for SPIDERMAN!"

Neither of these experiences, or any of the other dangerous situations he's faced—forty-mph winds pinning him against the side of a building, nearly getting hit by lightning, feeling glass fracture as he was suctioned to it, mistakenly pulling the brake release on both suction cups in mid-climb while inverted on an atrium—has made him reconsider his work. "Once you break the height fear factor, you learn to be able to push the limits and the envelope and not kill yourself," he told me at one point. "The key is that my body is very agile. I'm double-jointed. I can flip upside down. I'm a natural climber. People who aren't, they get locked up, they have so much fear. Me, two hundred feet up, I'm WHOOOOO—"

"Is there anything you can compare your work to?" I asked.

He paused, then shook his head. "No, because if there was, then I'd be doing that." He punctuated the thought with his squealing laugh, then rethought his sentiment. "Well, probably jumping out of an airplane but with that you jump and it's over."

He frowned slightly. "And you can't really make money jumping out of an airplane. With this, I get to find out what happened, I get to scale buildings. Jumping and climbing and scaling things as an investigator, I get to do what people only dream of doing. They sit there with their binoculars and—" here he mimicked the voice of what I took to be a shamefully landlocked investigator—" 'Wellll, I think that might be—'

"HA! I say let me find out AND I JUMP RIGHT OFF. Man, there is nothing I can't do on a building."

According to Plato, Socrates once said, "Thoughtful courage is a quality possessed by very few," while "rashness and boldness, and fearlessness which has no forethought, are very common qualities."

Where Spiderman fell in this spectrum, I wasn't yet sure.

HIS FIRST JOB SITE OF the day was the giant Portofino resort on the Pensacola coast, where the hurricane damage was worst. In my rental car, I followed Mulholland's white Dodge Ram 1500 V8 truck—identifiable by the MARINE CORPS SNIPER INSTRUCTOR sticker in the back window—and we were waved through various disaster checkpoints after Mulholland flashed his ID. The scene down by the beach was far more disturbing than what I'd seen on the drive up the coast, almost postapocalyptic. Everywhere the remains of crushed, denuded houses: mattresses, washing machines, plywood. The tops of palm trees had been eviscerated, leaving only brown stumps with a few stray dead leaves. Construction trailers had been picked up and deposited football fields away, where they lay on their sides, like dented aluminum cans tossed by the wind. Where before there had been lawns and sidewalks, now there was so much displaced white sand it looked like a snowstorm had hit. The roads were awash in it; it sat in giant drifts four, five feet high against buildings; it covered entire first floors of doorless houses.

My cell phone rang. It was Mulholland. "ONE HUNDRED SIXTY-SEVEN MILES PER HOUR."

"Huh?" I said as I drove.

"That's what the winds came in at. Just DEMOLISHED STUFF. All that sand, it used to be over there—" he stuck his arm out the window of his truck as he drove, pointing some two hundred yards away at the beach. "It's Spiderman's job to come in and fix things." It occurred to me that this would make him the only superhero who didn't avert disaster but rather cleaned it up. *Giant Monster Trashes City; Batman Arrives Next Day with Swiffer.*

We pulled into the parking lot of the Portofino, an upscale condo complex bordering the Gulf of Mexico that consists of five twenty-floor towers. Tower three of the hotel had been in the final stages of construction when the storm hit. The lower levels had been flooded, and there was some exterior damage, but for the most part it was in good shape. Mulholland was here to check out the roof. We parked and, as we headed past various foremen and workers, he turned to me and, in a tone that suggested I was about to attempt to bypass White House security, said, "If anyone asks, say you're my assistant for the day. Got it?"

I nodded and tried to carry my notebook in an assistant-like manner. I wondered if I should be wearing a hard hat. Apparently, however, "security" was rather lax, as we headed right into the deserted main lobby.

The elevator took us to the twenty-first floor; from there we ran up the stairs to the twenty-third floor—Mulholland is a big proponent of running stairs—and the roof access. A stiff wind and the shimmering Florida heat greeted us on top. From our vantage point, we could see all of Pensacola and to the south, miles and miles of coastline. The sun glinted off the water.

"Hold this," Mulholland said, handing me his camera.

Then he hopped over a railing and onto the sloped tile nape of the roof, which extended down and out thirty feet or so. At his request, I tossed him the camera, which he used to take both still and video footage for his analyses. "You don't," he said rather self-evidently, "want to lose your footing out here."

I was with him on that one. I have always hated heights. Ever since I was young, I've gotten a queasy sensation in my stomach when looking down from any distance above forty feet or so. Even though I stood

safely on the roof, as I watched Mulholland picking his way down to inspect damaged tiles, I felt that familiar intestinal free fall—call it sympathetic queasiness.

"I thought I was Evel Knievel when I was a kid," he yelled to me as
he went, turning his head to make eye contact, something I thought un-
necessary. "I busted my collarbone trying to become the first kid to flip
a swing all the way around. I got up top and it just dropped me straight
down and BOOMM!"

He paused to release one of his laughs, then descended further, with
no ropes to hold him in place, to the point where he was balancing himself about a foot from the edge, which dropped straight down to the asphalt 230 feet below. He steadied himself on the tiles, which were at a
forty-degree angle, and straightened up to film the damage (the photos
would fill out one of his binders). I was pretty sure he'd chosen such a
precarious perch for my benefit, but that didn't calm my stomach, which
was sending very strong signals to my brain that Mulholland should get
off the roof RIGHT NOW. A gust of wind hit him and he teetered for a
split second, then regained his balance. "All the other roof inspectors,"
he shouted to me, "their shots are from where you are. NOT ME
BUDDY! Heeehaaa."

Finished, he climbed back, hopped onto the roof, and hurried to the
stairs, which he descended at an alarming rate. So far, our day felt like
a continuous high-speed scavenger hunt. *Go! Go! Go! Go!* Clearly,
Mulholland hadn't quite let go of his Marine background, and turning
even the most mundane of tasks into a "mission" gave him satisfaction.
It didn't matter what we were doing; during our two days together he
tried to invest everything with a sense of urgency. Need to stop at a minimart? Gotta get in, get out. Gotta *refuel* with Gatorade. Gotta count the
change *quickly and efficiently.* Our ability to exit the 7-Eleven in a timely
fashion depended on it!

IT IS TEMPTING TO MAKE the comparison between Mulholland and
Peter Parker. Mild-mannered mold inspector by day, he morphs into a

wall-climbing daredevil who saves, if not lives, at least buildings, and if not buildings, at least insurance premiums. *Look, up there on the building, it's Deductible Man!*

Even Mulholland's life story, at least as he recounts it, is reminiscent of a comic-book superhero's origins. Many grow up as orphans, fighting the odds; Superman lived with adopted parents and the fictional Spider-Man, of course, was raised by his aunt and uncle.

Mulholland's story is darker, though it is tough to untangle the facts from an enthusiastic and potentially hyperbolic retelling by our hero. As he unspools the tale, Mulholland grew up in a fractured family in a suburb of Seattle. His father sold real estate and cars and split with his mother when Scott was young. Mulholland has memories of physical and verbal abuse, drug use and fights among his parents and his siblings (six brothers, two sisters, and two half-brothers). He dropped out of school after tenth grade and was placed in a foster home at fifteen, where he says he was beaten.

At sixteen, according to Mulholland, he was dispatched from the foster home and lived for a year and a half on the street. He told me he took to existing in a three-block area in downtown Seattle, where he ate from dumpsters, slept in a garbage can insulated with newspapers, and, eventually, sold his body for food. At one point, he said, he tried to intervene when he saw a prostitute being beaten in Chinatown and was savagely beaten himself. His attackers put him on a leash and made him a slave for twenty-four hours, after which he escaped. "I realized right then if I was going to get anything in life, I was going to have to get some guts, gall, and tenacity and obtain it. Because nobody was going to give it. All they were going to do was take me, molest me, beat me, shoot at me, hurt me, kick me . . ."

Scaling buildings, in this light, didn't scare him. "If you fall, you're dead," he explained. "It didn't bother me. I lost my mom, lost my dad, had a rough childhood. Life was pretty much in turmoil for me, so if I died it wasn't a big loss."

It was also during this time, and during his stint in the Marines, that he learned how to fight, becoming, in his words, a "killing machine" trained in street fighting and kung fu. The impetus was his father. "My dad said if I couldn't fight, he didn't want me. So I went out and purposefully got beat up to try to learn how to fight."

Though he doesn't fight anymore, he made it clear that he'd retained his training, performing a demonstration for my benefit. "If I did one move on you right now, I'd kill you right here," he said to me gravely as we sat outside a TGI Friday's, where we'd stopped for lunch (or at least I had—he had only a glass of water as part of his fast). "I'd crush your windpipe, I'd rip your eyes out of your head, I would LITERALLY DISMEMBER you right in front of you. Come across you right here"—he leapt to his feet and cocked his arm across his body to grab mine, as if reaching to start a lawnmower—"and take your arm and basically take your bones right out of your body."

But he didn't do any of that, of course. Instead he sat back down and continued his tale.

The turning point, he told me, came one day not long after his Marine days when he fell down in an alley and started speaking in tongues. Overwhelmed by religious fervor, he denounced violence and dedicated himself to the Lord, which meant giving up his lifelong dream of being a police officer.

"When I got the Holy Ghost, let me tell you, it changed me. From that moment on I never touched crack, barbiturates, acid, or LSD. I quit smoking marijuana, and I'd been smoking marijuana since I was nine years old. I put away martial arts. I had three thousand dollars' worth of samurai swords in my collection. Got rid of all them. Decided I didn't want to hurt people anymore. So I took my law enforcement career, and everything that I built my life for, the CIA or going in counterguerrilla operations or terrorist tactics. I canned the whole thing and became Spiderman jumping off the side of buildings. I make a whole lot more money, have a whole lot more fun, and I don't have to shoot people for a living. Which is cool."

He paused to unleash a big squealing laugh, then continued. "Ever since I was seven years old, I wanted to become a cop, get in the CIA.

Now the *CSI* stuff, I get to do it. I get to do the forensic stuff. It's a blast. I can walk on a multimillion-dollar building and have mold, water intrusion, roof blown off, or the building felled, or it's in lawsuit and the building has stopped construction. And I can walk up there and"—he snapped his fingers—"start back up the process. I help some of the biggest general contractors in America, by showing them how to fix their buildings. They can build them but they can't fix them."

Throughout, his wife has been alongside him. He first met her when, out of the military and unsure what to do, he was working at a supermarket outside Seattle, "baggin' groceries with sixteen-year-olds." She was cleaning hotel rooms at the time, and, according to Mulholland, her life was in shambles. "She was a broken violin and I pumped her full of self-esteem," he said. "It took sixteen years for her to get her roar back. Now she plays beautifully, LET ME TELL YOU, SON." The two got married in 1982.

Together, they have four children, all of whom are home-schooled. (Explained Mulholland: "They wanted to show them R-rated movies in the second grade about the Wizard of Oz and about magic and sorcery, and I thought, 'Where are these movies coming from?' ") Scott, twenty-one, is a minister in Louisiana; Michael, twenty, is unemployed but "fixing to be a clothing store manager in Birmingham"; and Sarah is finishing up her schooling. It is his youngest son, John, however, who has fallen hard for his dad's life. When he was twelve, John would steal his dad's rappel ropes and practice descending headfirst from twenty-foot trees. Just recently, Mulholland told me with obvious pride, John had done his first building rappel off an eleven-story office building in Pensacola, on a Sunday morning when no one was around. Mulholland pulled up the photos on his computer: a young, skinny boy, smiling like he had just met his sports hero. Mulholland's plan: when John is ready, he'll set him up with a $20,000 budget and marketing plan, then transfer his service trademark so that John can be the new hero: Spiderman's Professional Highrise Window Cleaning. It will be, Mulholland told me, the completion of a cycle of success that he initiated despite long odds.

"I get angry at people that will not take responsibility. You can become anything! I mean, look at me. My mom put me in the hospital when I was two. My dad was committed insane, I'm abused, I'm arrested and look at me! What's my excuse?" He mimicked a self-pitying voice. " 'Somebody cut me a check every month because I can't function. They took my mommy away when I was four.' That's a cop-out. I'm writing a book about it. I'm going to attack that Dr. Spock mentality. That stupid mentality. The psychologists who look at their mental anguish and say that they should be paid for the rest of their life. Oh, get a JOB! I'm sorry, Chris. I'm going to, I'm going to hit it hard. I'm going to rebuke the psychologists of our day in my book. God forgive them."

He shook his head, then laughed a righteous laugh.

LATER THAT AFTERNOON, WE HEADED to a seven-story condominium complex on the water to evaluate hurricane damage. Again, we raced up to the roof, only this time Mulholland had brought his "Felix Bag," a black roll bag about three feet by two feet. He unzipped it with a flourish to unveil a self-contained climbing kit that included a spaghetti-like mound of climbing rope (13,000-pound breakage) and all manner of carabiners and 9-inch suction cups that could withstand 525 pounds per square inch. Using solely the contents of the bag, he told me, he can reach any spot on the exterior of the building. For bigger jobs, he brings in more gear and, in some cases, constructs a new apparatus for unique problems (to go side to side, for example, he uses wheeled platforms that can roll across the building face).

As I watched, Mulholland ran the rope over the edge of the building so that it reached the ground, secured it with a bowline knot—"I use simple knots and use the same knot every time. That way I repeat it right every time," he explained—and tied it off to the metal piping at the bottom of two solar panel moorings, double-rigging for safety. As he worked he was uncharacteristically silent.

He stepped into a waist-slung climbing harness that bristled with an assortment of clanking metal belays and carabiners, pulled it snug up to his belt, and detached his cell phone. The sight provided a comical contrast: what looked to be a suburban dad in a polo shirt, Rockport easy-walking shoes, white socks, and a pen clipped to his shirt pocket jumping into a harness that looked sophisticated enough to take him up Everest. He clipped the climbing rope in at the front of the belt to a metal clamp that hung down like a big iron phallus. It occurred to me that, considering the pride and sense of self Mulholland derived from his rappelling, it was a rather fitting image.

Straddling the wall, he tested the line again and, as he went over, I thought I saw, if only for a moment, a trace of trepidation in his face, like a brief but telltale flicker of candle flame when a door opens somewhere in a room. He went over slowly, like an uncoordinated child trying to dismount a horse, which surprised me; it was the only ungraceful move I saw him make over two days. Once over the edge, he braced himself against the wall with his feet, knees slightly flexed, and breathed out audibly. Immediately, the brash Spiderman persona returned.

"WHOOOO boy. That's the hard part, stepping over the side," he said, breaking into a grin. "That's the moment where you wonder, am I going to die? Did my competitor cut my rope? You always have to have a little bit of fear. Always respect what you do, always be a little bit afraid. It makes you double-check."

Mulholland showed no fear once on the line. He dropped down, swinging back and forth from one side of the building to the other, throwing in some 360-degree spins for my benefit. As he went, he periodically took readings on the side of the building, snapped photos, and recorded notes with a dictaphone. A couple people in the adjoining building came out to the stairwell to watch. One woman looked up at me quizzically.

"TERMITES," I yelled to her with a serious nod.

She looked startled.

"JUST KIDDING," I yelled back. "INSURANCE EVALUATION."

She looked as though she thought this wasn't any more likely.

Mulholland is accustomed to peculiar reactions. While cleaning windows, he's seen babies born and had women walk around nearly naked, knowing he was there. He almost got shot at by a man who hadn't seen the flyer announcing Mulholland's window cleaning; when Mulholland descended onto his balcony, the man thought he was there to rob him and ran to get his gun.

It was an uneventful rappel on this day, however. Once he reached the bottom, Mulholland came back up the stairs. He was breathing hard and looked seriously amped.

"YEAH, MY BLOOD'S JACKED RIGHT NOW!" he shouted, pumping his arms as if inflating himself into a larger man. "A little seven-story building is good, but get on the big ones and GENTLEMEN, IT'S SHOWTIME! The traffic's stopped, people watching. Honking horns, they SHUT DOWN THE CITY. Sometimes I'll have a guy go out and stop traffic and I'll be up there ready and then I'll come flying out, running across the building. WEEEEHOOOOO! YES SIR, BUDDY!"

Mulholland may be more enthusiastic than his predecessors, but he belongs to a long lineage of wall climbers. Ever since man has built toward the sky there have been those whose job it is to construct, climb, fix, and clean these structures. Before there were skyscrapers, these men were known as "steeplejacks" (and before that, *way* before that, they were known as "slave laborers," the unlucky souls sent up to construct the Egyptian pyramids in 2000 B.C., believed to be the first rigging jobs in history).

Steeplejacks were the maintenance men of early cathedrals in Europe and the former Soviet Union, where no church was a good church unless it boasted a towering steeple and spire, presumably the better to be closer to God. The steeplejacks constructed smokestacks and towers, then clambered up their exteriors to paint them, make repairs, and, when needed, replace the crosses. They were a respected bunch and, to this day, are viewed with a fondness by many Europeans. In Britain, a charismatic steeplejack named Fred Dibnah became something of a celebrity during the late twentieth century. Dibnah, who passed away in 2004 at the age of sixty-six, was featured in a 1979 BBC documentary economically titled *Fred Dibnah: Steeplejack,* and later starred in a number of other documentaries. As he once said of his ascents up chimneys: "A man who says he feels no fear is either a fool or a liar. One mistake up here and it's a half-day out with the undertaker."

In the United States, skyscrapers, those hulking symbols of metropolitan power and prosperity, have provided an even greater challenge. Beginning with the first steel-frame buildings in Chicago in the mid-1880s and continuing with the behemoths of New York, ironworkers have risked their lives to build upward. Some of the most famous were the "skywalkers," Mohawk Indians who were instrumental in the construction of the Empire State Building, among others (many of the tribe are still ironworkers today). Adept at balancing and working at heights, a skill they learned by crossing streams via thin logs, they were said to refuse to work with anyone who was not afraid. Fear was not a sign of weakness but a necessity for survival.

LATER THAT AFTERNOON, WE PARTED ways and made plans to meet the next morning. Back at my hotel, I reflected on my day with Mulholland. He was certainly passionate about his work, more vocally so than anyone else I met while working on the book, and that passion was, if not contagious, certainly evident. On the other hand, I couldn't tell how much of it stemmed from a need to prove himself and how much of it might be part of his innate personality (or, someone more qualified than I might posit, a manic condition of some sort).

I also couldn't tell how much of what he told me was fact and how much was hyperbole. I had already become inured to the terminology he spit out in a fast and furious manner: aerosolization, microtoxins, bioremediation, and so on. Numbers were even better, especially if they involved the word "million." *I was 160 FEET UP, son! It's a FIFTY-MILLION-DOLLAR building.*

One thing had become clear: his marketing MO could be summed up as "Take a Look at Me!" Whereas some people might be embarrassed in certain situations to be named Spiderman, he loved the notoriety and pointed out that it's the best promotional tool in the world (even his wife calls him Spiderman). His stock line was "News media gave it to me about twenty years ago and it kind of stuck. Then I legally changed it. I kind of hang in there for a living." He took every opportunity to milk it; in the early days, he'd do speed rappels from the ceilings of civic centers during trade shows and at the halftime of local sports events. He said he paid to put up twenty-seven different billboards, that he signs autographs often, and that he appeared on a talk radio show on WCOA called *Ask the Expert* where he gave building advice. When we walked into a minimart at one point, he noted the signed photo of him behind the counter; he also suggested that it would be wise of me, as an author, to put photos of him in the book. "Me swinging from a building—that'd be NICE!"

He clearly enjoyed his relative fame, but even more, I think he reveled in the singularity of it. He'd had the chutzpah to find a way to make a living doing something most men either can't or won't do and he was proud of it, essentially finding a calling by following his idiosyncrasies. So he said stuff like, "Formal education will make you a living; self-education will make you a millionaire," and "You can't go to school to learn what I know." On his wall, there was a framed letter from the president of the Exterior Design Institute, for which he helped design protocols. It read: "Some are loners by nature. Others like yourself relish the challenge of soaring by themselves."

The following morning, we headed to his next job together in his truck. Much like Mulholland himself, the vehicle was immaculate and well organized. In the flatbed in the back, he had all his gear separated into plastic boxes: cordless power drill, flashlights, boots, buckets, WD-40, paintbrushes, an extended tool set, a hardhat that read VISITOR, Ziploc bags, batteries, a mobile mold toxin lab, and much more. Up front he kept his folders and files neatly categorized and had a phone log, in which he noted the date, time, purpose, and name and number of every cell phone call he made or received (even, I learned, while driving). A "New Car Scent" air freshener dangled from the rearview mirror.

As he drove, he took the opportunity to lecture me on business.

"You gotta outsource your weaknesses, Chris," he said. "And you gotta keep learning, always keep learning. I spend twenty percent of my time learning new stuff. You have GOT TO BE UP-TO-DATE." He estimated he'd spent $170,000 to $200,000 on continuing education, including travel costs.

As for sleep, he thought it to be, as the saying goes, overrated. He said he could go weeks sleeping only a couple hours a night and that his father had been the same way. I told him that, as a writer, I often went a single night, maybe two, with minimal sleep, but that beyond that I needed to catch up. Besides, I asked, what would make anyone want to stay up all night, night after night?

"PASSION!" he shouted (perhaps unconsciously), hitting the gas momentarily. "If you don't love what you do, get out of it. Because you'll never be successful. You'll always be halfhearted."

But what if it isn't so easy to find something you love, I said. Surely, when he was bagging groceries as a twenty-three-year-old, he didn't know that down the road he'd be scaling buildings and taking mold samples. He interrupted me.

"That never happened with me. I am what I am. Like Popeye said: 'I yam what I yam.' I know I'm doing what I'm supposed to do. And I love it. I get to go to work. I can't wait to go to work. I love what I do. If I ever get to where I don't love it, I won't do it no more. That's a real reality. You got to pick something you like because you never have passion in something you don't love."

He waved his hands to make his point, momentarily leaving the wheel unmoored. "If your passion is helping people and fixing people, become a doctor. If your passion is risking and knowing that every second your life is in your hands, then become a rappel specialist that climbs on buildings."

Still, he'd told me that he'd always wanted to be a cop, and certainly much about his mannerisms suggested that he still yearned for that type of conflict. How did he reconcile that?

He thought briefly. "Well, it's still forensics. Cops would go out and there'd be a bad guy. Or maybe a hit and run. Who's at fault? So in forensics, if you're dealing with law enforcement, same thing as counterguerrilla operations. Bomb blows up, what kind of a C4 was it, what kind of explosive? How many people sell this C4? It's similar to what I'm doing, only I'm trying to make the bad guy look good and bring everybody to the table with a win-win. And that's an art. And that's what I'm best at. I can take a situation where everybody wants to sue. When I'm done, everybody is happy and all the lawsuits are stopped and the building is fixed."

He thought for a moment. "I take horrible situations and fix them. A general contractor builds a fifty-million-dollar building, he's got brand-new condominiums, leaking like a sieve, he's got 150 people mad at him, each one of those has an attorney breathing down his neck. He calls Spiderman to the rescue. I walk in, I tell him to stop the attorneys, I find all the problems. I go to all those individuals and say he's willing to come back and spend $200,000 to fix everything, will you let him out? They say yes. Now that is fun. Now that is the crux of everything I do. I'm like a doctor. We have a sick building. Nobody knows what's wrong. I take blood samples, I take X-rays, I fix the problem. Whatever is good for the building, that's what I'm after. If I fix the building, it's good for everybody. Win-win."

Upon reaching the condo complex, a vacation retreat on the coast that had absorbed a lot of water during the hurricane, he once again ran up two flights of outdoor stairs and, predictably, treated his work as if it were a life or death situation. *This is not condo maintenance, this is a fricking adventure!* He heaved couches instead of sliding them, squinted at walls like they were suspects, ran his fingers over dust and then examined it like a detective and spoke rapidly into a tape recorder. He sniffed the air like a bloodhound, detecting various chemicals and types of spores. When he did find mold, he revealed it with force, as if ripping the mask off a thief: he'd punch through and tear off a small section of the wall with a screwdriver, then look up triumphantly at the landlord and declare righteously: "Like I said . . . MOLD!"

His purpose was to discern whether the building would qualify for insurance reimbursement, so he documented everything with photos. A picture of him with the moisture probe—anything above 8 percent is above normal and the reading at this building was in the 25 percent range—and of all the green spores. "This stuff is gold with the insurance companies," he explained to me. "You always want to shock them with the worst picture first. Show them THE HORROR. "Then walk them through the rest of it and tell a story."

As we continued through the day, Mulholland's stamina was remarkable. After six hours of inspecting apartments, I was tired, my knees were sore from squatting like a baseball catcher every time Mulholland discovered something of note ("LOOK AT THIS SUCKER!"), and I was feeling a bit ill from the mold fumes—and I was only watching. Mulholland, ever in the moment, was cruising right along. If one could bottle his enthusiasm and give it out in little doses—say to spike our breakfast smoothies—I do believe we'd all enjoy our jobs exponentially more. Hell, I'd take a dose before doing anything—attending meetings, riding the subway, conducting interviews.

As he packed up his truck at the end of the day, he explained to me, not for the first time, that he considered his work to be motivated by religion. Not so much in the sense of a Calvinist calling, but as a way to serve God. "I'm not a mighty man, but I'm a man of a mighty God. I believe you can do anything with His help. Everything I've wanted to do, I've gotten. I get a little worried because I'm running out of dreams. I don't really have any more dreams."

He paused, then corrected himself. He still had goals. He wanted a place in the *Guinness Book of World Records* for the longest upside-down speed rappel (he was going for 129 stories, which is taller than any building, so he planned to do it out of a helicopter once he designed a braking system that could handle the friction created by that type of drop). He wanted to write his life story, he wanted to be on Letterman ("I'll deliver him a pizza after climbing up the building!"), and he wanted to cut back on his hours (his plan was to work seven months a year).

As for his Christianity, he explained, "I don't push on nobody. I have my little testimony. But without Jesus Christ, I tell them you ain't got nothing."

We drove in silence for a second. He chuckled.

"Not that I haven't wanted to get into a little Bible study with you, mind you."

Then he told me about his father, Raymond Charles Mulholland, in what became more and more of a *Big Fish* moment as the conversation progressed. According to Spiderman, his father was a Golden Gloves boxer; spent eight years in the Navy; married a woman when he was sixteen in Japan not long before a mortar shell killed her; sang in nightclubs; worked on a top secret Navy ship called the USS *Polaris,* the existence of which the government never admitted; was in a wheelchair for four years and then willed himself out of it; threw sticks of dynamite at policemen; cut off a man's hand with a machete (while the man was pointing a gun at him); tied a ribbon to eighteen linked, open gas caps and threatened to light them; and might have beaten two men to death with a rubber hose.

Oh yeah, and one more thing. "My father could stop a watch with his mind. JUST LIKE THAT!" Spiderman told me. "He could also hypnotize people."

Of course he could.

Perhaps wary of these powers, Mulholland no longer stays in contact with his father. "I don't allow my wife and children around him," he told me as we drove. "He'll threaten you. I don't know if he's killed people, but there's a lot of stuff that he's involved in. The good thing is he's gotten old enough, it's forced him to slow down. He has a police file in Auburn, Washington, that I'm sure is a mile long. You can get the record."

So I did. According to a search of the Washington State Criminal History Repository, Raymond Mulholland went by two aliases—Roy C. Mudd and Rod McQuinn—and had one felony conviction (assault 2) in 1982. He was sentenced to ten years in prison. He now lives in South Dakota.

After my visit, I also learned that sometimes Mulholland's can-do attitude got the better of him, such as in 2003, when he was investigated on three counts of unpermitted construction and contracting without a license, all misdemeanors. Mulholland professed to be "shocked," and Shuman called it a "witch hunt, basically." Regardless, Mulholland was found guilty, and had to provide restitution to the clients involved and refrain from operating without a license.

WHEN I SPOKE TO MULHOLLAND again, nine months after my visit, he'd moved to Gainesville. The location was perfect for work, he said, because he could easily travel to Orlando or Tampa or Fort Lauderdale. He was building an office in the backyard, but hadn't worked much on it. "Too busy," he said, "GETTING STUFF DONE, SON!" A company called Rimkus Engineering had hired him to do building inspections. So he flew to New York, to Louisiana, wherever they needed him. "They said they'd been looking for years for someone who could scale buildings and then they found me," he said by cell phone while driving to a job site. "I told them they were lucky, because you better believe I'm the only one doing this."

That last sentiment is an example of what I found to be Mulholland's most enduring (and endearing) quality: the immense pride he took not only in his work but in his unique set of skills. I saw it in the way he treated each project as the be-all and end-all; he spoke of mold investigations as if he were a code breaker in World War II and the country's safety might be at stake. He confided that he liked stress ("Sometimes I wait until the last minute just so I can catch the stress. I *gotta* have the stress"). When I spoke to Shuman, the architect

Mulholland worked with while in Pensacola, he remembered being taken aback the first time he met Mulholland. "He came into my office and he gets real passionate," recalled Shuman. "I said 'You need to go sit down because you're about to hyperventilate here.' "

I'd met people like Mulholland before: Call them Amplifiers, for lack of a better word. By treating each aspect of a job, and his life, as crucial to the overall success of the endeavor—amplifying its importance—he is able to function in what borders on a constant deadline atmosphere. Some people would crack under this concocted pressure; Mulholland thrives on it. He truly does want to sweat the small stuff. He reminded me of an athlete who turns to drugs off the field to maintain the high he feels on it; only with him, it's re-creating the thrill of jumping off buildings.

That said, much of his job doesn't need amplifying. He's already risking his life on a regular basis, and, as he took every opportunity to point out, he works on multimillion-dollar projects. This is already rather stressful stuff, and would occupy most of us. But, even so, he searched for the rush elsewhere. At one point, for example, he nonchalantly told me that for eight years or so, he'd played paintball as a hobby, "you know, for the sake of my kids." Only it wasn't just his kids' gear he bought; he invested $3,000 a year in it and traveled to tournaments. I pity the poor weekend warriors who lined up opposite Mulholland. I can just imagine him crawling through the grass, "snooping and pooping," as he told me such sneak attacks were called in his marine days, belly pressed to the ground and camo paint on his face, only to pop up and drill some suburban father from five feet away. WHOOOOOO, indeed.

While many people struggle with the transition from military to civilian life, Mulholland had found a way to re-create that buzz in his work. More so than anyone else I met during the course of writing the book, Mulholland didn't just like his job; he *needed* it. It was almost a way of self-medicating, a way to channel all the unruly energy harbored inside of him. Put the man behind a desk and who knows what outlet, legal, savory, or otherwise, he'd find. But put him high above the earth, dangling from a cable in the midday sun, and he is sated. This may seem strange to some of us, but, as Mulholland told me at one point, "You have to be a little bit crazy to do this job."

And maybe, in his case, that's the best thing about it.

TWO

THE EYEBALL ARTISAN

MOST OF THE TIME, WHEN you ask people what they do for a living, they tell you in a sentence or two. If they're particularly proud of their work, or they sell things—especially something they could get you a great deal on tomorrow like a home appliance—they might produce a business card. That business card might even have a photo on it.

Then there are people like Willie Danz, whose identity is practically fused with his career. Here is what happens when you ask Willie what he does for a living.

> YOU (at cocktail party, making small talk): So, Willie, what do you do?

> **WILLIE** (smiling and plunging his hand into his left pocket rather suspiciously): I'm glad you asked that!
>
> **YOU** (wondering if he's going to produce some scary religious pamphlet): Okay . . .
>
> **WILLIE** (holding up an eyeball that looks disconcertingly lifelike): I make these!
>
> **YOU** (taken aback): What in God's name is that?
>
> **WILLIE**: I'm glad you asked!
>
> And so on . . .

Danz uses this trick because were he to say, "I'm an ocularist," (pronounced *ock-u-LAIR-ist*), people would probably assume he was a doctor of some sort. And, although many of his patients address him as such—perhaps because he wears a white doctor's coat, has a doctorlike office, and acts rather like a doctor—he is not a doctor. And if he said, "I make prostheses," which is the technical term for the artificial eyes, people might envision him working in a plastic appendage factory, fashioning fake arms. Then again, if he said he made glass eyes, the best-known term for the prostheses, it would be incorrect on two counts. First, the prostheses are no longer made of glass, and haven't been since the 1940s (at least not in the States). Second, what he makes aren't actually entire eyeballs, but rather, concave acrylic shells that fit on top of the eye muscle—or an implant made to mimic the muscle—sort of like a bike helmet over a child's skull.

But the main reason Danz carries around the eyeballs is because he really, really likes to talk about his work. Even among ocularists, a close-knit community filled with many second- and third-generation practitioners, he stands out. Not only because he's one of the most accomplished (though he is) and he makes all manner of unusual eyes for horses, dogs, and prisoners (though he does); but also because he is a fifth-generation ocularist (one of his distant relatives made the first glass eye). Some people rebel against the family business; I was curious what made him so passionate about his.

. . .

I FIRST MET DANZ AT 8:30 on a Wednesday morning at his twenty-second-floor office in downtown San Francisco, just up from Union Square (he has a second office in Santa Rosa). Previously leased by a dentist, the place retained the hygienic feel of its former tenant; I could picture the ghosts of nervous preadolescents fidgeting in the waiting area. A friendly twenty-seven-year-old named Rachael sat at a desk in the reception area. Rachael came in three days a week, she told me, mainly to do filing, billing, and, when she had time, extra painting on the prostheses (she was particularly good with the irises). Off the reception area was a lab room and a patient room, which had a barber's chair and two large south-facing windows. The orientation was important, Danz explained, because to accurately judge the color of the prostheses, indirect light, either northern or southern exposure, is preferred. ("A noonday northern light with slightly overcast sky is the absolute best," he told me, somewhat wistfully.)

Handsome in a nonthreatening way, Danz looks like he plays a doctor on TV. Though fifty-four years old, he could pass for a man in his forties; he has a full head of brown hair, which he keeps impeccably combed, smooth skin, and the upbeat manner of someone who just found a five-dollar bill in his pocket. He smiles a lot, has a goofy laugh that he uses to warm up his patients, and speaks in an even, reassuring tone, like an airline pilot pointing out the Grand Canyon below to your left. Every day, he wears some variation of dress shirt and tie, over which he buttons a white lab coat. Ever the professional, he keeps a pack of mints handy—"good breath is important"—and has a small mirror in his lab so that before patients arrive he can double-check the status of his hair.

His has been an illustrious career. Danz estimates he's made more than fifteen thousand prostheses in thirty years in the business. He has served as president of the American Society of Ocularists and is a charter member of the National Examining Board of Ocularists. In a field that numbers only 170 or so in the United States (and 400 in the world), he is renowned, both for his work and for his family name. His patients come from across the country for his services, the cost running between $2,000 and $2,400 per prosthesis. (The eyes are covered under "durable medical equipment," an insurance heading that includes wheelchairs, prosthetic arms and legs, oxygen tanks, and bedpans—a grouping that many ocularists believe does their "artwork" a disservice.) One woman, a fashion model, flew in from the Philippines to get a Danz eye; another regularly comes in from Washington, D.C., for checkups. Danz's work is so convincing that nurses at UCSF, where he spends two days a month working with children who have retinoblastoma, occasionally attempt to dilate the fake eye rather than the real one just prior to anesthesia. Some patients have a hard time convincing onlookers that they are indeed sightless; one woman with two striking green-irised Danz prostheses was accosted for sitting in the handicapped seat of a bus. After futilely pleading her case, she had to remove her eyes to prove they were fake.

On this morning, the first patient was Christina, a woman in her forties receiving her annual checkup. She'd lost an eye—I couldn't tell which at first—to glaucoma. Doctors had tried numerous surgeries to save it but to no avail. She took a seat in the chair and Danz made small talk for a couple minutes before picking up a small suction cup–like device.

"Let's have a look then, shall we?" he said.

Then he stuck the suction cup onto her eye and pulled it out.

Earlier in the morning, anticipating this very moment, I had spent a couple minutes in my hotel bathroom practicing what I hoped was a clinically detached facial expression—lips pursed, eyebrows slightly raised, *nothing to see here*. It came in handy.

The woman's orbital socket was moist and pinkish white. Imagine if one replaced an eyeball with an oyster and you'll get the general idea. The sight was not disgusting so much as disorienting. My brain wanted to fill in the missing space with something—without the twin markers of the eyes, I didn't know where to focus my gaze. Danz, as would be expected, was totally inured to the sight. He's seen so many eye sockets that they inhabit his sleep. "I had a dream that I went into the bathroom, looked into the mirror and saw that I'd lost an eye," Danz told me at one point. "At first I was freaked out and thought, 'Oh no!' Then I started looking around in there and trying to figure out how I was going to fit myself."

Like those who go into medicine, Danz has to be able to view a patient's anatomy in blueprint fashion. When I asked him if he was ever bothered by what he saw, he cocked his head for a moment and thought before answering, "People say, 'You *have* to look in eye sockets.' Well, I think there can be beauty in an eye socket. If the surgeon was good and there's good tissue in there, it can be beautiful."

This comment made me pause. Not only because it was unexpected but because of Danz's sincerity. It occurred to me that if one were to design a litmus test for whether someone had found a calling, it might be done with one easy question: do you see beauty in the details of your work? Certainly, this is easier if you're a florist, or an interior designer or, well, almost anything other than an ocularist. And even then, it would seem to me much easier to see the prostheses—the part of the job that could more readily qualify as "art"—as beautiful and maintain a clinical neutrality about the eye sockets. Then again, considering all Danz has seen and heard, he wouldn't survive long if he didn't feel this way. There are innumerable ways to lose an eye, and most of them, as I was to learn, are quite ghastly.

The second patient of the day was a good example. Forty-three years old, Brett accompanied most sentences with a self-conscious staccato laugh. He had lost the use of his right eye when he was five years old while playing with a dart gun in the backyard. When the gun jammed, he did what children do in such situations: he turned the pistol around and looked down the barrel to see if he could figure out what was wrong. Then, as he put it, "It went *POW!*"

He remembers screaming and then running into the kitchen to find his mother, who, upon seeing her son with a dart protruding from his eye socket and blood running down one side of his face, promptly passed out. "My poor mother," he said with a wan smile, "was traumatized for life."

And this is one of the less gory stories. Danz estimates that 40 percent of his patients lose their vision due to eye disease and tumors, the most common being malignant melanoma and retinoblastoma, a congenital cancer. Another 5 percent lose an eye to congenital anomalies such as congenital anophthalmia, when a child is born without an eye. The rest can be attributed to what is widely termed "trauma." This includes relatively mundane mishaps such as the female patient who was hit in the eye when her date tried to show her the proper golf backswing, and the young man I met that afternoon who had been shot in the eye with a BB gun as a fifteen-year-old (cue a thousand admonishing parents).

Then there are the more unusual cases. Such as the woman who was attacked by a grizzly bear on a hike in Alaska and, as Danz remembered it, "had a good part of her face torn off" when the bear moved to protect its cubs. Another woman was walking through a field when a great horned owl swooped down and landed on her head, clawing at her eyes. Then there was the local police officer who was playing paintball. Explained Danz: "He got taken out of the game, called himself safe, and lifted up his goggles when—poof!—he got hit in the face."

I also heard some disturbing, doubt-the-goodness-of-humanity stories. One woman I met lost the use of an eye when, as a grad student at Penn, she was attacked, raped, and stabbed in the face. Danz told of a husband who, in a fit of rage, reached in and pulled out his wife's eye, then held it up to her face and said, "Look what I did." Twice Danz has treated patients who tore out their own eyes. "Both of them were coming down off drugs," Danz told me. "The first guy, his girl had recently broken up with him. The second guy, he felt he'd developed an evil eye. You know the Scripture? Something like, 'If thine eye offends ye, pluck it out.' Well, he did."

It takes a certain type of person to enter a line of work that requires coming into contact, even if only secondhand, with this type of trauma. Months later, I was still disturbed by the stories Danz had told me (not to mention apprehensive around golfers). When I relayed some of the tales to my friends, many recoiled—except for my brother, who's an ER doctor. He pushed me for more details. *Interesting. Was the orbital bone damaged? Was there massive hemorrhaging?* But, like I said, the normal people were disgusted.

Danz's wife, Bobbie, a schoolteacher, tried to fill in for her husband once when he had broken his arm, but, as she told me, "My stomach doesn't do so well when you get to the socket." For many years Danz hoped that his son, Dave, would follow him into the business to create a sixth generation, but Dave couldn't deal with the emotional carnage. "I could embrace the paperwork, the lab work, and the patients, but when it came to the children, that was my downfall," he told me. "To see the pain and to constantly hear their stories wore on me."

Willie, on the other hand, sees the stories as part of the healing process, and his role as that of a listener. "I tend to just let them talk," he told me while resetting his lab in between patients. "Listen and not be judgmental. Agree, nod. The one thing ocularists provide that doctors don't is a chance to unload. Doctors often come in after other people have done a lot of the prep, and they are real busy. I really make an effort, and have the time, to let them talk."

As a result, he's heard some unusual stories, catered to unusual requests, and met all manner of people. His patients include lawyers, doctors, politicians, a commercial airline pilot, a federal judge, the elderly, and the homeless. He's done eyes for forty horses, including a show horse owned by Bo Derek that Danz estimates was worth "at least a million," and four dogs, including a police canine in Reno. When a Hispanic woman who'd always had brown prostheses came in asking for "Elizabeth Taylor eyes," he went looking through magazines to make them for her. He's made a Harley Davidson eye for a biker, an American flag eye for a veteran, a 24-karat gold skull for a man with an eye patch, and, once, a yellow and green cat eye for a man whose nickname was "Cat." One patient kept showing up with his good eye bloodshot. "He finally admitted he was smoking a lot of grass," Danz said, chuckling. "I asked him if he was going to quit and he said no. So I had no choice but to make him a stoned prosthesis with extra blood vessels. I said, 'If you ever quit the habit, let me know and I can take them out.' "

Another time, he helped catch a criminal. He used to work with patients at the California Medical Facility at Vacaville, which provides care for male felons. When one of the convicts escaped and burglarized a house, he lost his prosthesis while fleeing from a second-story window. The police found the eye, on the back of which Danz had written the patient's name, and took it to a local ocularist who identified it as Danz's work. Danz examined it and remembered the patient; not long after, Danz was on *America's Most Wanted*, explaining the case. A year after his escape, Aaron "Eyeball" Harris was apprehended.

During my two days in the office I met, among others, a peppy fourteen-year-old skateboarder who was born without one eye; a nineteen-year-old deaf boy who'd been coming in since he was three months old; Claudette, an African-American Pentecostal minister who, prior to coming into the office, had been preaching enthusiastically, unaware that she'd put in her eye upside down (the parishioners, Claudette recounted, thought she'd really channeled the Holy Spirit on that day); and John, who'd been coming in since 1977, when he'd lost an eye to shards of glass in an auto accident. Danz greeted each like a friend. With the help of a Polaroid—he snaps one of every patient—he says he can remember almost everyone he's ever worked on. "I feel like once I make a prosthesis for someone, I become part of their life," he told me in a rare moment of emotional analysis. "And they become part of mine."

OCULARISTRY IS UNIQUE IN THAT it straddles the line between art and medicine but qualifies as neither. Though he has the bearing of a physician, Danz refers to the prostheses as "the artwork," or "the painting," and labors much as a painter does over his work. One time, he told me, he spent two hours reworking a particularly tricky blue-green iris to make sure he got the color just right. Over the course of two days, I saw him make five prostheses, each the end product of months of work and three or four patient visits.

It is a painstaking process. Danz begins by taking an impression of a patient's eye with dental alginate—squeezing it into the eye socket and letting it set to the contours (though messy, the process is painless). Using that impression, he creates a model for size, which he checks against the patient on a return visit. If it fits, he then creates the real thing, using acrylic. To grind, polish, and shape the prosthesis, he uses all manner of instruments, from a volcanic pumice—"sort of like liquid sandpaper"—to a wet cotton rag wheel that looks like a miniature automated car wash to a dental drill used for grinding away excess plastic. This may sound rather laborious, but not to Danz. "One of the first things I enjoyed about the profession was the lab work, making things shiny and smooth," he said, in between happy bouts of polishing. "Plus, you get to get messy and have fun at the same time."

Next comes the painting, for which he moves to a small bench littered with tools: a scalpel blade to scratch away colors, an artist's pencil, tweezers for positioning the red "blood vessel" threads, a set of Windsor-Newton Series 7 sable brushes ("the best you can get"), and eight colors of oil paint: titanium white, cobalt blue, lamp black, alizarin crimson, burnt sienna, raw umber, Payne's gray, and raw sienna. He keeps a paper towel beneath the glass slab that he uses as a palette. "At the end of the day, it has all these colors and splashes and it's almost a work of art itself," he said, admiring it. "I've been tempted to frame it."

To create a base, he uses a mixture of monomer and polymer painting medium, a clear liquid that smells like a science lab gone horribly wrong. Think formaldehyde mixed with that Chinese food that's been sitting in the bottom of the fridge for six weeks. To combat the fumes, Danz keeps a small fan whirring next to the bench for "positive air flow." It wasn't quite positive enough for me; while watching him paint, I had to take discreet trips to the other side of the room every few minutes—"Hey, what's this over here?"—to keep from feeling ill. Whether through familiarity, cognitive dissonance, or sheer will, Danz has reached the point where he claims to enjoy the smell. "I miss it sometimes if I'm away from the lab," he told me. "I have been known to say," he added, "that I love the smell of monomer in the morning."

Once he's fashioned a prosthesis, he checks it again against the patient and then takes it to the lab to finish it up, adjusting for fit, color, and the patient's preference. If it's too large, he shaves away acrylic with a grinder as if using a carrot peeler.

If this seems like a terribly inexact science, that's because it is. Ocularistry remains stubbornly human despite attempts to digitize the process. So far, prostheses produced using computer models don't look as realistic as acrylic ones, and, more important, eyes produced digitally last only a year or two. So ocularists must paint. This makes ocularists happy.

When he's painting, Danz looks something like a surgeon, with the tweezers and the lab coat and the scalpel. And in a way I suppose he is: a surgeon for the disembodied. In society and mythology the eyes are often romanticized as the windows to the soul. Danz may not be able to replace an eye for the person who values it most—the patient herself—but he replaces it for the rest of the world. He holds a little piece of hope in his hand, in essence a person's self-esteem, and it makes him a savior of sorts. So he is gentle, caressing the polymer to find the imperfections and carefully examining it through the magnifying goggles he wears.

The most stressful part of his job, he explained, is the delivery of the finished prosthesis. "I try to be so careful but sometimes it doesn't turn out the way you want. Some people, no matter how good the product, aren't going to enjoy the finished result. But I know when I've done good work. If someone's not happy with it then I know it's psychological." And what of those people who aren't happy? Danz shrugged. "There are people who go from ocularist to ocularist searching for the

Holy Grail of eyes. These are the people who haven't dealt with the loss completely."

Like any perfectionist, he tortures himself over every last detail. His first reaction when he delivers a prosthesis is *what did I do wrong?* "It takes five or ten minutes before I can appreciate it and say, 'Hey, that's pretty good.' " He frowned. "I guess everybody has a certain amount of self-doubt in what they do."

Danz said this almost apologetically, but it is an important point. People who lack that apprehensiveness are less likely to be engaged by their job. In the author Mihaly Csikszentmihalyi's idea of "flow," that feeling of being "lost in the moment" that we all strive for in work, he describes being most drawn into an activity when it is perfectly balanced on an axis between being challenging, so as to engage us, but not so challenging that we become discouraged. Were Danz to see his work as monotonous, each eye merely another task to be finished, I imagine he wouldn't last long in the job. To him, however, each eye is a chance for expression. He proudly told me that each of his prostheses contains a "signature," a red thread that mimics a blood vessel at the six o'clock mark on the eye. All this means, really, is that he has placed a red thread where other ocularists don't, but its significance is that this marks the eye as Danz's. He also uses an indicator dot at the top of the eye, a blue star for boys and a red heart for girls, so they know which side is up. "Of course," he said while showing me an example, "if you put that in the book, other ocularists will start doing it."

It occurred to me, watching Danz at work, that the process of crafting an eye is not unlike the process of finding a career. When he initially examines someone, Danz pulls out a box with ten rows of five prostheses, fifty eyes in all, each a different color, each staring up blankly at the ceiling. One by one, he holds up the shades next to the patient's good eye, testing for the best color match. Sometimes he goes through the better part of the box, looking for something that fits perfectly for the person. Sometimes he thinks he's found the right match, commits to it, and invests the better part of a week making a new prosthesis only to find, once the patient returns, that he got it wrong. At that point, he has two options. He can make that one work or he can go back to the drawing board and start again.

Without exception, he chooses to start again and get it right.

ARTIFICIAL EYES HAVE BEEN AROUND since the time of the ancient Egyptians, who would place painted pearl shells into the sockets of the dead during burial. Such devices were mainly ceremonial until, in the late Renaissance, Venetian craftsmen began making glass eyes, which were fragile and uncomfortable; imagine choosing a seashell at random and sticking it into your eye socket and you get the idea. Still, they remained the standard until 1832, when a German glassblower named Ludwig Müller-Uri—a distant relative of Danz's—made a breakthrough in the fabrication of glass eyes, establishing the Germans' reputation as the masters of the glass replica.[1]

Glass eye production began in the United States in the 1850s, in response to German ocularists who were traveling the country, fitting and selling eyes from town to town. Local doctors took to buying full sets, which led to a haphazard, first-come, first-serve business; if all that was left in the set was hazel, you were getting hazel, even if your other eye was blue.

In 1903, Danz's father, Gottlieb Theodore "Ted" Danz, arrived in the United States as a three-year-old with his father from Lauscha, Germany, the cradle of ocularistry. When Ted was old enough, he went back to Lauscha for three years to train. It was a rigid, efficient process. As students worked, an instructor would walk around the room with a rolled-up newspaper. If Ted did something wrong, the instructor

---

1. Müller-Uri was originally a doll maker whose specialty was crafting realistic dolls' eyes with blown glass. When his seven-year-old son lost an eye in an accident, Müller-Uri was so devastated that he spent the next twenty years trying to make a perfect glass eye as a replacement. The finished product was so impressive that he was overwhelmed by people who wanted one of their own.

would whap him on the head with the newspaper. The teacher wouldn't tell Ted what he'd done wrong; Ted was supposed to figure it out for himself. "A little different," Willie joked, "from how they train ocularists today."

Ted established an office with his father in 1929, on the brink of the Depression. The two made glass eyes and sold them for whatever price customers could afford. If a patient had one dollar, then one dollar it was. To make sales, Ted traveled the country by train, stopping in small towns just as his forebears had done half a century before.

The next major advance in the field came during World War II, or, as the delightfully ocularist-centric book *Eye for an Eye* puts it: "In 1941 a global tragedy ultimately resulted in greatly improved artificial eyes." Cut off from the German supply of glass eyes, Americans were forced to make do. American Optical Company of Southbridge, Massachusetts, working with army and navy dentists, developed the first artificial acrylic eyes, which were essentially dental products reformulated to fit into orbital sockets (to this day, many of ocularistry's tools are dental). The new eyes were not only easier to make but more durable; today, the average glass eye lasts two to four years while an acrylic one lasts seven to ten years, or longer. (Glass eyes are still made in Germany, where, according to Danz, an influential glass eye union has managed to maintain the status quo.)

Ted Danz embraced the innovation and opened an office in San Francisco, where he lived with his wife, Vera, a beautician who, in keeping with the family's unusual career choices, once worked preparing corpses for funeral viewings (on her first week on the job, she learned the hard way that, without body heat, someone's hair will not naturally dry over night). The couple had four sons and each, at one point or another, dabbled in the family business.

As the years passed, ocularistry shed its traveling salesman stigma. In 1971, the American Society of Ocularists began to certify practitioners, and in 1980 the ASO began holding conferences alongside the American Academy of Ophthalmology in a joint scientific session.

(Ocularists must now pass board exams and be recertified every six years.) The field had finally gained an important measure of legitimacy.

Still, it is not hard to understand why eye doctors would hesitate to associate with ocularists (Danz said he had good ophthalmologist friends who used to pretend not to know him at conferences). "Sometimes we've been described as the morticians of ophthalmology," Danz explained to me. "Because when things go wrong, someone loses an eye. So for an ophthalmologist to acknowledge you in certain situations is to acknowledge failure. Doctors don't want to make mistakes." He laughed. "That's why they say stuff like, 'Complications occur.' " He paused. "Fortunately, that's no longer the case. The majority of ophthalmologists appreciate what we can do, just as we appreciate what they can do surgically."

Despite Willie's bloodline, he wasn't interested in a career in ocularistry at first. Instead, after two years of junior college, he enrolled at San Francisco State in 1970 intent on learning about computers because, as he quite correctly believed, "they seemed to be the future." Not that he was all that interested. "It was a choice that I made because I had to make a choice," he told me. "And I was a Trekkie, so I thought computers were cool." During school, he worked part-time in his father's lab with his oldest brother, Phil, also an ocularist. It was then that, with each acrylic eye he crafted, he began to feel drawn to the work.

How much of the attraction was the pleasure of meeting the family expectation, he didn't know at first. For a young man, it can be hard to untangle the desire for a father's acceptance from internal reasons to enter a career. The golfer Jack Nicklaus, for example, almost became a registered pharmacist. As recounted in *Sports Illustrated*, after winning the U.S. Amateur title in 1961, Nicklaus had to decide between making a go at golf—at the time, an unlikely way to make a living because of the relatively paltry tournament prizes—and running the family pharmacy in Columbus, Ohio, as was expected by his father, Charlie. Nicklaus was so flummoxed by the decision that when he finally did decide to turn pro, writing a letter to the USGA to declare his status, he couldn't bring himself to mail it. His wife, Barbara, fed up with his uncertainty, found it and mailed it herself. Nicklaus went on to win seventy-three PGA tournaments.

There are other forces at work in any such decision. For one, the promise of success. In a 2002 study, Arnold Chevalier at the London School of Economics found that sons who follow their fathers into careers are 5 to 8 percent better off in their first decade of work, a difference Chevalier postulated was due to the "transmission of human capital," which he defined as genetics and upbringing. Certainly, there is an advantage—whether it's transmission or nepotism or familiarity—but many children are inclined to rebel at first. In the controversial book *Born to Rebel: Birth Order, Family Dynamics, and Creative Lives,* MIT researcher Frank Sulloway concluded that firstborn children identify more strongly with authority and are more likely to be conformists. He found younger siblings, in contrast, to be more adventurous and rebellious, and therefore less likely to follow a father's lead. By this logic, Willie, the youngest in the family, was an unlikely candidate to be carrying eyeballs around in his pocket.

So what happened? There was a period, at the end of his college days, when he had no idea what he wanted to do. At the time, about all he was sure about in life was his own new family; he'd married Bobbie, his high school sweetheart, one month after graduating from college, and he'd only waited that long because of his father's stipulation that he couldn't get married without a degree. "I grew up really naïve," Willie told me. "I called them my fog days. Not until I got married and started working in the business did I see my future clearly."

So was there, I asked, an aha moment that pushed him toward becoming an ocularist?

"I think it was more a gradual realization," he said while sitting in his lab, painting a prosthesis. "This is what I want to do, but, even more, this is what I was born to do. I almost feel like this is a calling." This, of course, caught my attention, as I hadn't brought up the word yet. Danz stopped, took off his goggles, and looked up at me. "When I go some-where and patients or ocularists say, 'Oh, you're a Danz,' that's a great feeling. Obviously, my dad and brothers had a lot to do with that."

Willie apprenticed with Phil, was certified in 1975, and not long af-ter joined his brothers. For a slice of time, there were four Danz boys working in one office at 457 Sutter Street in San Francisco. This, as it turned out, was three too many. Willie started his own office in 1976, Phil eventually moved to Sacramento, where he runs a practice, and Ted has since passed away. Willie's twin brother, Walt, made a go at ocular-istry but, though he enjoyed the technical aspect, didn't feel comfortable dealing with patients, much as Willie's son Dave doesn't. Walt now owns apartment complexes in Vallejo, California.

These days, there are three Danzes (plus Ted's stepson who uses the Danz name, something Willie frowns upon) practicing in the United States, including Randy Danz, Willie's cousin, in New Jersey. Or, as Willie pointed out proudly, "one out of every sixty ocularists is a Danz." Still, Willie had yet to hire an apprentice when I visited, in large part be-cause he was still holding out hope that Dave would join him. "The door is closing," Willie told me. "There's still a slit but he's never told me he has an interest."

In 2003, Willie went to Lauscha with his brother Phil and his cousin Randy. He keeps a photo album of the trip in his office and, on my first day there, he pulled it out. There he was in front of the church where his father was baptized. There he was at the old glass eye factory. Clearly, Willie took great pride in his family connection to his work. This ex-plained why he first entered into it, but it doesn't explain why he stuck with it.

When I asked him about the appeal, one of the first things he men-tioned was the rewards of dealing with patients. Though he's not a doc-tor, his patients often treat him with a similar degree of trust and respect. (And that is no small matter; in a 2003 poll conducted by CNN, USA Today, and Gallup, respondents were asked to rate the honesty and ethical standards of people in different professions. The top five most-respected fields were medical in nature: in order, nurses, doctors, veterinarians, pharmacists, and dentists, all of which scored between 60 and 83 percent in the "very high" or "high" range. At the bottom were car salesmen, at 7 percent, followed by insurance salesmen [12 percent], and not that far behind, journalists [25 percent].) Danz receives Christmas cards and thank-you notes from patients, and, more immediately, some of the daily reactions he provokes are quite powerful. Claudette, the Pentecostal minister, began crying as she spoke about the transformative effect of her prosthesis. "It's amazing. I can't see out of it but the illusion of sight is so profound," she said. "When my lid was lifted, it lifted my whole spirit. Just the fact that I'm no longer looking like Quasimodo—I'm Claudette again."

Brett, the patient who'd lost his eye to the dart gun, was similarly encouraged. "Before the accident, I used to be the kid on top of the jungle gym," he said as the three of us sat in the patient room. "Then I withdrew a bit and became more shy. Now, even people who know I have one fake eye can't guess which one it is." In a month, Brett told Danz and me, he was headed to Europe to go deep-sea fishing and to climb the Matterhorn. He looked at Danz. "Thanks to you, I'm reversing my shyness."

Danz nodded and grinned just a bit. "From the top of the jungle gym back to the Matterhorn, huh?"

Brett laughed his staccato laugh. "I never thought of it that way."

I FOUND DANZ TO BE a prime example of how one's identity and one's work, even unusual work, can become intertwined to the point that the two are nearly impossible to separate. There is reason to think this is a rather enviable fate; according to a 2002 study done by Professor Barry Goldman at the University of Arizona, people who have a strong sense of identity tend to have not only greater work satisfaction but greater overall life satisfaction. Danz certainly fits the profile; this is a man, clearly, who likes eyes. His lab is a shrine of sorts to the sightless, full of inside jokes: a cup with a depiction of the Cyclops character from the movie *Monsters, Inc.*, a plastic skull into which he's inserted two prostheses, another skull wearing an eye patch. ("I tell people that was my last patient who didn't pay his bill. You know, the eye patch.") He has a dozen drawers full of glass eyes, some of which date back to the 1800s. There are wax eyes and giant horse eyes—looking at them, with them looking back up at you, is a creepy experience. I counted 117 eyes, in various stages of completion, on his counter (and I went home with my own—the best blue-eyed match he had in his collection—which I would use to great effect in social situations for weeks afterward). At one time, Danz even made earrings and cuff links out of eyes—as he said wistfully, "when I had a lot of free time."

It is a telling comment, as by definition "free time" usually means one is involved in something other than work. But for Danz, life is all degrees of ocularistry. Every day, he eats a "working lunch" or soup, scarfed down in between patients. As his wife, Bobbie, told me at one point during my visit, "When Willie goes to parties, he tends to get bored. But when someone asks about his work, well, he just lights up. Then he can go on for hours." Willie says the hardest part of his work is "over-scheduling," because "it's very hard for me to say no."

Danz was so proud of his work that he took to posing questions to himself if he felt I had neglected to do so. "People ask me if this takes a steady hand and I say yes." Or, "People ask me if I'm an artist and I say the only other painting I do is ceilings and walls with a big roller. My art is within the ocular world." He told me that he can examine a prosthesis and immediately know who made it. Once a year, he gives speeches at ocularists' meetings, where Bobbie is the registration chairperson. "She wishes I wouldn't lecture so much," he said. Countered Bobbie: "I'm trying to have weekends be free, to release him from the office."

I wondered if "extract" wouldn't be the better word.

• • •

AFTER OUR SECOND DAY TOGETHER, Danz and I headed to a local hotel bar with Bobbie for a post-work drink. Away from the office, and out
of uniform, he loosened up. He told stories of his early days in San
Francisco ("saw Zeppelin live"); of the wacky exploits of ocularists at industry conferences (including the "borrowing" of a medical vehicle for
late-night partying); and female patients who came on to him ("I guess
there's a certain appeal to being the ocularist"). Then there are ocularist
high jinks from his younger days. "Sometimes at parties," he said, swish-
ing his red wine, "after a few drinks we used to pour alginate on someone's face. We'd put straws in their nose and pour in stone to make a
casting. It would look like a death mask but it was really just a positive
representation." He chuckled. "Of course, sometimes we'd leave the
mask on for a while and pretend like we'd left the room, just to spook
whoever was wearing it."

He smiled at the memory.

"Hey," he said. "Wanna hear an ocularist joke?"

I nodded. Bobbie rolled her eyes.

"So this guy gets his eye enucleated, that is, surgically removed, and
gets a wooden eye. He's real insecure about it and for months he doesn't
leave the house. Then one Friday night he gets up the courage to go to
a dance. He walks in and sees this girl with a hunchback who looks just
as downcast. He gathers up his courage and walks over. 'Would you
dance with me?'

" 'Would I?' " she says.

"He points at her and yells, 'Hunchback! Hunchback!' "

Danz guffawed. He was in his element, and I found myself admiring the purity of it. Goofy and obsessive, he was proud of what he did
and how he did it. It made him feel good. Sure, to a certain extent he had
fallen into his work by following the family line, and this backfires on
some people, breeding a sense of emptiness and a loss of identity. For
him, the effect was the opposite; the job empowered him. He liked being good at something and being respected for it. He enjoyed the art, the
reward of the healing aspect, the independence of it, and the connection

to something bigger than himself, namely a tradition of family excellence. He was also a practical guy, so he saw it as a good living for his family, and satisfying that need made him feel good.

He was who he was. Not a doctor, an ocularist. As his son told me, "It takes a certain type of person to do what he does. This is my dad's calling in life and he owns it."

THREE

THE LADY LUMBERJACK

OCCASIONALLY, A PERSON WILL GO a good chunk of her life unaware of a latent talent and then—WHOOSH—like hearing a stereo suddenly switched from mono to surround sound, she realizes that, oh, that's what has been missing. Sometimes this revelation occurs while writing, or painting, or cooking. Other times, as in the case of Penny Halvorson, it occurs while assaulting a block of wood with an axe.

By the time you finish reading this sentence, Halvorson could have picked up a chainsaw, started it, and cut through a twenty-inch log of white pine three times: slicing down, up, and down again. This takes her approximately eight seconds, depending on the day and the wood and her technique. By the time you've finished this sentence as well,

Halvorson could have grabbed a saw and *manually* churned through a sixteen-inch log, something she can do in fourteen seconds. If she was having a really good day—like when she won one of her four lumberjack sports world championships—she could have done it in thirteen. Chopping through an eleven-inch-thick block of aspen with just an axe takes a little longer, because she has to attack it from both sides and swing from over her head in great sweeping arcs, but it's safe to say that she could have whacked through the entire block by the time you've read the last word in this paragraph, this one right . . . here.

Halvorson is many things—a forty-five-year-old mother of two and grandmother of five, a fourth-generation logger, a wood aficionado—but primarily and most passionately, she is a lumberjill. This means she competes in events such as the underhand chop, the "hot saw," and axe tossing, though she prefers the title "lady lumberjack" to "lumberjill" because it's less cutesy. And if there was one thing I learned during my time with Halvorson, it is that when she prefers to be called something, it's best to go along with her wishes. That tends to be the case when you're dealing with a five-foot-eight, 290-pound woman with biceps the size of baking hams, tattoos up and down her arms, and the ability to wield a sixty-five-pound chainsaw as if it were a feather duster.

If Halvorson has a defining characteristic in her work life, it is that she takes absolutely no shit. Sort of a no-shit, no-service policy. She got this quality from her mother, but it is also a product of being the first woman to compete in a traditionally, and overwhelmingly, male activity. The tales of her chutzpah have become legend: the time she picked up a tournament director by the tie and gave him a piece of her mind, the time she told off a radio interviewer who condescendingly asked how in the world a woman expected to compete against men: "Well if I can't," she said, "maybe I'll just lower my standards and go get your job." Or the time she responded to a male competitor who'd insulted her husband by yelling, "If I judged all the people from Ohio by you, they'd all be assholes."

But really, she stressed to me, she is just a big softie at heart.

. . .

I TRACKED DOWN HALVORSON THROUGH the U.S. Axemen's Association and headed to the home she and her husband, Rick, share in Alma Center, a speck of a town in Wisconsin halfway between Minneapolis and Madison. I arrived on a frigid winter morning in February.

In many parts of the country, one says it has been snowing for a certain number of hours, or maybe days. In Alma Center, it had been snowing since November. Icicles hung from roofs, snowflakes spiraled softly to the ground, and the surrounding farmland stretched out in vast tableaus of whiteness interrupted by occasional stands of trees. Driving through the "center" of Alma Center, which consists of one intersection bounded by Jan's Place and the Village Hall and Library, I didn't see another car. There were, however, plenty of cows just down the road, attempting to graze the icy ground.

The Halvorson home was hard to miss, even though there is no street address, only a fire road number. For starters, it was the only log cabin I saw in or near town, one built entirely by Penny and Rick, with some initial assistance from a team of Amish barn raisers. Secondly, there are only 446 people in Alma Center, so there weren't a lot of houses to choose from. Finally, the sawmill, timber loaders, and looming stacks of wood piled in the backyard gave it away.

Normally, Halvorson would already have been training for a couple hours by the time I got there at 9:30 A.M., but when I visited she was recovering from a knee injury. So the doctor had told her to take it easy for a while, a directive she was none too pleased with. "I'm not a soap opera type to sit on the couch and eat bonbons," she told me with some exasperation. "Sitting on my ass is driving me crazy."

She gave me a tour of the house as her two chow-mix dogs—Chopper and Sawyer—padded along behind us. The place was by all measures beautiful: polished oak floors, wooden cabinets (made by Penny), and a vast, high-ceilinged living room that felt like a cathedral.

Penny had spent the better part of six months working on the house with Rick. It was far longer in the making—they'd lived in a mobile home for the previous twenty years before Penny drew up the plans—and the only way they could afford it was to harvest the wood and build it themselves. "I'd always wanted a house built entirely of wood," she told me as we walked through the living room. "Ain't it nice?"

It was. It was also clearly the brainchild of a woman who really, really liked timber. Instead of a wine cellar, she showed me her wood cellar in the basement; there, next to a miter saw and an air compressor and a big table saw, were five neat piles of wood: cherry, pine, red oak, white oak, and ash. She ran down her preferences—cherry for cabinets, oak for the floors—and talked rapturously about one day buying a milling machine that could produce tongue-and-groove flooring. Using a drying kiln and her garage as storage, she told me, she envisioned starting a little business in woodworking. "It's just a dream I have," she said, caressing an oak board. " 'Cause I like making beautiful things out of wood."

At first, Halvorson struck me as every bit the friendly, matronly grandmother that she is. Polite and welcoming, she speaks in that slow, Wisconsinese in which "house" becomes *hoose* "about" morphs into *aboot*, and "you betcha" is a catchall phrase. A sturdy tractor of a woman, she has an incongruously thin, refined face framed by short curly brown hair and a pair of wire-rimmed glasses. Once she doffed her sweatshirt to reveal a black tank top, however—something she does at every opportunity—the grandmother look quickly gave way to more of a grandmother-who-rides-Harleys look. A brilliantly colored tattoo of a tiger intertwined with an axe curls down her left forearm; the insignia LADY LUMBERJACK is writ across her vast left upper arm; two large tigers bare their teeth on her back; and a phoenix—"because just when everybody thought I was done, I came back"—rises up her right shoulder. Her favorite tattoo, however, graces her right forearm: an image of a resolute-looking Statue of Liberty wrapped in an American flag and shouldering an axe. "I got that only a month before the terrorist attacks," she told me, running her fingers over it. "It has to do with winning the gold at the tournament in New York and fighting for women in the sport."

Her lower body revealed the dangers of her lifestyle. She pulled up her sweatpants to show me a thick, black brace on her left knee, the offending body part that was keeping her sitting on her ass, and, below it, a raised patch of skin the size of a paperback novel. The scar, she explained, came from a mishap at the Woodsmen's Field Days in Boonville, New York, in 1989. It is a story that tells you all you need to know about Halvorson's personality. While competing in the tree-felling event, her axe blade glanced off a cluster of knots in the log and veered into her left calf, nearly slicing off a thick, toastlike piece of flesh. "I didn't even know I'd cut myself, that's how quickly my body went into shock," she said. "I drew the axe back to chop again and my husband, who was behind me, said, 'Oh honey. I think you're cut.' I looked down and the whole thing on my leg was folded up and it was bleeding all over. I remember looking down, then looking over and seeing a lady sitting in the bleachers pass out and fall right onto the ground."

Immediately, Halvorson hit the deck to get her leg above her heart. Another competitor tore off his shirt to make a tourniquet while she waited for the paramedic. After receiving 120-plus stitches at a local hospital, she slept fitfully. The next morning, she attended the competitors' meeting, her leg swaddled in bandages and propped up on a chair. "They said, 'If anybody's going to drop out, we need to know right now,' " she said. She paused for effect and then harrumphed at the absurdity of such a concept. "Well, they all stopped and looked at me. I looked down at the prize money, looked around the room, threw down the book, and said, 'Let's PLAY!' "

Not only did she play but, along with Rick, she took second in the "Jack and Jill" two-person saw, in which a pair of sawyers teams up on a two-handled five-foot-eight-inch saw, yanking it back and forth as if engaged in a tug-of-war. Her leg almost gave out on her three different times but she stayed with it. "When I went up to get the trophy and the check, people were whooping and hollering." She paused and her face muscles relaxed. She smiled sweetly. "So would you like some more coffee? I got a whole pot."

WHEN I FIRST HEARD OF "lumberjack sports," my reaction was probably a rather common one: now there are two words that don't belong next to each other. But if you think about it, most anything can be a sport if you make it one. Challenge someone to a carrot-cutting contest, invite ten of your friends to watch, call it the Crudités Classic and, voilà, you've got a sport. Or at least a reasonable facsimile.

Who decides what is a sport, anyway? Before Abner Doubleday, James Naismith, or the first great collegiate football rivalries, the most popular "sports" in America were by and large outgrowths of jobs. Plowing, mowing, drilling, logrolling, tree cutting, firefighting, rail laying, typesetting, butchering, and bricklaying; if it required dexterity, endurance, and skill and, more important, lent itself to wagering, our forefathers competed at it (and occasionally our foremothers; quilting bees were popular in the 1800s). During the nineteenth century, miners held national "hand-drilling" contests, in which there was a very real danger of missing the tiny steel drill and instead pulverizing a partner's hand. And, as Dartmouth professor Frank Zarnowski recounted in a fascinating 2004 paper in the *Journal of Leisure Research*, firefighting competitions created heroes such as William W. Bush, a twenty-five-year-old who was crowned as the "Champion Fireman of American" and memorably described in the January 16, 1858, issue of the *New York Clipper National Police Gazette* as "in his glory at a fire, when he is in actual danger, or befitting mankind."

In each of these competitions, which Zarnowski termed "work-sports," records and stats were kept, just as they are in today's pro sports, and the results were breathlessly recounted in publications like the *Clipper*, the *American Turf & Register*, the *New York Sportsman*, and *Spirit of the Times*. In the days before TV, work-sports were huge draws. Corn-husking—a repetitive and arduous activity in which "huskers" wielding a hook grabbed, sliced, and extracted up to sixty corn ears per minute— drew crowds that topped out at 100,000, or twice as many as at an NFL game. By 1929, NBC Radio was airing the husking "nationals" live.[1]

Lumberjack sports were a natural, then. Wood was the most common building material and thousands of men lived in logging camps— particularly amidst the vast stretches of timber in Minnesota, Wisconsin, and Michigan. The first forest festivals were held in 1872 and the first recorded events in 1900. The loggers competed because, well, that's what a bunch of men living without women do, but also to hone their skills and, as logging lore has it, to cure hangovers. It was a rough-and-tumble culture; as former champ Bob Waibel, aka "the Rhinestone Lumberjack," described the lumberjack competitors of the mid-twentieth century in a newspaper interview, they were "the cussingest, rottenest bunch."

The sport grew as the century wore on but was still loosely organized and regionally based; the Lumberjack World Championships were held in Hayward, Wisconsin, and the Boonville field days, another big event, in New York. In 1985, that changed when the Stihl TimberSports Series began airing on ESPN. Suddenly, these gritty, grungy men in overalls were honest-to-God TV celebrities. Crowds of four thousand and more turned out to see them top trees and logroll and chop and saw. Many of the best lumberjacks came from Quebec, Australia, and New Zealand, where boys routinely grow up with an axe in hand. In the states, the top competitors were Wisconsinites and New Yorkers—or, I should specify, *northern* New Yorkers, as Manhattanites wouldn't know a "hot saw" from a hot dog.

As with all the work-sports, the competitions grew out of a simple desire: to make work fun. Spend all day husking corn, or setting type, or cutting down trees, and it is hard to see your work as anything other than

---

1. There are still work-sports, which account for half a million competitors by Zarnowski's count. They include, as he details, "Corn husking, oyster shucking, grocery bagging, grave digging (yes, there is a 'Cemetery Olympics'), plowing, shoveling, World Contest gift wrapping, chambermaiding, life-guarding, sheep shearing, and bike courier delivery."

grueling and monotonous because, well, it is. But add elements of competition and suddenly there is a reward system. As Csikszentmihalyi wrote in *Flow*: "The more a job inherently resembles a game—with variety, appropriate and flexible challenges, clear goals, and immediate feedback—the more enjoyable it will be regardless of the worker's level of development." I can vouch for this; for example, when I was a teenager, I spent three weeks working as a "car counter" on the Golden Gate Bridge. From 5:30 A.M. to 11 A.M. every morning, as the San Francisco fog rolled over me in lumbering gray drifts, I looked inside every car in my lane and, on a clipboard, checked off how many people were in it for a survey being conducted by the transit department. I would have passed out from boredom were it not for Danny, the guy counting in the lane next to me, with whom I entered into a daily contest to see how many of the four-person or more "jackpot cars," as we called them, came through our lane per hour. It got to the point where we'd be peering around the ticket gates, trying to subtly influence cars to our lane. Yes, it was rather pathetic, but it was a lot better than just counting.

Maybe I was just being American, though. One of the things Zarnowski found in his research was that the emergence of work-sports was predominantly a stateside phenomenon. As he writes: "The example of the typesetting 'Swifts' is insightful. Instead of rebelling against a piece rate system, long hours, and technological improvements that might hasten an occupational demise, the American typesetters decided to celebrate their speed by displaying it in contests. Rumble (2003) tells us that English and French compositors, similarly challenged, either boycotted or picketed. In the United States the typesetters raced."

I suppose this either makes us resilient and hardy or a bunch of doormats. I prefer to think it's the former.

OUR COFFEE CUPS EMPTY, HALVORSON and I bundled up and headed out to see the family business. On this afternoon, Rick was out in the woods just past Pigeon Falls, "thinning" a pine plantation they'd been working for fifteen years—they have a contract with the landowner for selective harvesting—by taking out diseased and dead pines, as well as carefully chosen "lines" of trees. We navigated a bumpy fire road into the heart of a pine forest, where we heard Rick before we saw him. He was at the controls of a Hydro-Ax machine, known as a processor, which looks sort of like a bulldozer with an enormous upright stapler on its front end. Rick was taking out a line of pine trees, each thirty-three to forty feet in height, by maneuvering the iron beast forward and back. Using large steel tongs at the bottom of the "stapler," he grabbed a tree and held it while a chainsaw blade flicked out like a tongue and cut the tree at its base. Then Rick turned the tree in the air, so that it was horizontal to the ground, and the machine ran it through the guts of the stapler to rid it of branches. Finally, the chainsaw cut the tree into premeasured hundred-inch pieces, which Penny's son Luke, twenty-three, would later come pick up with the "skidder," another bulldozer-esque piece of equipment that had a large arm in front for picking up logs. This was the part of the job Penny usually did—once again, her damn knee was keeping her from doing it. She watched, looking a bit envious. "I love being out here in the woods," she said to me, over the buzzing din. "And let me tell you, that skidder beats the hell out of using a chainsaw in the snow."

Rick cut the engine and stepped down. He'd been out since 6:45 A.M. He was a tall, solid man with a white beard and an easy smile. Like his wife, he had a down-home, midwestern charm: he talked of tractor parts being "mighty spendy" and worked in jeans, with a denim shirt, a camouflage hat, and a flannel coat. As he spoke, he reflexively picked the branches off one of the cut logs.

This is where the couple have spent much of the last twenty-odd years together, out in the woods, each tending to one aspect of the logging and then meeting up to eat lunch on a woodpile. The two have a comfortable patter, one that consists primarily of Penny talking and Rick occasionally nodding or offering a wry observation. When we went out to lunch together later, she absentmindedly picked tan flakes off his head, telling him, "Oh, you got woodchips in your hair, hon."

They kept some of the wood they harvested for projects and hauled the rest in their 1987 Freightliner semi to local paper mills, "you know, for all you office people to have something to write on," as Penny said. She said it with sympathy; she really did feel bad for people who spent their days hunched over a keyboard. Of course, she worked long, hard hours operating heavy machinery. It was cold, it was repetitive, it was heaven to the Halvorsons. "When you're logging, you're part of something bigger," Penny explained as we trudged back through the snow to my rental car. "Some people think all a logger does is come in and whack all the trees. That's not true. If you use proper forest management, you can maintain a beautiful stand of trees."

It was an unusual way to view logging; I'd always thought of it as inherently degrading to the environment. Penny, on the other hand, saw trees the same way Native American hunters do animals: she used every part of them and was grateful. Plus, she simply enjoyed being around lumber. "You don't get rich doing it but it makes a living," she said, looking out at the snow-topped trees. "And you won't get rich doing lumberjack sports either, but I do it for the love of it."

BACK AT THE HOUSE, WITH enormous mugs of coffee in our laps—I was starting to get a serious caffeine buzz—Halvorson explained how, in her mind, she was destined to do this work. Her father, his father, and his father before him had logged the trees of Wisconsin, first with axes, using horses to haul out the wood, and later with chainsaws. As a young girl, Penny would help her dad—measuring the logs and piling them—so it never occurred to her that it wasn't work fit for a woman. It did occur to her mother, Loretta, however. Loretta worked the forest for years as a young woman but found that life was easier, and the money was better, working on a factory line. In 1974, Loretta says, she became the first woman to work the line at the Nelson Muffler plant in Black River Falls. She encouraged her daughter to follow her lead.

So, after studying agriculture in high school, and briefly considering the military, Penny tried to make a go of it at the Nelson plant. She didn't enjoy it, though—too monotonous, too enclosed. Next, she tried her hand at a nursing home—her mother's second job—but wasn't cut out to withstand the emotional toll. "I couldn't get attached to these older people and then see them pass away," she told me. "It made me so sad. I'd rather work someplace where you're not so affected by somebody else's life."

Then, at twenty-five, divorced after an ill-fated first marriage, she met Rick. He'd been felling trees since he was six and working full-time in the timber industry since 1969. Just the year before, he'd tried his hand at lumberjack sports for the first time, successfully. So when he met Penny, Rick took one look at her strong arms and wide base and asked, right there on their first date at a bar in Black River Falls, whether she wanted to be his partner on the Jack-and-Jill saw. She was understandably wary, not only of the sawing, but of anyone who asked this sort of thing on a first date. But, what the hell, she figured, what did she have to lose?

So Rick coached and she learned, even though, as Rick told me later with a chuckle, "She don't like to be corrected very well." In their very first competition, in 1985 at the Hayward World Championships, they finished third. Rick was ecstatic; Penny was devastated. "She sat down and started crying," Rick told me. "She was so disappointed. She thought she'd let me down. It took a while to convince her otherwise." Penny agreed. "I sat down and cried like a little kid," she said. "Later I realized how well we'd done. This sport is a lot harder than it looks."

I followed her back out into the snow to find out.

THERE ARE NUMEROUS EVENTS IN lumberjack sports, from logrolling to tree felling, but Halvorson focuses on five in particular: the Jack and Jill, the single saw, the hot saw, the underhand chop, and the axe throw. We trudged out into her backyard so she could explain the finer details of each to me. And what a backyard it was; it looked like a cross between an obstacle course, a campground, and a junkyard. An enormous garage (built entirely of logs) towered on our right, a trailer (full of gear and trophies) stood beyond that, and, further back, the outdoor sawmill, two long metal tracks leading to an upright buzzsaw, rose out of snow drifts like an abandoned oil drill. To our left, an outdoor furnace sent underground pipes to heat the home, and her son's trailer stood amid a stand of thick pine trees, not far from a decrepit twenty-foot-high barn that looked vaguely foreboding—as if there might be a string of dead animal carcasses hung up inside (turned out the only thing lurking inside was a stray cat, which Penny shooed off). Straight ahead was a training area littered with various wood stands, targets, and blocks wrapped in garbage bags (to keep the wood dry over the winter). We headed first to her gear shed.

Inside, it looked like the coolest hardware store in the world—if hardware stores were stocked by a nine-year-old boy. The shed was full of chainsaws and two-man saws and five-foot-eight-inch-long, four-cutter "single saws" that looked like giant, sharpened combs (Penny imports these from a saw maker in New Zealand at about $1,500 each). Along one wall rested nearly forty axes of various sizes, each one sharp enough to cut arm hair—that's how Rick tests the edges prior to Penny's competitions—and all sheathed. ("If someone else even touches the blade," Penny said, "the oil from their fingers can dull it.") She grabbed one of the axes and I followed her to a block outside.

The idea of the underhand chop, she explained as snowflakes collected in her hair, is to stand on an eleven-inch-thick log and belt your way through it as quickly as possible by swooping the axe down from over your head. Sounds easy; looks hard. It demands not only strength and precision, but balance—especially when you're switching sides, which requires one to pivot on the log, rotate on one foot, and, all in one motion, swing the axe into the other side of the log.

Since her knee kept her from demonstrating, she had me straddle a practice log and directed me.

"So bring it down on the left side first and make two cuts, top and bottom."

Not interested in taking a chunk out of my left leg, I swung in super slow motion. The axe was top-heavy, and it picked up momentum as it came down, leading the way for me. Two cuts left, then two cuts right, then switch sides—the good ones can knock out the eleven-inch log with eight to ten hits on the front and ten to twelve hits on the back. It seemed about as easy as standing on a solid wood footstool while attempting to whack the love out of it with a baseball bat that happened to have a razor-sharp edge. The key, Penny explained, was to point the head of the axe at my opposite knee when chopping to get the proper angle. "The slightest turn of the axe blade can make all the difference in how that axe penetrates the wood," she said. She pointed at my stance. "The angle you have it, tip it just this way."

I could understand the gratuitous pleasure of the act, sort of like thwacking a piñata or pummeling one of those life-size weighted boxing dummies that bounce back upon impact. It was a test of skill, it relied on repetition and focus, and there was little in the way of strategy versus an opponent—more like golf than, say, basketball. "I think it's an art form," Halvorson said. "It's not just a matter of if you're big and tall, you'll be great. It's about technique, strategy, and matching up with the right equipment."

Next was axe-throwing. She lined me up twenty feet from a target—the end of a log with a bull's-eye the size of a soda can top painted on the end. I drew a double-sided axe behind my head and then, smoothly, gracefully, and quite powerfully, sent the axe soaring about ten feet over the log. It clanged harmlessly into the snow. I continued trying for another five minutes but couldn't hit the bull's-eye. By the end, I also couldn't feel my fingers. "That's not easy, is it?" I observed, rather obviously.

"Nope, you betcha it isn't." She smiled. "But it sure is fun!" She was getting into it. She hurried back to the shed and brought out a single saw. It was too cold to demonstrate with a block of wood—they were all frozen—but she led me through the technique, which was similar to a one-hand row. Reach, pull, weight on the back foot. She got even more excited as she watched me mimicking the motion. "We're always looking for an aspiring lumberjack!" she said, leaning down to see my weight transfer. "We have got to get you back here in the spring so we can set you up on this."

Finally, she showed me the "hot saw." These are not machines so much as bulky beasts of destruction: souped-up chainsaws with snowmobile or motorcycle engines, some of which run on airplane fuel, that weigh forty to sixty pounds and kick like a rifle when started. I picked up Halvorson's and my whole body immediately equalized against the weight. This one weighed "only" forty pounds; when she was younger, she told me, she used a Kawasaki outfitted with a snowmobile engine that weighed sixty pounds and had eighty horsepower (again, not cheap to come by; a good hot saw can cost over $5,000). In competition, you have to slice three discs of wood off a log, a task that requires strength, leverage, and a steady hand. I understood what she meant when she said it could "get away from you." After events, she often has a big black bruise on her thigh from resting the saw against it. She'd seen people lose control of the saw and topple over or, worse, lose a chain and have it wrap around their legs (hence the Kevlar safety pants competitors wear).

Though Halvorson has held the world record in four of the five events she competes in (axe-throwing being her weakest event), the hot saw is what sets her apart; for many years, she was the only woman strong enough to operate one, and she's still the only one to compete in the "unlimited," or "open," hot saw against men. When she first entered the sport in 1985, there was only one event for women—the Jack and Jill. This setup wasn't exclusionary so much as logical; there weren't a lot of women clamoring to run a chainsaw race. So when Halvorson did—and boy can she clamor when she wants to—the men didn't take it that well. Imagine for a moment a fraternity of the cussingest, rottenest men faced with the idea of a "lady" lining up across from them. At first, some thought it was cute. "They'd pat me on the back and say that's nice. But when I started doing well"—Halvorson paused to chuckle—"then it was, we *got* to get rid of this girl."

Through the late eighties, she challenged the system. Her first year at the Boonville field days, she says, she was told she couldn't compete in the hot saw and spent three days feeling frustrated. "I was like, 'What the hell does being a woman have to do with it?' I just didn't get it." On the fourth day, she got a lawyer and he called up the New York Axemen's Association. "It had nothing to do with my qualifications because I had better qualifications than three-quarters of men who'd entered," she said. "It was strictly because I was a Penny and not a Bob." So she threatened legal action—damages to her reputation of $1.5 million—if they didn't let her compete. "All I wanted was to hot saw like anybody else," she said, "I didn't want any advantage because I was a girl. All I wanted was to hear the bang of that gun and then do my best. If there'd been a women's competition, I would have done it. I never asked to have exceptions for me because I'm a girl." She brushed away the idea with her hand, like a pesky fly. "That's nonsense. If you want to play on an equal playing field, you should expect that."

She says the committee held an emergency meeting and—what do you know?—Halvorson was allowed to compete. In her first heat, she went up against a world champion, Mel Lentz, and not only beat him when his saw got caught up, but won the heat. "People were whooping and hollering in the stands, all these women jumping up and down."

Some of the men, she stressed, encouraged her, including several informal coaches she'd had over the years. Others weren't quite so supportive. "Someone would say you should be at home raising kids in the kitchen, and I'd say, 'Sorry, I've been there, done that. I already raised kids.'" What was sticking in the men's collective craw was that Halvorson was not just competing; in many cases she was doing quite well. She never placed first in an event against men, but she finished second in the Stihl TimberSports Series once and had numerous finishes of third, fourth, or fifth. "I didn't necessarily want to chop and saw against men," she explained. "I just wanted a place to chop and saw." Nonetheless, just by competing she delighted her mom to no end. "I'm so proud of her," her mother told me. "The best I could do was take a man's job at the muffler plant."

Halvorson may not have had the impact of a Billie Jean King, but don't try telling her that (her take on King: "She made a place for women in her sport as well"). She was very proud of advancing the "cause of women," bringing it up numerous times during our time together and using words like "pioneer" and "groundbreaker"—which, in her own corner of the sporting universe, I suppose she was. When I asked how she hoped to be viewed in twenty years, she drew in a breath. "Oh God, I hope it won't be all the records I set but that I fought so hard for all the women in the sport." When I asked if she saw herself as a feminist, she hesitated. "At first I didn't," she said, nodding slowly. "But down the road, yes. I didn't know I didn't belong there until it was explained to me."

Rick was a legend in the sport as well; for a good ten-year stretch, he set a world record just about every other time he went out in the hot saw. Together, they set a world record in the Jack and Jill event nine times at the Hayward World Championships. Buoyed by their success, they spent summers traveling to competitions. Living out of a trailer and bringing the kids, they drove the country in their pop-up camper, often going from Atlantic to Pacific in one summer. One of the highlights, Penny told me, came in 1994, when both made the finals in Virginia Beach—Penny being the only woman, of course—and they were chauffeured around in a limo ("You should have seen the kids' faces!") and went to a black tie gala, only it was a sequined gown for Penny ("Gosh, that was pretty"). Most events were far less glamorous; some contests paid $200 to the winner. The top events were worth $3,000, but even so, it was by no means a lucrative endeavor—in a good year, the duo made $30,000 from sponsorship and prize money. But as Rick told me: "Other people take vacations and have to pay for it. Whatever we paid, if we didn't make a profit, it was tax-deductible."

The sport did have its drawbacks. Not only did Penny slice her leg, she once broke her hand on a log while competing in the Jack and Jill when Rick pulled the saw through too far. For his part, Rick nearly cut off the first three toes on his right foot while competing in the underhand chop at a 1988 event. Eight hours of surgery later, doctors reattached the tendon. When they told me about this, both Rick and Penny laughed as if recounting the time when Rick got real drunk at the Christmas party and passed out in the corner. This was partly their outlook on life and partly, I learned, just how things are viewed in Alma Center. Just the week before, for example, two locals had gotten soused and tried to steal a bulldozer. As Rick told it, when the police showed up, each of the men took immediate evasive action. "One fella ran out into the woods and went straight into a tree and knocked himself out." He paused to chuckle. "The other guy, well he got out of his truck and hid under it. Only he'd forgotten to put on the brake. So it rolled right away and he was laying there on the ground."

This, the Halvorsons thought, was mighty funny.

WHEN I SPOKE TO PENNY'S mom, she told me she'd initially been skeptical of her daughter's career choice but had come around. "It's the perfect thing for her," Mrs. Halvorson said. "Not many of us get the opportunity to do what we really love." When I asked why this was, she cited what she thought were Penny's three predominant qualities: "She's powerful, she's caring, and she don't take no crap."

Really though, Penny didn't so much find her calling as it found her that winter night when Rick asked her out. What struck me was how enthusiastically she had taken to it, like a bess beetle to some downed oak. Being a lumberjill just felt right to her—it made her proud, it gave her a sense of importance. One could say it was her best self. By this, I mean that we all have different personas we show to different people; the eternal child to a parent, the witty and outgoing buddy to a group of friends. Some personas we like better than others—no one is fond of being the subservient employee. In Halvorson's case, she had tried on mother (which suited her) and factory worker and nurse's aide (which did not). It was only once she found lumberjack sports—a passion that'd been buried somewhere deep inside, underneath layers of motherhood, domesticity, and uncertainty—that she decided that she was not Penny Halvorson, but Penny Halvorson, the Lady Lumberjack.

This was a phenomenon I saw repeatedly while working on this project. So many of the people I spent time with felt their best when working. It was like they were donning a cape or changing in an occupational phone booth, only to emerge with superpowers. For example, the man you will meet in Chapter 7, Rex Swartzendruber, became remarkably more outspoken and confident—a different person, almost—when he was on the job. This is not unusual; expertise breeds confidence.

The question, of course, is how does one locate this best self? A lot of money has gone into figuring that out, or at least convincing you to buy a book that claims to have figured that out. One of the more popular, and illuminating, ideas comes from Marcus Buckingham and Donald Clifton, a pair of Gallup pollsters who wrote a series of books. In *Now, Discover Your Strengths,* they examined the way companies were training employees and came to the conclusion that instead of playing to people's strengths, the companies were trying to shore up their weaknesses. They cited one rather alarming stat: When asked, "At work, do you have the opportunity to do what you do best every day?" Gallup polls of more than 1.7 million people in 101 companies in 63 countries found that only 20 percent of people strongly agreed. The other 80 percent, presumably, are frustrated.

Sometimes, as with Halvorson, a person might not even be aware of what his or her strengths are. Again, there's a whole subeconomy of personality assessment tests such as Myers-Briggs out there to help one figure it out. Many are complex and involve all types of workbook exercises. A simpler concept comes from a group of researchers headed by Laura Morgan Roberts of the Harvard Business School, who built upon Buckingham and Clifton's findings. In a paper entitled "How to Play to Your Strengths" in the *Harvard Business Review*, they espouse using something they term "the Reflected Best Self" exercise. It is rather basic: ask eleven people from different areas of your life to write up what they believe your strengths are, then sift through and find common themes, which you organize in a table (it's a business school, so there has to be a table somewhere). Finally, use the information to write a brief self-portrait. The results are reportedly quite powerful; test subjects understood their strengths—"who they are at the top of their game," as the study authors put it. Furthering the sports analogy, the authors suggested the lesson behind the exercise is that there is no reason a third baseman should learn the tools of an outfielder.

HALVORSON'S BEST SELF WAS ON display at the 2001 Great Outdoors Games in Lake Placid, which she considers her crowning achievement in lumberjack sports. She became the first woman to win both the team relay and the endurance competition—a grueling tripartite race in which competitors run a hot saw, jog over to an underhand chop, and then run back to finish with a single saw.

As Chopper and Sawyer vied to see who could knock my notebook out of my hand—presumably so that I would be free to pet them—Halvorson popped in a tape of the competition. I was impressed; it had been hard to get a feel for the intensity of the sport out in the backyard. Here, the women were competing in front of four thousand fans, in the hot New York summertime, as ESPN announcers breathlessly described the women as "really laying the LUMBER!" and, "exploding the wood!"

After dispatching two lesser competitors, Halvorson advanced to the finals, where she faced Tina Scheer, another legend of the sport. Halvorson, dressed in sweatpants and a white tank top, her hair short and blondish, came out strong in the hot saw to take a lead going into the underhand chop. Perched on the block, she indeed exploded some wood, the chips flying off like timber shrapnel. Fifteen feet away, Scheer furiously hacked at her block, her bushy blond ponytail spraying outward with each blow. Halvorson finished first and, heading into the climactic single saw, again had the lead, but only barely. She looked gassed too; being an asthmatic and carrying 290 pounds doesn't mix too well with running and humidity. As she tore through the log, Rick frantically sprayed WD-40 on her saw blade to keep it lubricated. Scheer was sawing faster but Halvorson was eating larger chunks out of the wood with each stroke. Lopping off the final margin, Halvorson collapsed into Rick's embrace. "Your arms are just like rubber by the time you're done with the saw," Penny said while watching herself, shaking her head at the memory. "I was so glad it was over. Even if you win, you're so glad."

Halvorson is known in the sport for having good technique, remarkable focus—she routinely trains four hours a day in the off-season—and, most of all, immense strength. This, not coincidentally, is directly related to her weight, which she prefers to keep at 245 or so (the current gain, she told me, was due to the injury). "I don't care if they say that I'd do better if I lost weight, it's not who I am," she said, smoothing out her tank top. In fact, she tends to worry more about losing *too much* weight than gaining it. A couple years ago, she got down to 190 pounds. "I might have looked fabulous," she said, almost disdainfully, "but I couldn't control the saw. It controlled *me.*" No, she said, she prefers to stay north of 225 pounds. Then she chuckled at the folly of skinny girls. "You can't be a tiny woman and run the hot saw," she said. "Besides, I want to be healthy and not worry about being a size zero. If I'm strong and fit enough, that will make me self-confident. I tell some of the young girls who ask me for tips: if you feel like you need to put on twenty pounds for strength, then do it."

HALVORSON RESIDES IN A STRANGE limbo between sports celebrity and sports obscurity—famous to a certain subset of people but not famous enough to become wealthy from her sport. Both she and Rick are recognized occasionally at the mall or a restaurant, and asked to sign autographs. I could sense she was not quite sure how to view her limited renown. At one point, she said, "I talk to the fans and they like it much better if you talk to them like a real person, not a spoiled brat celebrity." Another time she said, quite seriously, "Rick and I never forget where we came from or who we are, no matter how much success we had in lumberjack sports or the media." Then again, she and Rick scraped for a living and spent years living out of a trailer. Dinners out, like the one we had that night at the Flying J Truck Stop restaurant, were not extravagant affairs.

While sopping up a giant plate of steak, potatoes, and fried chicken,

Penny gave me her take on her career. "In some ways I think I was des-tined to do this," she said. "I think fate was involved in it. In some ways it's a dream job. I get to go to work when I want and train when I want."

I couldn't help but be a bit envious. I played basketball for a year in college, but was never good enough to consider playing in any postcol-legiate league that didn't have the initials YMCA attached to it. How great would it be to be the best in the world at something, anything? I'd be ecstatic just to play in the NBA—I might shoot air balls but they would be *my* NBA air balls. In her arena, Halvorson was the best. How many of us can say we are even in the top 1 percent of anything?

When I asked if her success brought her happiness, she thought for a moment. "Hmmm," she murmured. "Sharing it with my husband has brought me the happiness. Looking over at his face when I set a world record and seeing the smile on his face, seeing all his coaching and sup-port paying off."

Her view of her work and life was beguiling. She loved what she did, did it with the man she loved, and mixed work with play. She didn't need a whole bunch of money—as Rick pointed out at one point, he knew a couple in a nearby town who started making money, "and you'd think they'd be better off but they just found new stuff to struggle with." She also felt as though she'd made a difference in the sport. Her life advice was short and simple: "Impress yourself first and understand that you'll never have enough money. So do it for the love of it."

There was another chapter to the story, however. When I visited, Halvorson was dealing with the uncertainty of her knee troubles. If she needed surgery, it would put her out for the summer competition.

This had happened once before, back in 2003, when she slipped on a patch of black ice and tore both rotator cuffs. At first she tried to ig-nore the pain but, when she found she could no longer hold a coffee cup, she went in to a doctor: she needed surgery.

She had a hard time during recovery. She broke down and cried at the Hayward World Championships while coaching a younger competitor—and this is not a woman who cries easily. Rick would wake up in the mid-dle of the night to find his wife pantomiming chopping motions in her sleep, a tendency so persistent that when she initially got a CAT scan, the doctor secured her arms behind her back so that she wouldn't start sleep-sawing and further injure herself. "I just really missed it," Halvorson told me. "The smell of the wood and the WD-40. It's funny how smell is like that." The only comparison to the thrill of competing, she told me, was marrying Rick and having children. "I know that sounds silly," she said, shrugging, "but that's how it is for me."

When I saw her, the knee troubles were getting her down. She felt like she'd already beaten one injury; she had come back from the shoulder surgery to reach the semifinals at the previous summer's Great Outdoors Games. More surgery seemed unfair. She tried to look on the bright side. "I could do some coaching and some announcing," she said, rather unconvincingly, of life after competition. "I've had a good run, after all."

Not long after I visited her, she called with some news. "The doctor said it's just dislocated," she said, practically singing the words. "I don't need knee surgery, just a minor procedure. I'm getting it done in two weeks."

She was so excited that she'd barely slept the previous night. With two good knees, she'd be able to compete again that summer against all the young guns, which gave her great pleasure. "Once in a while," she said, "Grandma has to go out and spank the little girls." Of course, she told me she was "driving Rick absolutely crazy" with her enthusiasm. He confirmed this, in his own laconic way. "She," he told me, "is pretty whooped up about this."

Now *that,* I thought, is the way all of us should feel upon learning we can go back to work.

FOUR

THE RAIL-AHOLIC

WHAT WOULD HAPPEN IF ONE'S hobby became one's job? For many of us, and here I speak of the divot-spewing amateur golfers and note-cracking shower chanteuses, it might be a disaster. For others, it is a tempting move: love something so much in small doses and, the logic goes, one would love it even more as a full-time profession. The origin of the word "amateur," after all, comes from the Latin verb *amare,* which means "to love."

But a hobby can rather quickly morph from love to obsession. In the case of John Nehrich, one day you're building model trains with college buddies, and, the next thing you know, it's thirty years later and you're attending Alcoholics Anonymous meetings. Not because you drink, mind you, but because you fear that you have become an incurable workaholic, unable to pull yourself away from a train layout that has become something far grander: a legacy. Everything else—money, friends, family—has taken a backseat to the layout, and what scares you most is the fact that, in the grand scheme of things, this might be just fine with you.

I HAPPENED UPON NEHRICH WHILE pondering the nexus of jobs and hobbies. It seemed an interesting area to explore, and model trains seemed the quintessential hobby. There is not much middle ground; either one considers model trains geeky, one considers them cool, or one professes to think the first but secretly believes the latter. Regardless, if you fall into the "cool" category, the chances are good that you are a boy. True, the rare girl falls for the hobby, but, by and large, it is a guy thing. According to the National Model Railroad Association, the hobby is 98 percent male, and, were one to browse a model train store, as I have, you would be doing so in the company of men. Though really, they are all boys at heart.

Even for boys, however, model trains are something of an anachronism amidst the current landscape of high-tech toys and video games. So I envisioned a model train expert who might be something of an anachronism himself (or, I suppose it was remotely possible, herself), in love with a bygone time and enraptured by the small thrills provided by patient, loving attention to detail, a reward largely overlooked in our ADD-addled world. There was only one question, however: Did people actually work on model trains for a living?

I called Terry Thompson, the editor of *Model Railroader,* and he assured me that there were indeed a number of people, "more than you might think," whose work lives revolved around train sets. Some built layouts, others designed parts, and still others, like Thompson, wrote about them. In one instance, he said, a modeler named John Nehrich even had something akin to a faculty position at Rensselaer Polytechnic

Institute, a school in upstate New York known for its engineering program. I was intrigued; Thompson, however, was hesitant. He paused on
the other end of the phone.

"John's an extremely talented builder and he's very well respected in
the industry," he said, and I could feel the "but" coming. "But he works
under, let's say, highly unusual circumstances." How unusual? It turned
out that the fifty-four-year-old Nehrich had been at the model train club
at RPI for over three decades, worked for a university stipend of something absurd like $10,000 a year, and was fixated on re-creating a stretch
of railroad running from Troy, New York, to the Canadian border
exactly as it stood in the year 1950. The *Los Angeles Times*, in a 1989
story, referred to him as a "living legend." This guy, I thought, stunk of
passion.

IT TOOK A WHILE TO set up an interview—the RPI PR department
made it seem like I was requesting an audience with the pope, not the
head of the model train club—but I finally drove up from New York on
a winter morning to meet Nehrich at school. I'd come prepared with
what I thought might be an ice-breaking opener.

"So," I said, moments after we met, "I'd just about given up hope
and was going to call your home number."

"Well," he said slowly and quite seriously, "you couldn't have."

I was missing the joke. What, he didn't have a phone?

"I have an unlisted number," he explained after a moment. "Some
years ago, I was getting so many calls from model train people asking for
advice that I ended up getting an unlisted number."

"Ha, ha," I said.

He wasn't laughing.

"You serious?"

"Yes."

Clearly, I was dealing with a man who valued his privacy. After all,
some people would love nothing more than to have fawning fans calling

them (Spiderman, for example, might set up his own 800 number to facilitate such calls). But not Nehrich. There are those who enter a room and instantly become the center of attention; Nehrich is not one of them. Rather, he slides through an environment, the quiet observer, content to be off to the side of the frame. His friends describe him as kind, thoughtful, sensitive, passionate, and dedicated (and, in the words of his sister, "very, very nonmaterialistic"). He prefers to work alone, or with those he trusts.

We strolled across campus together, Nehrich leading the way. Though a large man, he slumped his shoulders forward, as if to diminish his size, and moved slowly, the same way he talked. He wore a red RPI hat over his shaved dome and an earring in his right ear. Possessed of a big malleable face, he has a permanently furrowed brow to go with a permanently sympathetic expression, big intelligent eyes and a prominent dimple on his chin. I suppose on the scale of what I expected a model train buff to look like, he veered toward the less nerdy side (though apparently this wasn't always the case; in old photos he sported ties with sweater vests, a bristly mustache and thick glasses accented by a sweeping comb-over).

Following a web of sidewalks, we passed clusters of blocky brick dorms until we reached one that had a TRAINS THIS WAY sign posted, with an arrow pointing downward. We descended a flight of stairs into darkness, Nehrich unlocked the door and we entered what appeared to be a large, dank basement. Its three rooms were all standard issue for a college dorm: low-ceilings, concrete floors, and long fluorescent lights. Occasionally, water dripped down from the ceiling piping, and, to get to the nearest bathroom, one needed to prop a chair in the door—it locked otherwise—and walk down the hall. None of this really bothered Nehrich, however, for he saw the basement as merely a protective shell, safeguarding the treasure inside.

It was a remarkable layout, considered by many in the industry to be the finest historically accurate model railroad in the country. Stretching through all three rooms and doubling back on itself, the railroad is 500 feet from end-to-end. But in Nehrich's estimation it is closer to 2,000 to 3,000 feet of total track. It is a 1:87 scale model of a 190-mile railroad route from Troy north to the Canadian border exactly as it appeared on September 25, 1950, a date chosen because, as Nehrich explained while giving me a tour, "that's when trains last mattered." (As for why September 25, the original model train crew chose it, as Nehrich explained, "because we wanted to do late summer so it was still warm weather and early fall so we could justify the colors in certain places.") This means that everything on the track or around it—building stations, department stores, billboards—is re-created with historical accuracy. So if there was an Armour meat packing plant in Saratoga in 1950, there is a miniature sausage factory with a miniature butcher holding miniature sausage links in a miniature Saratoga.

The layout has been featured in hobby magazine spreads, and train buffs have come from as far as Japan and Australia and Italy to see it. The *Today* show featured it in 1989, and Vermont senator Jim Jeffords made a special trip to see it, as did the late actor James Doohan (Scottie on *Star Trek*) and Rod Stewart's manager. It has taken thirty-six years and over two hundred students, each coming in for three or four years at a time (and, in the case of a number who've stayed around after graduation, much longer), to build the track, but only one of them, Nehrich, has been there from beginning to end. In the process, he has devoted the better part of his life to it—by his estimation, he's spent 75 percent of his waking hours in the three rooms over the last thirty-six years. It is a staggering amount of time, especially when one considers the grim reality of the room—think of spending three decades in *your* basement. Perhaps, however, some would argue that a windowless cubicle isn't so much better.

We began in Montreal and headed south, Nehrich leading and acting as aerial tour guide. Small orange placards underneath the layout, similar to the kind you'd find at a museum, provided description and trivia. It was like walking through a history lesson, and I found myself getting lost in the layout; examining tiny bathers on Lake George who watched a scale-size two-and-a-half-foot hand-built Ticonderoga steam-boat go by; smiling at alley cats the size of an inkblot perched on fences the height of half a toothpick; fighting off an urge to try to operate all the cabooses in the train yards, which bustled with outgoing cars, each with an accurate route and number.

We headed to the final room. "And here," Nehrich said rather grandly, "is Troy." The city was clearly the jewel of the layout. There were the iron factories, the old Union Station, the water wheel, theaters, and, there, if one looked closely, a tiny prostitute advertising her assets on the stoop of a brownstone on Sixth Avenue, part of the red-light district, which drew customers from afar and was run by a madam named "Mame Fay." As we went, Nehrich narrated all this as if reciting a script.

One of the first thoughts I had as we went, and it would not be the last time I had it, was *What the hell is this doing down here?* The layout was nearly museum-quality, and would seem better suited to a prominent place of honor on the campus, not a dorm basement. Part of the problem, Nehrich told me, was that at this point it would be nearly impossible to move, unless enough money could be raised to reconstruct it. Furthermore, as became clear during my time on campus, the school was perfectly happy to have the railroaders where they were, down in the basement. There were other, more advanced—*more forward-thinking*—elements of the school to display to the world. Students didn't come to an elite engineering school to join the model train club.

The offshoot of this is that, since it's not on display—other than by appointment and during open houses—the room constantly looks like a science fair project the night before it's due. Around the layout—on the walls, on the floor—were the tools of the archivists' trade: Styrofoam, Cuisinarts for churning the mix of newspaper pulp and latex used to make rocks, wire mesh for use as a strainer, glue guns, wood screws, styrene, bags of paper scraps, an industrial-size jug of Elmer's glue. Satellite photos hung on the walls and artifacts and maps were tacked here and there, including one called a "Locomotive defect chart" ("complete with 199 defects!") from International Correspondence Schools in

Scranton, Pennsylvania. My favorite poster in the room, however, was the one that showed a train smashing into a seventies-style car; it read: "When it's a tie at the railroad crossing . . . You lose!"

As we progressed through the layout, Nehrich interspersed a history of the club itself, which was founded in 1947 by four male students (RPI is now one of a handful of colleges, including MIT, Purdue, and Syracuse, that have model railroad clubs). Nehrich joined in 1968 as a freshman and, four years later, the Rensselaer Model Railroad Society moved to its new location in the dorm basement. That's when the current layout was launched.

From his practiced cadence and smooth delivery, I could tell Nehrich had told this story, and narrated the layout's details, countless times—by his estimation, more than 250 times, at ninety minutes a pop. During alumni weekends, when the club runs the trains—a sight to behold, by all accounts—five hundred or so visitors file through per day. Nehrich is overwhelmed by such days. Shy by nature, he dislikes doing the song and dance routine—not to mention that he sees it as a waste of an hour and a half when he could be attending to a broken bridge trellis or some other pressing need—and he even jacked up the price to $45 per hour, thinking that might discourage people from coming. ("When you call a plumber," he said by way of explanation, "you don't expect him to work for five bucks, so why do the same here?") It didn't; they still came and they still expected on-demand service. "Just this week some guy from Canada called and said he wanted a tour at 10 A.M. this Saturday," Nehrich said, shaking his head at the nerve of such a request. "I said, uh, no! I've got other things to do."

Many of those who do come don't quite get it. They want to run the trains themselves, or see fantastical elements. "Some people are disappointed because it's not a toy train exhibit," Nehrich said, running his hand over the track. "It's too high for the kids to be able to see it." He paused. "But you know, that's sort of the point."

His work on the track has brought him renown within model railroading, or "the hobby," as he (at times disdainfully) called it. He has been a speaker at NMRA conventions, preaching the finer points of freight cars and scenery creation. He's been featured in various newspaper stories, has written over a hundred articles in magazines such as *Model Railroader* and *Mainline Modeler,* authored seven self-published books on the hobby, and is responsible for every one of the thirty thousand or so words posted on the sprawling, subscription-based RPI railroad Web site. Not that you'd ever know it. He is remarkably humble—the phone number comment, I learned, was not show-offy but genuine annoyance—and not disposed to talk about himself. When I spoke with Cynthia Smith, an assistant dean at RPI who has known Nehrich for fifteen years, she tried to explain it. "It's really a labor of love on his part," she told me. "He really, really believes that preserving this part of history is important, not just for model railroading."

IT IS HARD TO PIN down when, exactly, the first real train gave rise to the first miniature train, but the hobby came to national prominence in the early twentieth century, when trains were the roaring, steam-belching metaphors of progress and westward expansion. Those were the days of golden railroad spikes, when what amounted to train porn—publications such as *Railroad Man's Magazine* (later to become *Railroad Stories*)—romanticized railroad fiction, as did *Collier's*, the *Saturday Evening Post,* and books like Alan Chapman's *Ralph in the Switch Tower, or the Adventures of a Young Railroader.* These were stories of heroic switchmen avoiding imminent disaster, love on the tracks, and mail trains speeding "on the advertised." Hand in hand, hobbyist magazines such as *Model Railroader* and *Model Railroading* sprang up to serve the growing number of boys and men building their own little worlds in the basement. During this era, a layout such as RPI's would not have been confined to the bowels of a dorm building but displayed with great pride.

Over the years, the hobby grew, buoyed by various technological advances, in particular the 1982 introduction of cyanoacrylate glues (superglue to you and me) and in the early nineties the use of injection molding and laser molding. Today, some of the best-selling layouts are based on children's books: Hogwarts Express—from Harry Potter—and Thomas the Tank Engine, both of which are aimed at an audience a good half-century younger than men like Nehrich. For this reason, Nehrich and his RPI brethren profess a disdain for the hobby and its major organizing body, the NMRA. Nehrich has long since stopped attending conventions.

That afternoon, a number of RPI club members dropped in. They were the kind of young men who wear shirts with Apple computer logos on the front, who hold clipboards and make jokes about wearing gold foil on their heads to "communicate with the aliens," as club president Greg Snook did not long after arriving. As Nehrich and I sat in the middle room on a beat-up couch, the wooded ridgeline of the train layout stretched out before us, the club members hummed around us. Or rather, they did not hum. I'd never been around a group of people who could work in such silence, each lost in his or her own task, and by extension, world. Occasionally, they stopped by to ask Nehrich for direction. He answered efficiently. "No, we don't want to go with brass there." "Make sure you come back tomorrow to finish with the siding." "Take the switchers and move them to the L line."

Eventually, a number of them gathered in the middle room, including Snook; a couple of alumni members; one of the rare female members, Melanie, a nonstudent who got involved because her father loved trains (Nehrich said this is unusual, as most women who join do so because their husbands are interested); and Will Gill, a lanky recent graduate who looked like a younger, skinnier Tom Hanks. Intellectual and self-deprecating, Gill was a volunteer who essentially functioned as Nehrich's right-hand man in the club.

As they spoke, I got the impression that both Nehrich and the students considered the club to be less about model railroads and more about a scholarly pursuit of history. There was an elitist vibe; they spoke of "kit bashing," that is, taking apart premade modeling kits and modifying them to create accurate models (the implication being that manufacturers don't bother with accuracy), and their heroes were not model railroaders but rather professors like John Stilgoe (author of the railroading history *Metropolitan Corridor*) and James Howard Kunstler, the author of *The Geography of Nowhere,* a manifesto that argues that railroads represented a golden age of American society. "Not to be an elitist asshole," said Gill, leaning against a side of the layout, "but I really don't like modeling clubs. I feel like what we do here is so different from the average model railroader. I think of what they do as sitting in a chair and making a layout."

Nehrich nodded. "They make up all their own stuff, and it's all Disney-like stuff. Where's the skill in that?"

To spend a day with the club was to understand just how painstaking the layout construction was. Everything was researched, everything mapped out. Each tiny tree was actually a sprig of St. John's wort, chosen because of its bonsai look, which had been gathered from hillsides in Vermont, dipped in a mixture of Elmer's glue and water, and then dunked in ground foam rubber (chosen to represent the correct color of foliage), with more sprinkled on top, "like breading chicken," as Nehrich put it. The layout was the opposite of building a sandcastle—done slowly, methodically, and with permanence in mind.

Dredging up the historical details of forgotten times is not easy. For building layouts, the club relies on historical societies, old blueprints (including some from the Library of Congress), field research, and, of all things, eBay, which is a treasure trove of old postcards. "Texts aren't that helpful because we're not modeling interiors," Nehrich explained. "But eBay is amazing. You just type in 'postcards, Troy' and it's amazing what you'll find."

Why postcards? "Because they used to have postcards of industry back when industry was something to brag about. So there would be postcards of the city itself. Belching smokestacks represented prosperity." He smiled. "Now, it's like, 'Oh my God, that's pollution.' "

Will nodded. "It's *unreal* how many postcards you can get. A town like Proctor. It's a tiny little town, like ten people live there. *Nobody* lives there. And there are postcards of all four sides of their main plant from different views, postcards of hydrodams, tracks on both sides."

Around the room, murmurs of appreciation for eBay. "And best of all," Nehrich said, "you don't even need to buy the postcard. We can just use the low-res image." He laughed at the beauty of it all. They were co-conspirators; the world did not understand their goals.

Sometimes postcards don't do the trick, however. That's when the layout requires field work. So Nehrich packs up the students, or heads out by himself, and travels up the route. They stop at abandoned barns, at farmhouses, they take tours of manufacturing plants, pretending to care about the "tour" but really taking notes about the structure of the buildings. One time, a woman in Chatham thought they were with the highway department because they were measuring the area around her house (Nehrich had to reassure her). Most people, Nehrich told me, are nice once he explains their purpose. Still, "We once went to this place in upstate New York that used to be a creamery and now they make yo-gurt, and they acted like it was this high-tech yogurt and we were indus-trial spies. Yeah right!"

The more Nehrich and his charges talked about the research, the more animated they became. It was apparent that what drives Nehrich is the idea of preserving a piece of the world as it was fifty years ago. In many ways, he does what journalists and authors attempt to do—to record a time and place and give it context—only in tactile form. A newspaper reporter captures single snapshots, hastily rendering an in-complete picture of the world as it is on one day. A writer may spend years researching a book. Then there are those like Nehrich who spend the better part of their lives on a project.

By their nature, such projects are never-ending. As any author will tell you, no book is ever really finished. Even as you read this sentence, I'm probably sitting somewhere wishing I'd written it a little more elo-quently. There is always more research that could be undertaken, more calls that could be made, more documents that could be scoured. For some, this open-endedness is part of the lure. I sensed that this was the case with Nehrich; he loved the process more than the result.

So when I say that Nehrich was a stickler for details, I do not mean in the sense that if Troy used to have fire hydrants, he makes sure to put in fire hydrants. No, he wants to know what brand of fire hydrant, its color, and how many dogs peed on it. Well, not really, but close. When he bought miniature geese, he painstakingly repainted them to be Canadian geese, because those are the breed that would be flying over in the fall. To accurately re-create the fire alarm boxes of Troy in 1950 was a research project that took him to three libraries and for which he traced the 150-year history of fire alarm devices (bells to alarms to phones to, now, cell phones). Then he checked with a fire buff and searched out available photographic evidence from the era.

And Nehrich does that for *every aspect* of all of the cities on the route. When I finally took my leave of the club that night, I told him how impressed I was with the layout and its intricacies. "That's funny," he said, appraising me, "because all I see are the parts that aren't done, where the imperfections are."

AS A YOUNG BOY, NEHRICH loved two things very much: trains and Gilbert and Sullivan operas. Had there been an opera about trains written by G&S—*Pirates of the 5:09 to Boston*—he would have been in heaven. As it was, his younger sister Helen remembers many a family "vacation" centered on visiting trains—as she told me with a laugh, "We took steam locomotive tours in Vermont. We'd go to Pennsylvania to see trains."

Nehrich's father, Walter, was born in the United States but studied art in Germany and made a living colorizing black-and-white photos— including the Breck shampoo girls—before World War II. He later taught arts and crafts and worked in a lumberyard. John's mother, Marjorie, was a secretary who'd been crippled by polio when she was eleven—her right arm and leg were weak and she had a limp. The family lived a modest life in Jackson Heights in New York City; John took the subway into the city and attended Stuyvesant School of Science. In 1966, when John was sixteen, Marjorie got mugged and Walter, upset by the incident, moved the family to the small town of Chester, New York. It was quieter but the countryside posed new challenges. For example, Walter didn't drive—he didn't see the need to—so Marjorie acted as family chauffeur. (John grew up to mirror his father's distaste for automobiles. To this day, he doesn't drive—both because he doesn't find it necessary and because he's opposed to the infrastructure of the automobile. He walks everywhere or takes public transportation.)

Nehrich entered RPI in 1968 intent on becoming a chemist but was quickly sucked into the model train club; he'd finally found a like-minded community, one who understood his passion. By his senior year, he was loath to leave the layout. He took a job nearby as a chemist with GE, but after finishing the training program, found himself inexorably drawn back to RPI. He decided on a trade-off; he would only take jobs that allowed him to work on the layout. So he wrote articles for modeling magazines—which paid poorly and sporadically—and took odd jobs to feed his habit. He worked as a night watchman, a clerk, and, memorably, as a security guard at the building where they dropped the numbers for the lottery.

Openly gay since after college, Nehrich believed his sexuality affected his ability to be hired, but that, in retrospect, this wasn't such a bad thing. "I was sidetracked from a professional job with the state," he explained, "and thus wasn't stuck with making so much money that I never would have been able to drop my income level to take the job with RPI. Which I guess was a good thing in the long run."

For the better part of two decades, Nehrich wasn't even getting paid for the work he did on the layout; it was a true hobby, if an all-consuming one. Then, in 1989, RPI put him on payroll, giving him a salary of $10,000 a year as a part-time employee. His life was the layout; there was little else. He was spending so much time in the basement that he used his tiny $190-a-month apartment in South Troy primarily as a bunking house. He would leave early in the morning, eat all his meals at work, and return only to sleep. He saw no reason to buy a refrigerator when the only cooking he did at home was to make coffee in the morning, and for that he found he could stomach dehydrated milk. Likewise, he found it cheaper to buy an electric blanket for his bed instead of heating the entire apartment. During the brutally cold winters of northern New York State, Nehrich would spend his nights curled up under an electric blanket alongside his alley cat, Angie, while Angie's water bowl froze over on a nightly basis. "I remember once counting out twenty-six dollars in pennies that I had while waiting for a check to come from a model train magazine," he told me. "I was living off a can of tuna fish and a can of pork beans one day and the next day it was chicken salad sandwich. I would roll the pennies and take them to the bank. The chicken sub was like $1.25 and the tuna fish was fifty cents a can."

And you believed, I asked, that all this was worth it for the layout?

"I kind of felt it was important and, again, I was willing to make the sacrifice," he said. "Even now, I don't really like to travel. I don't own a car. I don't care about fancy clothes. Money doesn't seem to matter that much. As long as I have something to eat and a roof over my head, that's okay."

It was as if Nehrich was following Candide's advice—to give up on the world and cultivate your own little garden. He'd go stretches where he rarely left the layout. "I think he lived there," Cynthia Smith, the assistant dean, told me. "I would go in and I wasn't sure if he'd gone home for a while. He would stay there forever, just working."

It reminded me of a story recounted in *Sports Illustrated* about Dick Vermeil, the workaholic pro football coach who is known to regularly sleep in his office. Once, while coach of the Philadelphia Eagles, Vermeil heard what sounded like explosions outside Veterans Stadium. Concerned, he sent an assistant to determine the source of the sounds. Upon returning, the assistant told him that the strange noises were actually fireworks. It was, the man reported, the Fourth of July.

Nehrich's passion was impressive but also seemed to be workaholism—if not escapism—of the first order. I asked Smith for her take. "He loves what he does," she said. "He really does. Is he a workaholic? I would say yes. I would say sixty hours is light for him." When I asked Helen, his sister, this question, she paused. "He mentions he is. But if your hobby is your job, where do you cut it off? I always tell my kids you want to do something you love, that you'd do it for free."

This brings up the question I mentioned earlier: Can you love your job too much? The historian John Hope Franklin once said, "You could say that I worked every minute of my life, or you could say with equal justice that I never worked a day. I have always subscribed to the expression 'Thank God it's Friday' because to me Friday means I can work for the next two days without interruption."

But Franklin also taught classes and traveled the world and wrote books. Nehrich's life is different, even if his hours aren't unusual; by many measures, we are a nation of workaholics. According to a 2004 report by the International Labor Organization, Americans work more hours, 1,835 per year, than any advanced industrial nation other than Australia (Aussies, somewhat surprisingly, logged 20 hours more than Americans): we work 245 hours more than the French, nearly 353 hours more than the Germans, and a whopping 459 more than workers in Norway. The Italians take two-hour lunches; we try to scarf down a grilled chicken sandwich while typing e-mail messages. Paul Romer, a professor at Stanford, makes the argument that there is a "time famine" occurring because, even if people aren't actually working, they are thinking about work and calculating in their head the value of every minute they are "wasting." We end up with the perception that we are more pressed for time than we actually are.

Nehrich, however, is far from the typical multitasking stereotype of a workaholic. Nor was he driven to long hours by the need for money or by the need to escape a bad home life—the startling possibility suggested in a 1997 book called *The Time Bind*, in which Arlie Hochschild concluded that work, rather than home, had become the escape for many modern parents. So what drove Nehrich? And was he happy? I headed back to RPI a few months later to accompany him on some "field research" with the aim of finding out.

. . .

I MET NEHRICH ON CAMPUS and we headed into downtown Troy. Once upon a time, the city was a thriving hub of trade and industry; as the terminus of the Erie and Champlain Canals, it was the fourth wealthiest community in the United States per capita in 1840, and by the turn of the century it led the country in iron and steel production (the shell of the warship *Monitor* was made in Troy). These days, however, the city's shoreline, factories, and gritty look draw enough movie producers—*Scent of a Woman, Ironweed, The Age of Innocence,* and *The Time Machine* were all filmed partly in Troy—that it has gained the nickname "Hollywood on the Hudson." While gritty may appeal to location scouts, however, it doesn't appeal so much to real people.

After parking, we made our way on foot into the downtown area, if you could call it that. It looked as if a citywide fire alarm had sounded and nobody had told people it was safe to come back—boarded-up storefronts, sparse lunch crowds, empty shopping areas. I noted this and Nehrich nodded. "It's not a pedestrian-friendly area anymore," he said. "Everything they've done in the city, from making broad curves at the intersections to limiting parking, has encouraged cars to drive faster and made it less safe for pedestrians."

He said the word "cars" as if spitting out a piece of rotten food. "I'm not really opposed to cars on an individual basis," he explained. "What I'm opposed to is the way that society makes the infrastructure to accommodate them at the expense of the pedestrian."

He continued as we walked. "So it's not cars, just the way that we have allowed them to become . . ." He paused, then furrowed his brow. "I almost feel like the Constitution has changed and you don't have any rights as a pedestrian, but you have a right to a car and a right to a parking space. If you can't find a legitimate space you have a right to take any place, because God forbid you're without a parking space. Drive up on someone's lawn and you can be, like, 'Well, there was no other place to park.' "

Trains, on the other hand, encouraged city centers as well as human interaction. The reason he'd told me earlier that 1950 was when trains "last mattered" was that this was when railroads were just getting the first diesel locomotives but had yet to scrap the steam ones—which didn't happen until 1953—and the gradual shift from trains to planes, cars, and trucks had yet to fully take hold. "To give you a perspective," he explained, "in 1915, the Troy station was served by 130 passenger trains a day plus there was regular trolley service to as far away as Lake George. The trolleys went out in 1938. In 1950, there were still about forty trains a day to Troy. The last train to Troy was 1958, and since that time, there has been no train service whatsoever."

He shook his head, then stopped to point out an important land-mark. We'd reached Fifth Avenue. "This is where our model ends," he said, drawing a horizontal line in the air, "so every time we go past it we say we're going two-dimensional." I told him that this sounded a bit nerdy. He smiled shyly and nodded. "I know."

We walked into the heart of the city, eventually arriving at the site of the original railroad station, which was now, somewhat absurdly, a Sushi King. After a stop at the Visitors' Center, where Will proudly showed us an antiquated half-hour slide show on the history of Troy, we headed back to my rental car. On the way, a disheveled-looking man with a bushy beard and a questionable number of teeth passed by.

"Hi George!" Nehrich said sprightly.

"Hi," the man said.

We kept walking. Finally, I asked, "Who was that?"

"Oh, that's George, from AA."

Or at least that's what it sounded like Nehrich said. He'd told me he didn't drink and never had, so I must have misheard him. "I'm sorry," I said, "did you just say AA? Is that a train acronym?"

He looked at me as if I were a little slow. "No, it's Alcoholics Anonymous."

"But you told me you don't drink. . . ." I said.

"I don't," he replied, "but I've been going to the meetings. It helps." He paused. "I also go to Narcotics Anonymous on Thursday nights. That's easier. I say I'm an addict. People relate to the experience."

"An addict?"

"Well, I work so much. I should be doing it basically forty hours a week or forty-five. But I have to really watch myself that I don't do it on my days off. I'm kind of learning that that's what I have to do, force myself to do other things. But it's a struggle. It helps to relate to people."

This, I'd never heard of: a man so enraptured by his work that he was going to AA meetings. It had begun, he explained, during the previous summer. The job was so isolating, and he was spending so much time doing it, that he became depressed. It didn't help that he'd cut off ties with many in the model railroad community. He'd found that, instead of going to conventions and having to answer a lot of what he considered dumb questions, he could just exchange e-mails with the handful of people he respected. Beyond those like-minded souls, he found few people in the hobby who understood his point of view. "I kind of wound up in this special situation—you know, the stereotype where you go to the cocktail party and the doctor is always being asked for free advice and the lawyer and everything like that? Well, at least they make big bucks. We had to make money for the club. So you resented doing anything for free. Say a school group wanted to come—it would be taking up time when we were supposed to be making money."

So instead he'd get lost in the work for hours and then, suddenly, realize it was 11 P.M. That summer, he went to see a counselor, who recommended AA and a second, antithetical, outlet. "There was a bar on the way down to my house and he wanted me to start going in to talk with people. So I was like, 'You're telling me to go to a bar and AA meetings at the same time.' It was real ironic." The bar idea didn't work; it's tough to bond with drunks, Nehrich pointed out, when one is sober. So he stuck with the AA meetings. "Most of the people who go to AA use alcohol as a coping skill. I used working on the computer and the layout. I get so engrossed in that. It's like my own personal blackout."

He didn't share his stories at the AA meetings, he explained, but mainly listened. "I don't drink, so I couldn't talk about that," he said, "And I can't talk about relapse, because I kind of think that I'm relapsing every time that I spend my day off on the computer doing research. But it's not like when you drink and you relapse and you keep going for days and days. It's only six hours' worth. So most of the time I don't share, I just listen."

We'd arrived at the car, signaling the end of that conversation. He pointed the way as I drove to our next stop, the site of the old railroad line through Green Island.

We followed the tracks northwest through a working-class neighborhood bristling with American flags. It was a warm, windy day and dandelion spores were heavy in the air, like summertime snowflakes floating by the boxy houses with aluminum siding. A blue Honda STR parked on the side of the street boasted tricked-out lights and a sticker on the back that read IF IT'S TOO LOUD, YOU'RE TOO OLD. Nehrich noticed none of this; he was concentrating solely on the architecture. "A lot of these buildings date back to the period we're modeling but we have to look past the remodeling. It can be tricky."

He pointed to a brick house. "See those windows on the second story? They used to be taller because you needed more light. You can see where they reduced the height because you don't need the light as much anymore."

This led to an impromptu history lesson, one of many I received. Fluorescent lights, Nehrich explained, were first sold in the United States in 1938, but since most of Troy's buildings were constructed prior to that time, they reflect the electric-light era, when it was difficult to illuminate a large area without producing a lot of heat and using a lot of energy. Also, until air-conditioning and Freon came into use, almost all buildings needed scores of windows for ventilation alone. This all related, of course, to model train layouts. "I get frustrated by people in the hobby who model and base it on today and don't put in windows." He shook his head, becoming uncharacteristically animated. "You've got to have windows everywhere! It's like a room today without an electrical outlet!"

He headed off behind a house through a backyard—unconcerned that we might be trespassing—to reach an old set of tracks, the Waterford branch of the D&H line. The line runs under a hulking concrete overpass for Route 7. Above us, cars and rigs rumbled by, but down in the shade it was quiet and lonely, mainly gravel, trees, and hardy shrubs. Weeds sprouted along the iron tracks, weaving their way through old tires, abandoned shopping carts, and rusted-out trash cans. It was a sad place, a forgotten place. Progress had passed it by, rumbling on like the trucks overhead. Nehrich, however, saw something beautiful to be preserved. He bent down to examine the tracks lovingly. "This would be on the edge of our layout," he said, "but it's on there."

WHEN I MET NEHRICH, HE was in a transitional period. Only two months prior to my first visit, he'd stopped working on the layout full-time and begun working in the student union. It was menial work; overseeing the area, keeping an eye on things, helping whoever needed help. He told me this was a breakthrough, however, for two reasons. For one, he no longer needed to "justify" his work at the model railroad club by raising money. For years, he'd had to meet a budget to, in essence, pay his own salary. So he'd sold memberships and given tours. At one point the club was making its own models and doing $100,000 a year in business. But it was exhausting work and, more important to John, it wasn't the work he wanted to be doing. So when he made the move to the student union—where he had a salary of $31,000 (as opposed to the $26,000 or so his model train salary had risen to) and could still work on the layout—it was like a cloud had lifted. He was a man coming out from the dark, in more ways than one.

Secondly, he was now out of the basement and interacting with people. The average adult spends one-third of his or her waking time alone, but Nehrich was spending far more time than that by himself. The Hindu sage may have found comfort in solitude, but few are cut out to be Hindu sages.

The inherent contradiction of Nehrich's life was that he clearly yearned to help others—he took great joy in mentoring students at the club and seemed to be as interested in helping others at AA meetings as in getting help himself—but he still chose to spend most of his time alone. When I spoke with Cynthia Smith, the assistant dean, I learned that when Nehrich walks back from work—no cars, remember—he passes a homeless shelter. "He'd stop at the convenience store at 11 P.M., or whenever he'd finally make it home, and buy donuts and drop them off," Smith told me. "Then he helped them develop and manage a Web site. And he didn't tell anyone about this; I only just found out. I think that's pretty monumental. I think he really believes in people."[1]

Disengaging from the layout, at least financially, had given him a certain perspective on how he related to it. As we headed across town, to an urban area he wanted to photograph for modeling, he tried to explain it to me.

"For a long time, I really felt that what I was doing with model railroading was really significant and so it seemed okay to make sacrifices because it was important. And I think . . ." He paused, looking out the window as Troy passed by. "It seemed like it was real important to document this stuff, and maybe it is, but we started out with the idea that we would be sort of a tourist destination. But the school did not come through with their side of it."

We stopped at a red light. I sensed that, after years of toiling without acknowledgment, years when the layout was enough, he was saying that a love can go unrequited only so long, that maybe for something to be a calling you need the world to value what you value. "So," I asked, "do you still see it as significant?"

He thought for a moment, rubbed his chin. "Not enough to sacrifice for it. I think that's one of the reasons I'm now in the transition. To find something so that I feel I'm doing something important, and I haven't found it yet."

This was a matter of opinion. Some might say he was deep in the throes of a boy's hobby, while others might see him as creating a visual,

1. After Nehrich's original push, the Web site, josephshouseandshelter.org, has since been taken over by a webmaster involved in the shelter.

tactile history, preserving information that might not otherwise be pre-served. Ideally, all that would matter is how Nehrich himself perceived it, but it is the rare man who can survive on his own accreditation alone. I asked how the work made him feel.

He thought for a moment. "I feel really good until I get home. The eight hours of work are good, but it's also good to have something in the other hours. If it's been the work that has kept me from doing the other parts of my life, then that's bad. The rest of it is good."

We had reached our destination, but I had another question to ask. He sounded so conflicted about the layout—or at least what his love for the layout had done to the rest of his life. "Do you think," I asked, "that you find meaning through the work?"

He paused for a good ten seconds. "I don't know. A year ago, I would have said, yeah, this is kind of my purpose in life. This is my legacy and I'm happy with it. I'm kind of going through this transition and maybe a year from now it will be a totally different transition."

"But what about right now?"

"No. I guess it comes back to the point that so many other people don't see it that way and I buy into their feelings on it. They trivialize it and therefore it's easy for me to trivialize it. There are people who I would not tell what I really did for a living because it was too hard to ex-plain, and if I just said I worked for a model railroad their initial reaction was, 'Oh Lionel four-by-eight layout and how could you spend a whole . . .' And it was easier just not telling them."

"What would you tell them?"

"I work up at the student union, I work up at RPI. I had this one guy who thought I was a janitor and I didn't bother correcting him."

I was shocked. "So you'd rather be considered a janitor . . ."

"Than someone who plays with trains? Yeah."

WE'D ARRIVED AT OUR NEXT stop, off of Third and Madison in Troy, where Nehrich wanted to examine period buildings. Toting his digital camera, he headed off the main streets and down alleyways.

He broke into a grin and pointed to the back of a row house that looked as if it had been constructed by a kid with Legos, all misshapen additions and diagonal outdoor staircases. "Now that brings joy to a modeler's heart," he said. "It has character. You got the phony siding. You got the staircase that comes out. You got the windows all over the place, all different sizes."

"So that's a period building?"

"Pretty much. It looks like aluminum-sided windows went in there, so you'd have to take them out of that. This building here," he pointed to a decrepit shack that slumped to the left, "is clearly an old one. The carriage houses had to have a second floor where they stored the hay. The difference between a garage and a carriage house is that it wasn't one story. If you start making this stuff up, it all looks the same in the modeling because you have a limited imagination."

It was not a scenic area. Dogs barked as we navigated a terrain of discarded couches, busted folding chairs, overgrown weeds, and old potato chip bags. Suddenly, he stopped, animated. "Now *there's* a back I would love to model!" He pointed to a patchwork two-story building and started snapping pictures. "It's all ratty and kind of angled. I wouldn't want to live there though." The snapping continued; I wondered if anyone on the block was concerned that an excited fifty-four-year-old man was taking photos of their backyards. If they were, they hadn't come out yet. "It's easy making them look all pristine," Nehrich continued, "but making them weathered is tricky. That's where the challenge is."

As we went, he became more animated. I found it hard to believe that he was going to give this up. He was in his element, as alive as I'd seen him. As he hurried over to another house, talking as he went, he looked like a man who couldn't help himself—not so different from the alcoholic in a room of free drinks. I told him that for a man who claimed this wasn't his purpose in life, he was becoming awfully enthused. He gave me a melancholy smile. "I guess I just want more people to listen."

Two months after my second visit, I heard from Nehrich again. He had decided to make a change. "Since we last spoke, I realized I wanted to become a drug counselor," he wrote in an e-mail. "I just got accepted (on Friday), and I should be starting classes in a week or so. I figure once I'm done, I would like to counsel in my spare time, while still remaining in my current job full-time. Since I don't need the extra finances, I can even work as a volunteer. I feel in some ways like a jigsaw and the final piece is falling into place so one can see the entire picture."

I wished him luck with the counseling program. It sounded, I told him, like a natural fit. I suspected, however, that he would be drawn back to the layout like iron filings to a magnet. I wondered whether he would be able to balance the two.

SEVEN MONTHS LATER, I CALLED Nehrich to check in on his progress as a counselor. It had stalled. He'd also stopped going to AA meetings. Regardless, he sounded excited. He told me that, because of a new position—he was working at night at RPI, overseeing the student union, so he had more free time during the day—he had been able to really get back into modeling again. More important, he said, the club had voted to close the layout to the public. Now it would be for students and members only; anyone else would have to go to the Web to see it. No more tours, no more cleaning up for visitors, no more kids running around derailing trains. Despite the fact that this most likely meant he would have even less human contact, he sounded blissful. "It's like a weight off my shoulders," he said. "I kind of felt like I had a thousand bosses—everyone could call up and say I want this, I want that. I've gotten back to modeling which is nice, because I hadn't done it. Now I'm getting my hands dirty, covered with paint, styrene, sawdust. Which is good. I've got a whole bunch of projects going at once. The place is a mess, but that's good."

I asked about the rest of the crew. Greg Snook, the club president, had graduated and moved to New Jersey; they didn't hear from him much. Will was still working nearby and spending as much time as ever at the club—his newest project was to build a working steamboat (to scale, of course). The Green Island area of the layout—the part of town I'd visited underneath Route 7—was almost done and they planned a spring "dedication" to which they intended to invite the mayor, the historical society, and the media.

But what about him and the idea of counseling? "I'm still going to do it; it will just take longer. I think the AA meetings and the classes were good for me. It helped me realize a few things. But I got tired of never talking at the meetings. After a while, everyone was supposed to lead one, and what did I have to say?"

We talked a while longer. It was a weekday morning and he was in his office, at school. I asked what he had on tap for the day. "Well, now that I have my own office, I've found that I can actually do modeling in here during the day. So I'm working on something right now, a carriage house. It's coming along pretty well."

When I'd first read about Nehrich, in various newspaper clips, I'd noted that he had made varying estimates of when the model railroad would be finished. In 1989, he guessed another ten years; in 2000, it was five more. I asked him what the current time line was.

"Well," he said, "I don't know. We keep making progress but then we rip up certain sections. I suppose we've been at it thirty years, so . . ." He paused. "Another thirty years is not unreasonable."

I smiled. I was reminded of a Shel Silverstein poem about a search for a pot of gold. The narrator looks far and wide and, finally, finds the treasure. It is exactly as he had hoped. His response: So what do I search for now?

FIVE

THE TIME-CLOCK

PHILOSOPHER AMID

AN INDUSTRY OF

ANSWERS

TO BETTER UNDERSTAND THE QUEST for a calling, I thought it would be wise to talk to those who study it for a living. So I headed to Sacramento for the International Career Development Conference, where thousands of career counselors and would-be counselors and those who cater to them had gathered to discuss the Holy Grail of the business: how to find happiness at work.

On my first day, I found myself sitting in a room the size of an airplane hangar, at a table with five other people who, like me, were wearing nametags. Each of them was holding his or her hands about a foot apart, vertically, with fingers pinched as if sprinkling salt. They were all focused forward, toward a distant stage, where a career counselor named Rich Feller, who is also a professor at Colorado State, was exuberantly exhorting the crowd of fourteen hundred, who were exuberant in their willingness to be exhorted. He was holding a rubber band stretched tall, which he said served as a metaphor for the job search.

"You can either slowly move up to the dream"—he held the top of the rubber band in one hand and lifted the bottom up toward it with the other—"or"—and here he held the bottom in place while letting the top contract down—"you move back to the reality of now and give up."

There were murmurs of approval; if people didn't stretch for their dreams, they were lost. Feller, an energetic man with an athletic demeanor onstage, used lots of catchwords and slogans, such as *focused effort looks a lot like polished talent.* After his speech, he left to thunderous applause. You could practically smell the inspiration wafting through the room. "He was amazing!" a woman near me said, clasping her hands together. "Thought-provoking!" answered a middle-aged man with a coat and tie and a fistful of his own business cards. From the reaction, one might have thought Feller had struck gold and all career counselors would join ranks and follow his lead. But, as I learned, in career counseling there is no such thing as a right or a wrong answer, because everybody has his own solution.

At the conference in Sacramento, these answers could be bought in the form of personality tests, which ranged from the intimidatingly complex (the popular Myers-Briggs Type Indicator instrument breaks down personalities into a set of paradigms) to the intuitive (a deck of cards designed to make people free-associate their way to a new career). One could buy answers on audiotapes, in video seminars, in workbooks, and, most of all, in self-help books. Nearly every attendee, it seemed, had a book to hawk, and most of them were laid out on tables in booths. Feller was signing his book—*Knowledge Nomads and the Nervously Employed: Workplace Change and Courageous Career Choices*—at booth number 34. Many of the books looked remarkably similar—thin volumes with large print and, often, numbers in the title. Almost every topic was covered; titles included *Jobs and the Military Spouse, Married,*

Mobile and Motivated for Employment (which bore a cover photo of a sultry brunette holding a camera), *Ten Steps to a Federal Job, Can I Lie on My Résumé?, Get a Raise in 7 Days,* and *Take This Work and Love It.*

Attending the seminars was like being bombarded by relatives, all of whom have picked out *just the right girl for you,* regardless of whether or not you two have anything in common. I sat in on "Career Education Lithuanian-Style," "Don't Just Vent, Reinvent" and "4 New Tools for Faster Job Search and Better Salary." Some of the career strategies were question-based; Feller, for example, espoused the 3M test:

1. Mission—What's the core thing you're trying to
   do with your work life?
2. Model—Whom do you admire? Whom would
   you like to emulate?
3. Mirror—Am I proud or embarrassed of myself?

A presenter named Brian Weeks suggested making an "I Love It List" that will lead to finding "Your Truest Self," which in turn leads to "PURPOSE." Another duo endorsed using a "life metaphor" to find direction (for example, if you're like a subway train, you just need to get off at the right stop). One presenter examined "Why is it that career counseling has such little prestige?" while a Bay Area counselor named Marty Nemko claimed he could complete a "career makeover" in three to five minutes that 97 percent of his clients were satisfied with. (The key? "I am listening my butt off from the first nanosecond.") John Krumboltz, a droll, likable Stanford professor, gave a presentation along with Al Levin, a Cal State professor, in which he declared that career counseling had it all wrong. Instead of focusing closed-mindedly on one goal or "calling," he said, we must leave ourselves open to opportunity and recognize it.

It was a mind-numbing array of strategies. Just as management theory has offered up endlessly conflicting concepts in the last thirty years— from "team building" to "empowered autonomy," from "distinctive corporate culture" to "multicultural corporate culture"—so too has the career counseling business collectively thrown its ideas up against the wall to see what would stick. To be successful an idea doesn't necessarily need to be good, just new.

No one seemed particularly concerned with coalescing the ideas, or pruning them, much less critiquing others. Near the end of the conference, I sat in on the talk given by the "parachute guy," Richard Bolles, author of the bestselling *What Color Is Your Parachute?* and the reigning deity of the career counseling world. Afterward, I sidled up to him, introduced myself, and asked the question that had been bugging me: How can there be so many solutions, and little apparent standardization, in the field? A big, friendly man with a football coach's presence, he frowned for a moment. "It can be a problem," he said. "The only career counselor I trust is the one who has been out on a job hunt himself. They get too excited about every new idea without trying it out."

Then he asked if I owned his book.

I LEFT SACRAMENTO FEELING OVERWHELMED. I had no doubt that most of the counselors I'd met were sincerely trying to help people, but I was more interested in *why* some people find a calling than a million suggestions of *how* to go about it. It was in the pursuit of this why that I came upon Amy Wrzesniewski. An assistant professor of management and organizations at the Stern School of Business at NYU, Wrzesniewski studies how people feel about their work. When I contacted her, I hoped that she would provide an interesting perspective on the people I'd met; I didn't expect her to qualify as one herself.

We met at her office on the campus of NYU one winter afternoon. Wrzesniewski (pronounced rez-NES-kee), who is in her thirties, is slender and friendly, with shoulder-length blond hair that is a tad unruly and a wide, trusting face that brings to mind the actress Maggie Gyllenhaal. Amiable and attentive, she has an unhurried midwestern manner of moving and talking that makes her seem out of place amidst the streaming humanity of Manhattan. Despite her outward calm, she harbors an underlying organizational drive that is stunning in its manifestations; for example, before each school year, she posts notecards in her closet listing every lecture of the semester and which outfit she will wear that day. That way, she guards against, in her words, "forty-five minutes in front of my closet."

There is probably no better place in the world to people-watch than New York City, and no better part of the city than Greenwich Village, a mélange of hipsters, students, young professionals, artists, freaks, and beatniks. From her office window, Wrzesniewski looks down on West Fourth Street as it passes through the NYU campus and could, if she were the type to daydream, pass the time wondering about the lives of all those ants marching by, bookbags slung over their shoulders, their futures open and unknown.

Her office was small and neat. Textbooks lined one wall, research books another, and above her desk she'd pinned badges and other mementos from various work conferences. She also had a stunning array of houseplants; four lined up along the office's large window, one perched on a bookcase, its tendrils trailing past textbooks, and another striking lime-green, purple-veined specimen on a side table. When I asked about them, she smiled sheepishly.

"I'm embarrassed to admit I have no idea what kind of plants they are," she said. "Only one of them is mine, the orchid on the shelf."

The other plants, she explained, had been brought in by the office janitor, a gregarious woman in her sixties named Maria. Not only did Maria bring in the plants, but she took clippings, potted new ones, watched over those of other professors who were on vacation or sick leave, and, without notice, rotated the greenery to brighten up other offices. "Some mornings I'll come in and there will be a new plant," Wrzesniewski said. "Other times, one of them will be gone and then I'll see it down the hall in someone else's office. I've had people in other departments ask me if they can borrow Maria for their floor too."

In addition to taking care of the plants, Maria was also meticulous in her janitorial work. She had a system for cleaning the offices, and, after she took vacation, she inevitably returned annoyed that someone had not only messed up her system but had done an inferior job—not cleaning in the handle grooves on the filing cabinet, for example (those amateurs). Obviously, this was not a woman who saw her job as "just" an office cleaner.

To most of us, this would be an uplifting story about a conscientious janitor. To Wrzesniewski, it is research fodder. She saw Maria as a prime example of a phenomenon she calls "job crafting." In a 2001 study published in *Academy of Management Review,* Wrzesniewski, in collaboration with Jane Dutton at Michigan, looked into this concept by interviewing twenty-nine office workers. She found that her subjects, by voluntarily changing the duties and boundaries of their jobs—becoming not just a cleaner, for instance, but a caretaker and hence part of a community—could imbue their jobs with meaning (and, not incidentally as far as companies are concerned, provide added value to the bottom line). The moral: it's not the job that matters but how the person doing it *defines that job* that matters.

This is the kind of stuff that makes Wrzesniewski excited. Since graduating from the University of Pennsylvania in 1994, she has published or collaborated on almost a dozen studies about how people relate to their work. Considering that the average human spends more than one-third of his or her waking life working, this wouldn't at first blush seem a particularly novel or unusual field of study. Surprisingly, it is. While many psychologists and pollsters have studied work as a big amorphous beast—looking at how it affects our stress, health, and overall life contentedness (one study pegged work satisfaction as capable of altering overall "life satisfaction" by 20 percent)—few researchers have attempted to look at the topic of how each of us views our work—and sometimes the same job—in a different manner. Maybe this area of study is too specialized, too subjective, too anecdotal, too irreproducible—or maybe it just sounds too unscientific. Whatever the reason, it has been underrepresented and this worries Wrzesniewski. "This is a critical area," she told me as we sat in her office, "and I don't know why people haven't done much work on it."

She seems to be trying single-handedly to rectify this. Wrzesniewski works up to eighty hours a week and had spent a recent Christmas break in Ann Arbor going over data for an upcoming study, a trip she described as "taking a break from my work to take a look into a fun subject."

FROM NYU, WE WALKED THROUGH the Village to Café Reggio, a quaint coffeehouse that feels like it was lifted off a Parisian street. Over chai tea, she told me about her career trajectory, which she described as "embarrassing because it sounds made up." She grew up in rural Brookhaven, Pennsylvania, where her mother worked (still does) as a registered nurse and her father loaded trucks at a refinery. Her grandfather on her father's side immigrated from Poland and no one in her immediate family had gone to college until Amy and her brother went. Determined that their daughter would break the mold, Amy's parents emphasized schooling to what she called "an almost freakish degree." They often told her, "Our job is our job. Your job is school." By the time she was ten, she'd developed a keen interest in psychology.

When she was sixteen years old, she was walking down the hallway at Sun Valley High School in Aston, Pennsylvania, when she saw a flyer for what she called "essentially a weeklong psychology summer camp" at nearby Lebanon Valley College. She enrolled and, for one glorious week, she was immersed in psychology, spending each day on a different specialty. They trained a rat in a Skinner box and went through the old perceptual exercise in which one puts on headphones, reads a passage, and has one's voice fed back with a slight delay (it becomes impossible to continue speaking without lapsing into gibberish). But it was when the camp focused on industrial organizational psychology, a rather stilted term for the psychology of work, that it all clicked for Wrzesniewski. "I thought to myself, *This is it*. I was done," she told me, chopping the air for emphasis. "People always say, 'You were that young and you already knew you wanted to do this?' But growing up, I saw such a huge span of what work can mean. I was fascinated by the amount of variance in joy, heartache, and importance that people got from their jobs, even when they were doing the *same* job."

So she went to Penn, which made her parents ecstatic. While there, she worked for a professor named Marty Seligman, a giant of the psychology world whose specialty is the idea of "positive psychology," essentially the study of what makes people happy. (Colloquially, he is known as a "happy-ologist.") She was honored. She was inspired. She was mostly opening mail and making photocopies.

Her sophomore year, she began working under another senior professor of psychology, Paul Rozin. She eagerly worked long hours and Rozin took her under his wing, impressed by her work ethic. (In four years at Penn, Wrzesniewski says, she missed one class. She also held a second job at a local high school, teaching marching band fifteen to twenty hours a week.) She had planned to get a job after graduation and then go back to grad school, but Rozin convinced her to make the jump right away. While at the University of Michigan in 1997, she collaborated with Rozin and two other colleagues on the paper that first drew my interest: "Jobs, Careers and Callings: People's Relations to Their Work," which was published in the *Journal of Research in Personality*, with Wrzesniewski as the lead author.

Employing a classification system first proposed in the mid-eighties by a psychologist named Robert Bellah and his collaborators, Wrzesniewski and company surveyed 196 employees at two work sites: a state university student health service and a small liberal arts college. Those interviewed included nurses, physicians, computer programmers, librarians, supervisors, administrators, clerical workers, and health educators. Most fell into middle-class or lower-middle-class designations: over half made under $35,000 a year (these being 1993–94 dollars, because that was when the surveys were taken).

The goal was to see if people, either consciously or subconsciously, separated themselves into three categories: those who saw their work as a "Job," those who saw it as a "Career," and those who saw it as a "Calling" (in the secular, popular sense of the word).

Along with her collaborators, she came up with three paragraphs, which she had each subject read and rate as to how closely it resembled his or her life. The first person, "Mr. A," represented the "Job" mind-set (though the words "job," "career," and "calling" were never mentioned). He was described, among other things, as follows: "works primarily to earn enough money to support his life outside of his job . . . if Mr. A lived his life over again, he probably would not go into the same line of work. . . . Mr. A's job is basically a necessity of life, a lot like breathing or sleeping."

Mr. B, on the other hand, "enjoys his work but does not expect to be in his current job five years from now . . . has several goals for his future pertaining to the positions he would eventually like to hold . . . for him, a promotion means recognition of his good work." Mr. B was the "Career" archetype.

Finally, there was Mr. C, who sounded like the perfect employee. "Mr. C's work is one of the most important parts of his life. . . . [It] is a vital part of who he is, it is one of the first things he tells people about himself. . . . Mr. C feels good about his work because he loves it and he thinks it makes the world a better place. . . . He tends to take his work home with him and on vacations, too."

Next up, the subjects answered a survey of eighteen true-false questions that read as follows:

1. I find my work rewarding.
2. I am eager to retire.
3. My work makes the world a better place.
4. I am very conscious of what day of the work-week it is and I greatly anticipate weekends. I say, "Thank God it's Friday!"
5. I tend to take my work with me on vacations.
6. I expect to be in a higher-level job in five years.

7. I would choose my current work life again if I had the opportunity.

8. I feel in control of my work life.

9. I enjoy talking about my work to others.

10. I view my job primarily as a stepping-stone to other jobs.

11. My primary reason for working is financial—to support my family and lifestyle.

12. I expect to be doing the same work in five years.

13. If I was financially secure, I would continue with my current line of work even if I was no longer paid.

14. When I am not at work, I do not think much about my work.

15. I view my job as just a necessity of life, much like breathing or sleeping.

16. I never take work home with me.

17. My work is one of the most important things in my life.

18. I would not encourage young people to pursue my kind of work.[1]

What Wrzesniewski and company found was that, in matching each score with the paragraphs, workers were unambiguous in seeing their work primarily in terms of one of these three categories. There was no middle ground, no hazy in-between, no one was conflicted—at least by the standards the testers had defined. Perhaps more surprisingly, the differences in the respondents' relations to their work could not be reduced to demographic or occupational differences. In other words,

1. For those interested in testing themselves, the true-false questions that associated a "true" answer with "Job" were numbers 2, 4, 11, 14, 15, 16, and 18. "Career" correlated with 6 and 10 (and a neutral response to the rest). The "Calling" group answered "true" overwhelmingly to numbers 1, 3, 5, 7, 8, 9, 12, 13, and 17.

those with high-paying or more "prestigious" jobs, such as college administrators, were no more likely to see their work as a calling or career
than those doing work stereotypically deemed less demanding or fulfilling, such as secretarial work. Wrzesniewski also found that the "Job"
and "Calling" people were inversely related in all their responses (for example, "Job" people didn't take their work home with them while
"Calling" people did).

So what did all this mean? Being a researcher, Wrzesniewski professes not to be an interpreter—she sees herself as someone who asks
questions rather than answering them—but her findings reinforce the
concept that people can find meaning in most any type of work. My father, for example, tells the story of a stenographer who worked with
him at UCSF Medical Center. She would take tapes dictated by the doctors in the nursery and type them up, day after day. Some might see this
as repetitive, boring work. But my dad remembers being stunned when
one day he walked in and saw the woman crying while typing. He asked
what was wrong. She explained that she was just so happy that a baby
had made it; she had been following the progress of a sick premature in-
fant via the tapes. In her mind, she had completed a cycle of care.

One of the things Wrzesniewski's study didn't address was the value
that others ascribed to professions. The cross section of people she focused on represented a range, but, I wondered, what would it be like if
she looked at, say, one hundred Peace Corps volunteers (the stereotypi-
cal "Calling") and compared them to one hundred investment bankers
("Career"), and, finally, one hundred people who run the drive-in at
McDonald's ("Job" in the sense of J.O.B.). I mentioned this to her and
she told me about the new study she was working on, the one that had
taken her to Michigan. "We decided to choose nurses, because it's one
of those jobs that by its very definition is almost a calling," she explained. "We wanted to see if people chose this type of occupation or
just landed there." While she wasn't able to compile significant data on
that particular question, she did happen onto another, surprising, finding. As she explained, "A significant number of nurses went into it as a

calling and because of the health care system became disillusioned." In other words, they were actually *losing* a calling rather than finding one.

WRZESNIEWSKI WAS UNEQUIVOCAL ABOUT HER job: She loved it. She complemented her research by teaching undergraduates, grad students, and executive MBA students, many of whom were very successful men ten or twenty years her senior. "It's harder but I'm superengaged," she explained. "These are people in their forties with high-powered jobs in charge of global positioning." Many of them have a hard time considering their work idealistically. "One of the first things I do is put a Power Point presentation up with a list of questions. The third one is: 'Do you feel like you're doing something good for the world?' When I ask that, I often hear snickers. Some of them ask, 'Does harming the world count?' It's very sad."

At each step in her career, she worried that she would wake up one morning and—poof!—the joy would be gone. "I kept on wondering, through college and grad school, *What if I hate it now?* It was my biggest fear. Some people get deeper and deeper into a field, past the doctoral level, and they get to that furthest level, with all the other obsessives, and then they realize—*this is too weird.*" She paused, smiling. "Not me. I love it. I think it's absolutely—I feel like if I won the lotto I'd . . ." And here she thought for a second. "Well, I'd stop teaching but I'd still be doing this research."

Wrzesniewski's enthusiasm might sound a little suspect considering her field of study—*I'm not just the president of the Hair Club for Men. I'm also a client!*—but she didn't strike me as disingenuous. Rather, I noticed a number of "tells," to borrow poker parlance, that she displayed when she talked about her research. She spoke quickly and in incomplete sentences, waved her hands in little circles in the air, and, as she talked, a vein protruded on her temple, as if her brain required more blood to express her excitement (in one of our later meetings, she even teared up when speaking about the profound effect her mentor, Rozin, had had on her).

She'd found a group of like-minded people, a core of young researchers at Michigan, Harvard, Illinois, and Emory, who functioned as
her community of "obsessives." In describing the feeling, she referenced
an old music video by the band Blind Melon called "No Rain." Those
who grew up in the early nineties surely remember it; a forlorn-looking
girl in a bee costume wanders through the world. As singer Shannon
Hoon warbles, "All I can do is just pour some tea for two . . ." we see the
girl trying to find her place in the world. Finally, at the end, she discovers
a meadow where everyone, like her, is wearing bee suits. Wrzesniewski
mentioned it offhandedly, but it struck me that this was something that
tied many of the people I met together: they'd found their bee people.
For Halvorson, it was the lumberjack community, for Danz it was other
ocularists.

Much time has been spent examining this phenomenon from an organizational perspective. In something called the "attraction, selection,
attrition model," people are said to shop for companies and organizations in various settings that fit them. The idea is that people know
pretty quickly if there is a fit. The concept of bee people, however, extends beyond just the job one has, to an outside community of people.
There hasn't been a lot of study of this phenomenon, but it is especially
prevalent in the computing world—open source programmers are a
good example of people who work for one firm but have a deep involve-
ment in an extracurricular group that is stronger than their work tie. In
Wrzesniewski's case, her group provided a powerful bond. "It's a great
feeling," she said, "knowing that these are my people."

SO WHAT IS IT LIKE to analyze other people's livings for a living? I put
this question to Wrzesniewski as the afternoon wore on. "Those of us
in the department joke that we get to choose the eighty hours of the
week that we work," she said. "It's meaningful autonomy. I can choose
which ideas and puzzles I want to look into. You can't get more au-
tonomous than that."

The downside, she explained, was that if her ideas aren't any good, or if they are too obvious, her work will be discounted. So she abides by the same advice she gives her students: if it doesn't pass the grandmother test, get rid of it. "If your grandmother could have told you what you're finding, is it really an interesting theory? At that point, you need to rethink your assumptions."

In her opinion, much of what passes for popular "career literature"—the vast expanse of how-to job-search guides, many of which I'd encountered at the conference in Sacramento—could come straight from the mouth of your grandma. "I once got deep into the corners of that literature and I was surprised at how atheoretical it was and how it wasn't really based on a lot."

She stayed away from doing any prescribing herself. "I see myself as asking the questions: What does this mean?" She thought for a moment. "I actually don't think about how people can find their calling. I think about what callings *mean*, where do they come from and how do they affect interactions with the companies these people work for. Sure, there's probably a bit of the ivory tower thing, but the holy grail for us is publishing in the academic journals."

Her success is measured not only by getting her research published, but by where it gets published. In the past, she had tossed out a year's worth of work when a paper wasn't accepted at a high-profile journal. As she saw it, it was better to publish less frequently and be placed at better journals than to publish more often but at a lower-prestige journal.

SOME TIME PASSED BEFORE I saw Wrzesniewski again. In the interim, I tried applying some of her theories to my life. Or, more accurately, my friends' lives. On nights out, I became a barstool interrogator. I didn't just ask what you did, I asked why you did it, how you felt about it, and whether you felt you were making a difference. The poor bastards I cornered thought they were out to make conversation over a beer, just a bunch of the guys out to watch a game, and then I'd start grilling them during their off-hours about exactly what they were trying to forget by coming to the bar: work.

Despite some initial reticence—people aren't accustomed to someone not just perfunctorily asking but actually wanting to know about their job—the conversations became very intimate very quickly. It was almost as if I were asking about the details of someone's love life, or the state of his marriage. I found myself listening—a lot—because, after not knowing what to say at first, once people got going they couldn't stop. It was as if I'd cracked open an emotional fire hydrant and everything was just shooting out. After a while they'd invariably stop and say, "I must be boring you to death."

But they weren't. I couldn't get enough. One night I was talking with a friend I'd known for two years who never really talked much about her job other than to say she loved it. I asked why and pestered her for something other than platitudes. "Well," she said, "I have a great boss and I really like my coworkers. The salary allows me to live the lifestyle I want and I have time to study on the side." And on she went, giving me eight reasons why her job was great. And none of them—not one—had anything to do with what it was she actually *did* all day. I pointed this out.

Three days later, she sent an e-mail to tell me the conversation had "sent her into a whirlwind" thinking about her professional future. The upshot: she was changing jobs. This had clearly been brewing for a while; she just needed a reason to think about it. I'd given her one.

THE NEXT TIME I MET Wrzesniewski it was a Saturday afternoon. She'd just finished teaching her executive education class and was still "on an adrenaline high," even though she'd been up since 5:30 A.M., when she'd risen to go over her notes. At the end of each class, the researcher in her came out; she had all the students prepare a "one-minute memo" in which they gave her feedback. As we once again walked through the Village to grab lunch, she told me about her students.

"It's tough because they're executives so a lot of them have this professional listening face," she said as we navigated the landscape of Bleecker Street. Wrzesniewski could have passed for an executive herself; her hair was pulled back in a tight bun and she wore a black suit. "It's tough because I'm used to these undergrads who are like open books."

Earlier in the week, while arranging lunch, I'd asked if we could do some "field research," an idea she had warmed to immediately. So she took me by a few businesses that she thought were interesting. After stopping at an eyeglass store where she'd been impressed by the proprietor's memory for customers and willingness to fix glasses gratis— "clearly not a 'Job' orientation"—we headed down a long block to a wine store run by two older gentlemen.

"I've been going to this place for six years and they've never steered me wrong," she said as we walked. "I can go in and say, 'I need this kind of wine for this kind of party at this price,' and it's always a good choice." More impressively, she said, the proprietors will steer customers toward cheaper wine if it's better. "Clearly, the guys know what it means to be a neighborhood guy. All the faculty I talk to know them."

We reached the store and headed in to find one of the two managers, a bushy-haired gentleman who'd been working there since 1976. As an experiment, I asked for a not-too-sweet Pinot Grigio between $15 and $20 for a date with my wife. As Wrzesniewski had predicted, he recommended a $12 Pinot, a Furlan Castlecosa, which he deemed just as good as the ones in my price range.

As we headed out, Wrzesniewski analyzed the encounter. "In terms of engendering trust and long-term relationships with people, it's a brilliant strategy," she said excitedly. "If he'd said, 'Oh no, you can't get a good Pinot for that price,' he'd drive you away. And by the same token, if he'd sold you a crappy $7 bottle of wine, you wouldn't come back either. And he'll remember stuff that you like. It's almost like Amazon.com. 'People who bought what you like also like this,' except they're human repositories. Talk about job-crafting!"

Wrzesniewski sees much of New York through this lens. Cab rides are an opportunity to quiz drivers about how they come by their "skill sets." ("I've found that when they ask which way to go, if I say, 'I trust that you know the better way to go,' that this opens them up because I'm acknowledging their expertise.") Restaurants allowed for covert observation of waiters and waitresses, who in her opinion must multitask as much as anyone in any job. "The level of complexity is astounding," she said, shaking her head. "A good waitress will anticipate a table's needs, remember who is having what drink, know how fast they're drinking, read the situation, and know when not to bug diners. It requires multiple lines of action and, at any moment, they have to recalibrate. It's not just practice, it's an orientation." (Even her home life provided perspective; recently married, she lives in the Village with her husband, an architect, and she watches as he trades "necessary jobs" that aren't challenging for the opportunity to do the ones he wants, like a movie star who alternates indie pictures with big-budget ones. "He loves it when he can express himself," she explained, "but a lot of the time he is boxed in by the dimensions of the jobs he has to accept.")

As we made our way through the streets, it was like accompanying an anthropologist on an excursion, only the exotic locale was my own city. It made me think of the people I knew who invested in their jobs: the woman at the Chinese restaurant who took pride in knowing our order every time my wife and I called ("It is you, my friend, of the Chicken with Mixed Vegetables!"), the basketball league commissioner at my gym who often called to dissect the previous night's game.

Over lunch, I forced Wrzesniewski to switch sides of the microscope. "So what do you see your contribution being," I asked. "What would you like to have accomplished in twenty years?"

"Oh my," she said, taken aback a bit. Amazingly, she'd spent all this time asking other people such questions but rarely had anyone asked her. I felt like I was back at the bar, grilling a friend. When she spoke, it was slowly, as if creating a mission statement for her life. "Well, . . . if I could have my druthers . . . I would like to change the way or open up . . . the way that both scholars and organizations think fundamentally about work. What it is, how people connect . . . that domain of their lives and what the implications are."

I pointed out that it seemed unusual that she wasn't accustomed to thinking about this. She agreed. "Even in my department, we all spend all this time teaching but we never talk about what we do," she said. "It's almost this religious sermon type of thing. We talk to the class, then we talk to each other about what texts we teach, but not what we *do*."

Wrzesniewski picked at her tuna sandwich for a moment, then decided to revisit her mission statement. "You know what it is?" she said, "I want to know what people do all day. As I told you earlier, very few people study the work; there's so much focus on the organization. I'm interested in what people are actually *doing* when they're working." As she spoke, she made little chopping motions with her hands, slicing imaginary apples. "It's almost like the organization be damned for me. For my money, I can't think of many other questions that are more important in this realm of study than how work affects people's lives."

Not surprisingly, then, she was fascinated to hear about the characters I'd met. I told her about Danz ("remarkable sense of identity"), Halvorson ("she would make an intriguing case study"), and Mulholland ("Oh my goodness"). I asked her for her thoughts on them, and, instead of bringing up some complex theory or invoking a research study, she simply said, "Maybe your people are just doing that thing. They've found *that thing*."

The term couldn't have been more vague, yet at the same time more fitting. I called for the check and headed out in search of more of that thing.

SIX

THE SIXTY-SECOND

SALESMAN

ON LAFONTAINE BELIEVES THAT WHEN he was four or five years old, he was blessed with a gift. As he sees it, there is an invisible energy that swirls around us, and, at some indeterminate time, it swirled down and smacked right into him, whereupon he was imbued with a unique talent.

I first experienced his gift via a voice mail. LaFontaine returned my call and left a mundane message. I listened to it about six times. If I could have framed the message and put it on the wall, I would have.

It was a thing of beauty. LaFontaine's voice rolled out of the phone on its own red carpet, rich and husky and powerful. He pronounced his name in three quick, rising beats—"La-Fon-Taine"—as if he were a sommelier triumphantly presenting a prime Margaux. It was the voice of a king, a voice that could move men's hearts and bring a flush to women's cheeks. It said: "Hear me for I am important." It was commanding yet somehow familiar, even comforting. It was a voice I'd heard thousands of times but never before addressing me personally.

And this was all from one message. Imagine what this man's voice could accomplish if amplified in stadium seating by Dolby THX and accompanied by sweeping visuals and a blasting sound track. It might move one to do wondrous, perhaps even foolish, things. Like go see *Dr. Doolittle 2*. Or pay eight dollars to sit through *Entrapment*.

Those are but two of the more than 3,500 films for which LaFontaine has narrated trailers over the last forty years. He was the rumbling bass behind the previews for everything from *Doctor Zhivago* to *2001: A Space Odyssey* to *There's Something About Mary* to *I, Robot*. In 1984, he told moviegoers about the imminent return of a futuristic cyborg that, for all its advanced technology, inexplicably spoke in an Austrian accent. The spare refrain of *Terminator 2*—"This time he's back . . . for good"—immediately entered the pop culture vernacular, as so many of LaFontaine's taglines have. He helped write the much satirized opener, "In a world where . . . ," something he is decidedly ambivalent about (the way, one imagines, Don Mclean must feel about singing "American Pie" for the ten thousandth time). In the industry, LaFontaine is known as "Thunder Throat" and—in what may be the coolest nickname in history—"The Voice of God."

From our modern, media-saturated perspective, his career choice doesn't seem all that unusual; man has amazing voice so man does voice-over work. But half a century ago, when movie trailers were relatively low-budget affairs and NBC didn't need to record two dozen promos a day for its hot new fall lineup ("This Thursday, it's the one *ER* you *cannot* afford to miss!"), there was no blueprint for LaFontaine to follow, much less a role model. There was radio, but that was an entirely different world, one in which the best route to success was either as a DJ or as a character actor. LaFontaine essentially created his own profession and now, at the age of sixty-four, embodies it to the extent that most voice-over artists working today sound eerily like him.

As I flew out to Los Angeles to meet him, I thought back to something he'd said to me on the phone: "I love my job, but this really is a silly way to make a living." He'd said it with a breezy laugh, but it had sounded to me like practiced self-deprecation. I think he knew that, to the outsider, his job *did* sound silly; he basically talked emphatically for a living. But, I wondered, could someone have a calling yet feel his work wasn't important? I suppose if his balance in life tipped toward other aspects—family, maybe—but it seemed unlikely that anyone could spend his life doing something, and doing it exceptionally well, and consider it silly.

If that was the case, then LaFontaine was one hell of a salesman; as it is very hard to sell something you don't believe in, as I learned during my Kirby days. Rosser Reeves, a legendary copywriter in the 1950s whose creations included an ad for Anacin in which a hammer clangs an anvil as a gentle visual metaphor for the sensation of a headache, used to hold up two quarters as a way of explaining the business. The goal of advertising, he'd say, is to make the consumer believe that the two quarters are different and, more specifically, that one of them is worth more than the other.

Some people have a knack for this transformative dance and others don't. Those who do often wind up in sales, politics, or some other creative venture. LaFontaine ended up scripting and voicing movie trailers. It is a highly specialized job, and one for which he is uniquely qualified, or, as he would suggest, "gifted." It has brought him great wealth—and all the baggage that goes with it—a strange form of celebrity, and many admirers in his field. I wanted to know how he felt about it.

I ARRIVED AT LAFONTAINE'S HOME on a warm winter morning, one of those rare, nearly smogless Los Angeles days when the city seems to stretch out forever. Perched high on a hill in the Griffith Park area of Los

Angeles, near the top of a narrow one-lane road that twists and turns past assorted breeds of luxury automobiles, his house jutted up from the street like a three-story tan-colored fortress, smooth, gleaming, and impenetrable. It looked like the house of someone very important, or at least very wealthy. I buzzed through to an intercom, which was answered by his assistant, Jeff. Moments later, Jeff arrived at the door and cordially led me down, out of the light, to LaFontaine's basement recording studio.

The studio was not a particularly pleasant place to be. It was small, windowless, and crammed with all manner of electronics—a four-foot-long audio/video mixing system, a Power Mac, a small colony of hard drives, and all manner of monitors and TV screens. One end of the room was consumed by LaFontaine's soundproof recording chamber—a booth roughly the size of a handicapped bathroom stall and about as charming. Inside it there was only a stool, a microphone, and a music stand to hold the ad copy. His agent calls it "his dungeon." It was a no-frills, things-are-getting-done kind of place. It's where he spent every weekday recording dozens of spots using an ISDN line.

LaFontaine was in the middle of recording one such promo when I arrived.

"Okay Don, can we try it again, just a little punchier this time?"

LaFontaine adjusted his "ears," as he calls his headphones, and shifted forward on his stool toward the microphone. There were three beeps, then he sprang into action.

"The Monday night finales on Fox are shaping up to be HUGE!" he practically shouted, his voice deep and textured and instantly familiar. The tendons in his neck bulged, his eyes widened and he punctuated his sentences with his left hand, which he held as if gripping an imaginary chopstick. He looked like a juiced-up symphony conductor.

"First, at just four feet five inches, he's America's biggest sensation. Now *The Littlest Groom* must choose between women who range from small"—he paused a beat for dramatic effect—"to TALL! Does size matter? Find out on the finale of *The Littlest Groom*. *THEN!* The moment of truth has arrived, and you are cordially invited to attend Randi and Steve's Big Fat Wedding. Will the *CON* go *ON?* Or will her parents go *OFF?* It's the series finale of *My Big Fat Obnoxious Fiancé!*"

LaFontaine leaned back, as if pushing away from the table after a large meal, and adjusted his reading glasses.

The disembodied voice came back, piped through the speakers. "You the man, Don! That's it. Thanks."

LaFontaine disconnected the call and turned to me. "Real poetry, huh?"

LaFontaine looks nothing like he sounds. I don't know what I expected—perhaps a strapping, thick-forearmed type to match the muscular vocal cords. Short and thick in the middle, he has a shaved head accented by a finely trimmed goatee and an amazing set of eyebrows, which angle upward at the tips like Spock's and give him a permanent air of bemused skepticism. He was wearing faded jeans and a baby blue short-sleeve sweater-shirt that both matched his eyes and traced his sloped midriff. I couldn't help but think of the Wizard of Oz booming forth from behind his curtain.

He spends most of his day here in the studio, reading everything from TV promos to movie trailers to DVD intros. Over the next hour, I heard him do spots for Fox, the TBS movie showcase, and CBS. ("Tonight on a new Justice for All Tuesday: A body bag just arrived at the NCIS lab, but what's inside *isn't dead!* Mark Harmon, *NCIS.*") His agent sets his schedule and he receives his scripts by fax, often only minutes before he reads them. Most of the time, he's forgotten each one within fifteen minutes of reading it—a technique he said he found necessary for preserving his sanity, considering the volume of work he churns through. One year, as an experiment, he decided to keep all his scripts; by the end of December, the pile was three and a half feet high and included over nine thousand jobs.

Before technology allowed him to work from home, LaFontaine used to have a limousine and a driver ferry him from studio to studio throughout the day. During the early eighties, when he had a virtual monopoly on the industry, recording eight out of every ten movie trailers and working twelve-hour days, he'd cruise around town and make grand entrances at Paramount, NBC, and other recording studios, popping in to record for an hour, then heading on to the next place. Of course, he was also doing cocaine by the boatload, but I'll get to that later.

When I visited, he was the picture of domesticity. He took his daughters—Elyse, nine, and Skye, thirteen—to school in the morning, ate lunch whenever he wanted, and padded around his house like a king. (His not-so-obedient subjects were Duchess, a nine-month-old poodle mix given to peeing on the carpet; Dina, a seventy-five-pound, rambunctious one-year-old black Labradoodle; and Jack, a small seven-year-old black poodle who appeared resigned to his fate as Dina's play toy.)

When there was a break in the recording, LaFontaine took me on a tour of the house. It was quite a contrast from his grim, subterranean workspace. Sprawling and opulent, it was 8,000 square feet ("17,000 if you include the deck," as LaFontaine was quick to point out), cost over $10 million to build, had an elevator from the first floor to the second ("because it got annoying to keep carrying luggage up and down"), a small basketball court, a spillover pool, beautiful views east toward the San Bernardino mountains, and, in the backyard, a gigantic mural of him, his wife, his three daughters and his (now-deceased) golden retriever, Roseanne Bark. Upon first seeing it, I didn't immediately recognize the people in the painting, probably because Don was depicted in full Shakespearean garb, addressing an unseen audience, while his wife wore a gown and a giant set of butterfly wings. His daughters likewise had butterfly wings and sat on toadstools. The dog had no supernatural qualities but did look very happy.

Clearly, it was good to be the king.

SO OFTEN WE SPEAK OF people who are "gifted" at something, often deifying them culturally, whether it is a child prodigy, a star baseball player, or a mathematician. Rarely, however, do we focus on the circumstances of their success. David Henry Feldman, a psychologist who wrote a 1991 book studying six child prodigies (*Nature's Gambit: Child Prodigies and the Development of Human Potential*), argued that a prodigy must be gifted not only in a particular field but at the right time in that field—for example, could Einstein have made any contribution to science had he come along in Galileo's time?

Nor does being a gifted child, by itself, guarantee success or immunize one against failure. In the 1920s, Lewis Terman, a professor at Stanford, began a groundbreaking study of exceptional childhood intelligence, following some 1,500 kids with IQs above 135 to adulthood. While most went on to be very successful, none reached the kind of fame or recognized genius that he'd hoped for. Scientifically, he found no correlation for this, but many of his subjects battled alcoholism, twenty-two committed suicide, and some had trouble holding a job altogether. Of the students his study passed over, two became Nobel laureates, whereas none of Terman's 1,528 attained such a high honor.

These results suggest that in many cases, it is not whether you are gifted that matters, but what you do with that gift (and, in some cases, being "gifted" might actually be a burden, something I'll come to later). In LaFontaine's case, it's clear that he capitalized on his gift, and the story of how he did it explains much about the man, not to mention the industry he works in. It is a story he told me that afternoon, in the breaks between recording, which were sometimes fifteen minutes and sometimes an hour. Full of twists and turns, his life might make a good movie itself.

If that's the case, the establishing shot would be a cramped second-story studio apartment in Duluth, Minnesota, in 1949. Noise filters up from the 18 East Bar one floor below as a nine-year-old boy is setting the table for dinner. Only it is not a table but a piece of plywood balanced on a bathtub. His younger sister, Sandra, sits in the corner, on one of three chairs in the room (there is also an icebox, a toilet behind a curtain, and one bed, which the children share with their mother). Rubie, the mother, is not home yet, and Dad left when the boy was two years old. Rubie works long hours as a waitress at the Zelda Bar & Grill, so Don watches out for his sister and listens to the radio.

Don spent much of his youth seated in front of this radio with his chin cupped in his hands, lost in his own little world. *Peter Potter's Jukebox Jury, The Jack Benny Program, The Lone Ranger, Sergeant Preston of the Yukon*: he tuned in to them all. He loved the stories, the cadences, and the rich voices, even if they were nothing like his own, merely a squeak at the time.

When he was thirteen years old, however, something changed inside him. He woke up one morning to find that a large, gravel-throated forty-five-year-old had hijacked his vocal cords. Or so it sounded. "It literally happened in mid-sentence," he told me. "One morning it was 'Mom, I'll' "—and here he modifies his voice from prepubescent boy to pure bullfrog bass—" 'HELP YOU WITH THE DISHES.' I was about four and a half feet tall, this little tiny guy with a deep voice." So Don did what any thirteen-year-old would do in such a situation: he called his school pretending to be Mr. LaFontaine and said his son was sick. "Immediately, I became everybody's dad. I'd get on and say, 'Billy can't come in today, he's feeling very ill.' "

As a teen, he loved the spotlight. Slim and handsome in the photos I saw, he had a tremendous brown pompadour and a ducktail. A natural performer, he became a minor celebrity as a dancer on KDAL-TV *Bandstand*, "Duluth's own weekly dance show." Each week, he and his friend Dino LaTour would head to the studio and, along with some other kids, break into the lindy and the modified jitterbug to bands like Bill Haley and the Comets, Junior Rodgers, and Dion and the Belmonts. The ladies loved him and he loved the ladies for it. He was such a hit, he told me, that, even after graduating and heading into the army, he received duffel bags filled with fan mail.

The next five years were a blur (cue the feel-good musical montage). Fort Carson, Colorado, for basic training, then Army Signal School in Fort Monmouth, New Jersey, where he learned basic radio recording techniques (not to mention advanced ones like how to meet women by "practicing" interviews on the Jersey boardwalk in his uniform). Next up was Washington, D.C., where he was selected to work as a White House Signal Agency engineer, a title that sounds daunting (and would be today) but back then meant you essentially set up microphones on the lawn and in the Rose Garden for press conferences and piped the music through the White House. Despite passing six months of McCarthy-esque background clearance, however, he was instead routed to the official Army Band and Chorus, where he spent two years. The band was stationed next to Arlington Cemetery, so every morning he would see Blackjack, the horse that, riderless and with boots turned backward in the stirrups, later paraded in John F. Kennedy's funeral procession.

Once out of the service, LaFontaine moved to New York with dreams of breaking into the entertainment industry, walking out into the enormity of Grand Central Station in 1961, a young man bursting with ambition. At first, he channeled that ambition into one menial job after another. He sold liquor at Gimbel's department store. He ran paper at a music publishing house. He sold encyclopedias or dictionaries, he doesn't remember which, but was so bad at it that by the end of the first week, he actually owed the company $17 because he'd "invested" in his materials but had yet to sell a single book. The nadir came, he said, while he was living in a $14-a-week room in a boardinghouse on Ninth Avenue. He got food poisoning and lay there for a week, doubled over in bed, unable to leave the room. And since both the bathroom and the phone were down the hall, by the time he could walk again he was both out of a job and in a particularly fragrant living situation. "I threw all my trash out in the hallway and started laughing," he said, smiling at the memory. "I laughed because I realized I couldn't go any lower. I had no job, no money, and knew nobody in the city. I had nothing."

With help from his mother—who sent $30 in the mail—and a friend in New Jersey, he eventually got a job as an engineer at National Recording Studios. Not long after, he was hired by a producer named Floyd Peterson, who had his own company. While with Peterson,

LaFontaine met his first wife, Joan, who was a secretary at the office. He also had the opportunity to work with all manner of rising Hollywood stars. He teamed with a pre-*Graduate* Dustin Hoffman ("he was scruffy and modest") on an ad. In 1964, he worked on the campaign for *Night of the Iguana,* a movie starring Richard Burton and Ava Gardner. The studio wanted an unusual sound so they hired a young actor working on Broadway named James Earl Jones who had a deep voice but a horrible stutter. Said LaFontaine: "He came in and was very nervous, which only made his stutter worse. That's why he talks so precisely." Jones nailed the recording and went on, thirty years later, to give voice to probably the most famous heavy breathing recorded on film, the tortured wheezing of Darth Vader. (Less memorably, he also wore a leather skirt in *Conan the Barbarian* and read lines such as "Infidel defilers. They shall all drown in lakes of blood!" But, hey, it was the seventies.)

LaFontaine's first real opportunity behind the microphone came by accident. He'd started writing trailer copy with Peterson and had a natural knack for it. One day, they needed someone to do a take so he tried a hand at voicing his own script. The movie was a low-budget western called *Gunfighters of Casa Grande,* an MGM film so obscure that today it is not even listed among the nineteen thousand entries in *Leonard Maltin's Movie Guide.* His delivery, which he duplicated for me, was more nasal than it is now, and his reading more staccato and less nuanced, but the rumble was still there.

In a blur of speed their hands flashed down to their holsters and came up . . . spitting fire. Gunfighters of Casa Grande!

The tempo, the rush, the surging life in the words. This is what he'd been waiting for, building toward. As a teen, he'd toyed with the idea of being an actor, but, as he told me, "I rapidly found out that I had neither the talent nor the skill to be one or the ability to absorb the blows that actors absorb in order to make a career." At various points he'd also considered radio, but radio couldn't compare with voice-over. With trailers, he found a forum for his combination of dramatic talent, natural speaking skills, and knack for writing a clever phrase. "I was lucky in that, along with a very small group of people, I stumbled upon this form of advertising that was more storytelling, more fun, more risqué, more dramatic, more punchy, more poetic," he said, leaning back in his chair. "I've been very, very lucky. No one can ever be in the position of being on the ground floor of an industry and be lucky enough to have an affinity for writing this kind of stuff and be stupid enough not to know that he's breaking every rule in advertising so therefore blindly going about breaking all those rules but at the same time helping to create a whole sort of a new art form."

Indeed, LaFontaine came into the business just as it was beginning to morph from a cinematic afterthought to an industry in its own right. Trailers had been around for fifty years, but up until the sixties they were relatively crude, and rather obvious, pieces of advertising. The first known preview was shown on a white sheet at Rye Beach, New York, in 1912. The movie was a silent-film serial called *The Adventures of Kathlyn,* and at the end of the reel Kathlyn was tossed into a lion's den. As the spectators gasped in horror, a piece of film "trailed" asking, "Does she escape the lion's pit? See next week's thrilling chapter!"

Four years later, Paramount became the first studio to regularly produce previews for its most highly anticipated films. Many of these were merely the first reel of an upcoming movie, shown at the end of the main feature. Not long after, noting the success of Paramount, the vaguely sinister-sounding National Screen Service was founded expressly to make trailers, and for the next half century the NSS churned out nearly every preview. Lacking today's technology, the NSS instead turned to grammatical fireworks. Trailers were overridden with exclamation points, which accompanied virtually every snatch of text—"Amazing!" "Colossal!" "Spine-tingling suspense!"—or made promises that a movie would be "The Greatest You've Ever Seen!" Even when sound was added, the previews remained languorous affairs. The original trailer for the *Ten Commandments,* for example, featured director Cecil B. De Mille walking onscreen with stone tablets tucked under each arm, at which point he proceeded to read from an oversized Bible. A deadly game of cat and mouse it most certainly was not.

By the time LaFontaine entered the business in the mid-sixties, studios were beginning to consider trailers as mini-movies in their own right. This process was accelerated when a young film executive named Andrew J. Kuehn cofounded Kaleidoscope Films. As a boy growing up in Chicago, Kuehn used to edit tape using an ice pick and Scotch tape and had remained fascinated with the splicing process. His breakthrough idea—which, like car cupholders, seems blatantly obvious in hindsight—was to use quick cuts, "voice" talent, and snappy writers to pen his scripts. As he told *Variety*, "A trailer has but one goal: to draw audiences out of their houses and into a theater. To do that you have to set up a sense of urgency."

Kaleidoscope went on to produce more than a thousand trailers, including the campaigns for *E.T.*, *Star Wars*, *The Exorcist*, and *Jaws 2*, which boasts one of the most memorable tags ever: "Just when you thought it was safe to go back in the water." Kuehn passed away in February of 2004 but left a heavy imprint on the business.

LaFontaine first met him in the spring of 1963 and, five years later, Kuehn recruited him to Kaleidoscope, based on the steady trailer work LaFontaine had done since his *Gunfighters of Casa Grande* breakthrough. LaFontaine's stature grew during his seven-year partnership with Kuehn, which lasted until 1975. In October of 1978, he took a job at Paramount. While there, he had occasion to write, produce, and announce a trailer that he considers one of his proudest moments ever.

The movie was *The Elephant Man*. It was Mel Brooks's first venture into serious movies, and Brooks was working with John Hurt and a little-known actor named Anthony Hopkins. "From the moment I read that script, what I wrote was never changed," LaFontaine said gravely. "The movie was three weeks into shooting and the trailer was written. It was, I'm trying to remember it . . ."

He leaned back in his chair and looked upward, then closed his eyes briefly, an actor getting into character. He started, slowly, in a low-register monotone that sounded nothing like his Fox promos.

"At first you will want to . . . turn away from him, to avert your eyes, your face. But if you come to know him, you will see beyond the perversion of his form and discover the beauty in the beast. And finally . . . perhaps for the first time, you'll come to understand the true meaning of dignity and human courage."

LaFontaine paused, lost in a screening room in his mind. His eyes were wet.

"It was just a beautiful piece. It had all these cuts in between. The whole thing was just panning across him with his head down. One long shot, with shots of other people reacting to him. Then Freddie Jones, this incredible English actor, says, 'Ladies and gentlemen, the incredible Elephant Man.' And then we just zoom in on this incredible shot of Anthony Hopkins, never moving. He just stood there and stood there, his expression never changing. And then a tear rolls down his face.

"I showed it to get John Hurt in to redo his line, which was, 'I'm not an animal, I'm a human being.' I needed him to do it quietly. He came out to Hollywood and saw the trailer and he wept."

LaFontaine squeegeed his own eyes with the back of his hand and apologized for getting teary, saying, "I'm so old I cry at supermarket openings now."

Even though I was sitting in a dank basement room without visuals, I could feel the passion and the humanity in LaFontaine's voice, and, I was a little surprised to find, I was moved by it. It was like hearing a stranger read a particularly moving eulogy and, even though you don't know the deceased, feeling a connection.

We sat in silence for a moment, contemplating the beauty of it all. Then, as if to provide the starkest contrast possible, a producer called through to record a television promo for the movie *Planet of the Apes* (the remake) that began, "In a world where freedom is history . . ." and ended, "only one species can rule the planet!" Even though I had already seen this movie, and knew that it was without question a very, very bad movie, I was again helpless up against LaFontaine's enthusiasm. And goddammit if I wasn't wondering which species *would* rule the planet?

When he finished, LaFontaine emerged from the booth and sat back down. How, I asked him, could he summon the same emotion for *Planet of the Apes* or *The Littlest Groom* that he did for *The Elephant Man?*

He smiled. "We're all salesmen. Whatever your passion is—if it's writing, if it's skiing, whatever it is—if I draw you into a conversation about that, within three minutes, your voice is going to change, your skin is going to be different, your eyes are going to be different. Your whole body is going to be different; it's going to lean into your passion. You're going to want to drag me into it, you're going to want me to understand the thrill you get, the fun you get out of it. You'll be talking a bit faster, you'll be looking for words. Passion is a different thing than conversation. All this is is turning passion on."

I was skeptical. "You can manufacture passion?"

"Certainly, everyone can. We're just big bags full of passion. Aren't we?"

For some reason, this brought to mind a sleeping bag stuffed into its sack, all that metaphorical passion bunched up inside, just ready to pop out.

"Sure," I said, "but I might not be passionate about *The Littlest Groom*. I might not be able to summon the passion for it—"

"Let's put it this way," he interrupted me, "in that thirty-eight seconds, I made $350. Could you summon up some passion for that? Since you've been sitting here, I've earned about $5,000."

He waited for me to provide the appropriate eyebrow-raised nod of appreciation, and do some mental math (for those who'd like to play along at home, at this point I'd been sitting there for about five hours). Then, satisfied that I was sufficiently impressed with his earning power, he continued.

"That's part of it, obviously. The financial rewards are great. But I also love what I do. *I love what I do.* What I do is go in there"—he points to the booth—"and I manufacture—though it's no longer manufacture anymore, that's what's so funny about it. It's a genuine passion. It's like I'm giving this gift to someone. And for that moment, I give them this—this pleasure, this wonder, this revelation."

As he saw it, there was an audience out there, somewhere, for every movie and TV show, regardless of whether it's an Oscar winner or a base reality series. He felt he owed it to that person—the one who really loved *Battlefield Earth*—to invest his reading with as much emotion as possible. In some ways, he was almost like a preacher—notice he used the word "revelation"—bringing salvation to the entertainment-deprived masses. This is not such a stretch either. Many of the great advertising men of history had ties to religion. Bruce Barton, cofounder of the ad agency Batten, Barton, Durstine & Osborne (and discoverer of Norman Rockwell), was the son of a Baptist minister, and in 1925 wrote a bestseller called *The Man Nobody Knows* that characterized Jesus as the first great salesman. Artemas Ward, a pioneer of outdoor advertising while running the textile company Sapolio, was the son of an Episcopal minister. And our friend Rosser Reeves, he of the anvils and quarters, was himself the son of a Methodist minister (another ad great, John Wanamaker, who virtually created the modern department store, was not sired by one, but rather once thought of becoming a Presbyterian minister). It makes sense that these men would succeed. They'd learned from their fathers the art of persuasion, a healthy respect for the English language, and how to catch (and keep) someone's attention.

After lunch, served on trays in the studio by the housekeeper, LaFontaine continued with his life story, moving on to what he called the "really fat days" of the mid-eighties when he had started spitting out his "revelations" at a furious pace.

After Paramount, with his marriage breaking apart, he moved to Los Angeles in the fall of 1981 to set out on his own and see if he could make a go doing solely voice-overs. He was an immediate success.

His income doubled, then quadrupled in the space of a couple years. He was paid per reading, rather than a salary, the same setup he uses to this day (by his count he is the busiest "actor" in the Screen Actors

Guild's history, having signed more than 100,000 contracts). At one point, he told me, he went to the theater and heard himself do all of the six movie previews. It was around this time that he earned the nickname "The Voice of God" on account of his omniscient sound (ironically, he has actually been the voice of God in local church plays).

It wasn't that LaFontaine was the only voice in the industry, but then, as now, Hollywood was a copycat business (see *Daredevil, Catwoman, The Punisher,* and all the other god-awful comic-book movies spurred on by the success of *X-Men, Spider-Man,* etc.). So if LaFontaine's voice did the trick for someone else's movie, you had to have him for yours. He also had the advantage of being both a writer and a narrator, so he understood the rhythms and lulls of the trailer. "His great skill is that he interprets copy from the writer's standpoint," said his agent, Steve Tisherman, when I spoke to him on the phone. "So writers started writing expressly for him, in that cadence. A lot of times, the producers would bring in a guy who sounds like Don and he wouldn't work, so I'd get a call. 'Can we get Don?' Because that's all they know, what's successful, and that's Don voice."

LaFontaine also has a unique ability to cut through background noise, in the same way that a mother learns which (usually high-pitched) register will always catch her child's attention. "There's something in the timbre of my voice, where my voice sits, nothing else lives there," LaFontaine explained. "Explosions, gunshots, crashes, nothing lives in that particular range of sound. So *Terminator 2* is very soft, very quiet. I was one of the first guys to do that, to go very soft on action movies. And when I do horror pictures I'm always on the side of the bad guy. It's much more effective to be from his side."

To practice, he used to recite Edgar Allan Poe, specifically "The Raven" and "Annabel Lee," though his favorite book for such purposes is *Cyrano de Bergerac* (he recommends the Brian Hooker translation). "It's just musical, beautiful writing," he said, nodding slowly for emphasis. "There's a philosophy of life in his whole speech, when he's speaking to the patriots and asks, 'What would you have me do?' At the end of it, he says—" and here LaFontaine took off his glasses and looked past me, perhaps mentally inhabiting that Shakespearean garb he wears in the mural—

> "But to sing, to laugh, to dream, to walk in my own
>   way and be lone, free with an eye to see things as they
>   are, a voice that means manhood. To cock my hat
>   where I choose. At a word, a yes a no. To fight or
>   write. To travel any road under the sun or under the
>   stars nor doubt. To never write a line I have not heard
>   in my own heart. And with all modesty to say, my soul
>   is not satisfied. I stand, not high it may be, but alone."

He stayed in character for a moment, then put his glasses back on. "Now that's good writing. You read that and it will bring tears to your eyes. It will just kill you, the love that he has for Roxanne, the unrequited love. It's just marvelous."

It was marvelous, but one line in particular struck me as ironic: "To never write a line I have not heard in my own heart." I wondered how many of the thousands of lines LaFontaine has written, to say nothing of the hundreds of thousands he's recited, were ones he heard in his heart.

"As for reciting reading," he continued, "I tell anyone who wants to come into the field that all they have to do is recite something that has meaning to them to find the power of words, whether it's a song lyric or a poem." In lieu of that, he said, one can recite the inscription at the base of the Statue of Liberty or the Pledge of Allegiance. Of the latter, he said: "Say it as if you mean it, not just as a rote reflex, and you get an idea of what it means to find the glory in the words." (Later, on the drive back to my hotel, I tried this out with the Pledge of Allegiance and I would recommend this to anyone. I found it both chilling and empowering to recite the words: chilling for I had recited them so many times in my youth without ever thinking about exactly what it was I was saying—it is a *pledge* after all—and empowering because of the un-expected patriotism it stirred in me.)

During his career, LaFontaine has had to find the glory in some un-usual pronouncements. He's read, often tongue-in-cheek, for weddings, amateur movies, jokey corporate videos, countless answering machines, dozens of nonprofit commercials, and even, once, a wedding proposal. A young man called him from Ohio with a request and LaFontaine, be-ing "a big softy," as his daughter Lisi described him to me, agreed to pro-vide the narration. So this young Romeo rented his hometown theater and cut together a trailer, which started with a love story/mystery voiced by LaFontaine. Then, suddenly, a picture of the couple came on-screen and LaFontaine's voice rumbled forth. "And then he turned to her and said . . ."

At which point the young man turned to her and said . . .

"Will you marry me?"

These are just two of the many lives he's changed, some more tan-gentially than others. A whole generation of voice-over artists has grown up on LaFontaine. These days, there is a core group of a dozen or so men who do the majority of the trailers and TV spots. And they are almost exclusively men. One of the first women to record an action trailer was Melissa Disney (yes, of that Disney family), who did *Gone in Sixty Seconds* in a breathy voice in 2000, but she remains one of the few women working in the business. The reason may have less to do with sexism in the industry (though it may have had in the beginning) and, as with much in Hollywood, more to do with money. LaFontaine says that in focus groups, studios have found that, even with movies aimed at women such as *Sleepless in Seattle,* women prefer a man's voice. So men it is. "It's a shame," LaFontaine said. "There should be more. But no-body wants to be the guy who blows a ninety-million-dollar picture by taking a chance on something different."

LaFontaine serves as dean of the voice-over community, as well as combination mentor/living legend. He has worked with just about everyone, counseled most, and jump-started the careers of many current talents, including Ashton Smith, a onetime agent in Tisherman's office who is now one of the busiest voice-over talents in the business. Smith is tall, gray-haired, smooth, and outgoing. Like LaFontaine, he has a driver (LaFontaine gave him the idea when he lent him the limo), a deep action-movie voice, and has followed a winding path to get where he is: he was a documentary filmmaker in college, did a stint in PR promoting Surf detergent at baseball stadiums, worked as a sound engineer, as the struggling voice of "Movietime" (which is now E!), and finally became a big-time artist. As he told me over lunch in New York when we met, "I was really good at getting fired at first. But I was just too stupid and naïve to quit. I don't know why I didn't. The odds are one in five thousand in this business. Five guys do ninety-five percent of the work. It's like trying to make the NBA."

Unlike players in the NBA, however, even the most successful voice-over artists are nearly anonymous. There are announcers who are recognizable such as Michael "Let's Get Ready to Rummmmmble" Buffer, and a certain number of DJs such as Rick Dees and Casey Kasem. But if a legend of the trailer industry walked past you in the grocery store, you'd never know it. Unless, perhaps, he had reason to choose paper or plastic ("PLASTIC PLEASE") and you recognized the voice. In a town where self-worth is often measured by the number of paparazzi staking out your house at any given time, such anonymity is both the benefit and burden of the craft.

LaFontaine professed not to mind. He said he enjoyed being able to go to the store and not be bothered. Even when he speaks, he is rarely recognized. The one time it did happen—and I know this will come as a shocker—he was identified by a *Star Trek* fan at a bookstore in Chapel Hill who remembered him as the voice of *Deep Space Nine, Voyager,* and *Enterprise.* "It's because I don't use The Voice, or a version of The Voice in normal conversation," he explained. "But when a friend has me do it in a social situation, and I say"—and here he switched tones, like an engine being revved—" '*Coming to a theater near you,*' then they go 'Oh yeah.' I just tweak it a little bit. It's an attitudinal change, a meter change, more singing than speaking. It's all very subtle, but the totality of it creates this voice that all of a sudden becomes very recognizable."

Recognizable but not necessarily recognized. The Oscars seem to honor every technical achievement possible, but there are no statues for previews. Even the Key Art Awards, which honor the production side of movies and honor trailers in general, don't give awards for voice-over work (though, LaFontaine told me, they were supposedly going to start the following year). So people like Smith and LaFontaine exist in a limbo of sorts, known by most in the industry, from actors to directors, but as technicians rather than artists.

This lack of accolades may in part explain the lavish lifestyle of LaFontaine, as well as a little something called *The Sandman,* which we viewed that afternoon. LaFontaine pulled a video off his shelf and told me it was a home movie for the children that "got a little out of control." To call it a home movie, however, is a bit of a stretch, unless your idea of a home movie includes CGI effects, five musical numbers, multiple cameras, and a cast of at least a dozen, including one girl who'd been on a network drama. From what I could make out, the eighty-minute plot revolved around giants and nymphs and two children (his daughters, Lisi and Skye) who can't get to sleep. LaFontaine provided narration and played one of the main roles. The whole thing, he told me, ended up costing him more than $150,000 to make.

It was an amazing display of, if nothing else, disposable income, which continues to be, for many, the light at the end of the workaday tunnel, regardless of whether it necessarily makes us any happier. The mindset starts early; a survey of children ages ten to thirteen, as quoted in *Born to Buy: The Commercialized Child and the New Consumer Culture,* by Juliet Schor, found that their primary goal in life was to make money. Gobs and gobs of it. In response to the statement "I want to make a lot of money when I grow up," 63 percent agreed. Only 7 percent disagreed.

Certainly, everyone strives for financial security; it is the emphasis on "a lot of money" that is striking. A recent Associated Press poll showed that people who make more than $75,000 a year are far more likely than those who make $25,000 or less to say they are "very satis-fied" with their lives—56 percent of the higher-income group compared with 24 percent of the lower-income group. However, once you can pay the rent, more money doesn't necessarily mean more happiness. Again and again, studies and surveys have shown that, once people can live at a comfortable level, their happiness tends to level out.[1] After a certain point, the theory goes, we just enter onto a "hedonic treadmill," always wanting the next step up: the slightly bigger house, the better car, the $150,000 home movie. In fact, studies show that we're better off getting relatively small raises each year than receiving one big promotion, be-cause it is the feeling of moving forward that is gratifying, not the actual big bump in salary.

Then there's the matter of comparison. When I spoke to Wrzes-niewski, the NYU professor featured in Chapter 5, she mentioned some-thing called "equity theory," which holds that people want to get as much compensation out of a job as they feel they are worth, relative to those they see as peers. This holds true not just with monetary compen-sation, she said, but also with every other signifier: who gets the corner office, who gets the perks, who gets his or her name mentioned promi-nently. This goes a long way to explain why pro athletes and movie stars, for example, get into pissing matches because, "Will Smith gets $20 mil-lion a movie so I should too."

One potent example of this comes from a 1998 study in the *Journal of Economic Behavior and Organization,* in which Harvard students were asked to choose between the following two situations: a) living in a world where they were paid $50,000 a year while others on average got $25,000, or b) living in a world where they were paid $100,000 but others

1. Incidentally, despite what the lifestyles of certain celebrities might lead you to believe, rich people aren't having more sex than the rest of us, either. A recent study by the National Bureau of Economic Research, based on a University of Chicago database of 16,000 Americans from 1988 to 2002, found that there is no correlation between house-hold income and frequency of sex or number of partners. (There was, however, a correla-tion found between how often people have sex and how happy they are, which makes perfect evolutionary sense.)

got $250,000 on average. A majority chose the first scenario, the relative income, over the real income.

This is not to say I found LaFontaine to be fixated on money; I don't think he was. But I did suspect that, at times, he relied on it to provide a sense of self-worth, as surely many of us do, if not on the same scale. As for the home movie, his perspective on it was "It was something I could do for the kids. And anyway, it's better than the way I used to blow my money."

WHICH BRINGS US BACK TO the cocaine.

During LaFontaine's heyday in the early eighties, he entered into full-on, live-the-stereotype Hollywood mode. His first marriage had disintegrated and he was living alone, with a lot of money, in a large house (his first daughter, Christine, was living with her mom on Long Island). So he did what most males do in such situations: he partied like a rock star. Women, drugs, alcohol—it was Mötley Crüe time. "I'd finish work, come home and pour a tumbler full of vodka like that"—he held his right hand about ten inches off the table. "I'd go off to the clubs, bring people back to the house. I'd suck a Mercedes right up my nose chasing a high."

He looked the part, too. By this point, he'd lost all his hair on top but was wearing a realistic brown toupee that, with his prominent eyebrows and handsome face, made him look a bit like Burt Reynolds. Which isn't all that surprising, considering that, according to LaFontaine, he was wearing the exact same toupee, down to the sizing, that Reynolds wore.

Despite all the trappings of fame and the psychological rewards of a skyrocketing career, however, LaFontaine was emotionally miserable. "Ultimately, it was self-destruction. There's a reason for it, a reason why I was fucking with myself. In my case, I was unhappy. My ex was after me, my daughter was going to shit, and I had no purpose other than work. I was fifty and the job was great and I was making nice money, but I was lonely. I'm not Mr. Single Guy. That was my rationale. I was literally trying to kill myself."

In 1986, the sinner met his angel. He was at the Rose Tattoo, a cabaret in West Hollywood, judging a singing contest, when he first saw Nita Whitaker. A contestant in the competition, she was tall, had an amazing voice, and was gorgeous (in 1984 she became the first African-American Ms. Louisiana, as Don proudly pointed out). He was, well, short and old. But he was also charming and, more important, persistent. He badgered her for a month and finally got a date. At the end of the night he kissed her. As he told it, after she left, he got on the phone and called every woman he was seeing and told each one, "I met *her.*"

Whitaker went on to win *Star Search* thirteen times, and he kicked both the coke and cigarettes at her behest. As he recounted it, "She said, 'I wish you wouldn't do the cocaine.' I said, 'Okay, I'll quit on March 15.' I was watching a show and went into the bathroom to do a little coke. And I was like, what am I doing? I'm doing this until the fifteenth, which was in two weeks, so I'm going to spend whatever on this every day and then I'm going to quit? I said screw this. I had two grams of coke and I poured it in the toilet. Flushed it away. Never touched it since. Haven't missed it."

The two married in 1988, named their house "the Voicebox," and produced two beautiful daughters. When I visited, LaFontaine was clearly still enraptured with his wife. In addition to the outdoor family mural, he commissioned a six-foot-high painting of her that hangs in the foyer of the house, produced and financed her first album, and talked of her with the type of brain-dead grin usually associated with seventeen-year-old boys intoxicated by their first crush. Here's a sampler: "Nita is the most compassionate, thoughtful, sweet, considerate, wonderful, consistently beautiful woman I've ever known." So enthusiastic was he about it that he returned repeatedly to the subject of *my* wife, whom he wanted to know all about as at that time we'd just gotten married. "Women are incredible, incredible beings," he told me as we sucked on Sprite-flavored Popsicles made by his younger daughter. "You will see." He smiled beatifically.

Obviously, his family brought him great joy and his home was a testament to that, with all the photos and paintings of Nita and the kids.

What was interesting, however, was that for a man as successful as he was, there were few artifacts of his actual work, much less any type of homage. Sure, he had a wall of photos of him with famous actors (among others, Clint Eastwood on the set of *Escape from Alcatraz* and a signed photo of Arnold Schwarzenegger inscribed to Don with the message: "When you talk, people listen. I like that") and some industry mementos, but the rest of his work life was relegated, just as his workspace was, to the basement, pushed aside and boxed up. When I asked him if he had any CDs of trailers or recording sessions I could listen to, he spent a while looking and then apologized. He didn't have any. All that work he'd done was ephemeral; completed and forgotten.

I asked him about this, in an indirect way, as we sat there on the deck. "What would happen if you could no longer work," I said. "Let's say you lost your voice. Would it affect your identity?"

His answer was immediate. "Not at all. I could write or draw or something. What I do does not define me. I define what I do."

AFTER MY TIME WITH LAFONTAINE, I headed back to New York but found I couldn't stop thinking about him, and not just because I started listening intently to every TV promo and movie trailer I heard.

He *did* have a gift, that was clear. But was he shackled by it? His reasoning was that, when he's making $5,000 in a morning to use his gift, why should he be doing something else? It is a fair point, but wealth, status, and power are but symbols of happiness, not proof. It is telling that, at the height of his earning power, LaFontaine was miserable, killing himself with cocaine. It took balance in his life, specifically a wife and family, to make him happy. Some people may be capable of relying completely on their work to provide happiness; LaFontaine wasn't one of them.

SIX MONTHS AFTER MY FIRST visit, I saw LaFontaine again at his house in Los Angeles. Not all that much had changed: Nita got a prominent part in the L.A. theater version of *The Ten Commandments* alongside Val Kilmer, and LaFontaine had been seeing an uptick in movie trailer scripts.

On the afternoon I stopped in, he was recording a trailer for a new movie produced by MTV and created by Matt Parker and Trey Stone.

"From the creators of *South Park,* intrigue, espionage, disaster, and . . . Puppets??? This fall, meet the NEW American heroes. They're taking the *terror* out of terrorist. TEAM AMERICA: World Police. Rated R."

LaFontaine shook his head and said to the producer on the other end of the line: "We're being attacked by ists. . . ."

The producer didn't get the joke. All business, he asked LaFontaine to "take it bigger," something that I thought was impossible. LaFontaine complied, booming away, "THEY'RE TAKING . . . THE *TERROR* . . . OUT OF TERRORRISST."

After he finished, we headed out onto his deck.

"You told me before that you consider your skill to be a gift," I said. "In light of that, do you believe you have a duty to share it?"

He thought for a moment, uncrossed his legs and leaned forward.

"I consider myself the caretaker of it," he said, gravely. "I did nothing in the world to get this voice, at all. The spirit that resides in me I sternly believe just grabbed it out of the cosmos and it has been recycled a number of times, so I'm not responsible for it. It's capable of giving me a terrific lifestyle and a wonderful career and all the perks that go along with it, but I can't have that unless I use it. I can't have any of those things. This gift, it's not yours to keep, it's not yours to hoard. If you're a great artist, you can't paint something and hide it in your closet because you want to hoard it. You have to give it out to the world. You have to share that."

I asked him if he had any regrets—if he felt that his gift had constrained him.

He patted the younger of his poodles, who had helpfully launched herself onto his lap. He said he was a big believer in destiny though he sees it as eminently changeable. "That's one of my philosophies of life," he said. "If you are successful at what you do, no decision you ever made is wrong. If you are not successful, virtually every decision you made could have been wrong."

Just then, the phone rang. It was Tisherman, his agent. LaFontaine had to record a promo for Fox's *King of the Hill*. Our conversation would have to end.

So we headed inside, to the basement of his enormous house, the one his gift built, bought, and refinanced, so that LaFontaine could preach the brilliance of the Sunday night Fox lineup. The Voice of God had to be heard.

SEVEN

THE FUNGUS

PROSPECTOR

REX SWARTZENDRUBER PITIES YOU. Not you personally, as he's probably never met you, running in the circles that he does, but you as a collective—the conference-call-taking, mass-transit-riding, casual-Friday-abiding You whose life is ordained by schedule makers, middle managers, and the other authority figures of the work-aday world.

Swartzendruber, on the other hand, lives by his own rules, on his own clock, and answers to no one. Or at least that's how he sees it. To him, the autonomy inherent in his work is invaluable. But what I discovered about Swartzendruber, aside from his tendency to talk to squirrels, was that, if anything, he actually has less freedom than most of us. As is the case with many of the people in this book, however, it was the *perception* of autonomy that was important. If you're forced to do something, every moment can feel like torture; choose to do something, however, and working sixteen hours a day isn't so bad. Even, apparently, when those sixteen hours involve slogging through bogs, digging through topsoil with your hands, and navigating a shadowy world of competitors.

I first heard of Swartzendruber through a friend who'd read about "some mushroom hunter with a sixth sense up somewhere in Oregon." Somewhere turned out to be Salem, not far south of Portland. I arrived on a Tuesday night and called Swartzendruber to confirm our plans for the next day. He asked what type of "rig" I'd brought. When I replied that my "rig" was a two-door Pontiac Grand Prix from Avis, he sounded disappointed. "I should have told you to rent a Subaru Outback or something with four-wheel drive because one of my trucks has been in the shop," he said. "Oh well. We'll make do."

I ARRIVED A LITTLE AFTER 9 A.M. at the house Swartzendruber shares with his wife, Marcy, and the three boys from her first marriage. They live in South Salem, at the end of a cul-de-sac on a quiet tree-lined street, the kind where kids are always out playing some game or another. Swartzendruber emerged and eyed me a bit suspiciously. Or at least I thought he did; maybe it was just the tinted glasses.

At first glance, he didn't look the part of an outdoorsman. For a man who spends so much time outside, he is remarkably pale, thanks to an ever-present baseball hat and the fact that, by virtue of where mushrooms grow, he's always in the shade. At forty-four, he's gone a little soft in the middle and he walks gingerly at times, the result of a back injury he suffered in his teens. He has a prominent, droopy nose, thick eyebrows, and his fallback facial expression could be described as Deeply Cynical. As I learned, however, when he gets out in the woods, he can become tremendously animated, even giddy.

At that moment, though, he had on the Deeply Cynical face and was directing it at my bare legs. "I presume," he said, "that you brought some jeans, right?"

When I said I hadn't, he frowned. "We'll have to go back to your hotel."

Apparently, for a mushroom picker, walking around the forest in shorts is akin to Rollerblading down a gravel driveway naked. Swartzendruber also prefers to wear rubber hiking boots, extra long socks (to keep out the ticks, and the bees if he steps in a nest), a bright orange hat (so hunters don't mistake him for deer, which has been known to happen to pickers), and monsoon-grade rain gear (precipitation never stops pickers). He also keeps a stack of mycology guides in his "rig," though he rarely consults them.

From years of experience and study, he is able to name upwards of 200 mushrooms on sight. This constitutes only a fraction of the 28,700 known fruit-forming fungi, but, and here is what matters, those 200-plus constitute every commercially viable variety found in the Pacific Northwest. The woods there are home to truffles and morels and porcini and matsutakes—the celebrities of the fungal world—but also a whole gourmet market-in-waiting of less glamorous mushrooms such as *Catathelasma ventricosa* (known as "cats"), lobster mushrooms, and a number of "secret" mushrooms that Swartzendruber made me promise I wouldn't tell readers about. (Because, who knows, maybe you will read this book and decide to head out to Oregon to make a go of it on his secret patches, and then where would he be?)

Once he picks the mushrooms, Swartzendruber sells them in a number of ways. A good percentage goes out through his Web site, truflezone.com, and, for a number of years, he also sold on eBay. He sells another chunk to gourmet chefs in the Portland and Salem area (including good friend and local celebrity chef Jack Czarnecki). Others he takes to upscale supermarkets and organic markets, or sells himself via booths at farmers' markets. He dries them and freezes them, and, if all else fails, sells them at low profit to the mushroom wholesalers who provide an outlet for pickers who, for one reason or another, can't or don't sell them directly themselves. Loners, drifters, drunks, and junkies, I learned, tend to be drawn to the solitary nature of the mushroom business.

It is a patchwork, hustle-it-out type of existence. Some months, Swartzendruber barely breaks even. Other times, especially during the high-volume winter truffle months, he can barely keep up with the demand. It is enough of a living, however, that he was able to send Marcy back to school and can support his family solely on the mushroom income. The previous year, he boasted, he'd brought in $160,000 before expenses from his picking and other assorted mushroom income. What's more, he stressed, it's the best job he's ever had. "It is kind of an addiction," he told me at one point. "I haven't found anything else that does it for me like this. And it isn't like a stockbroker—you're actually adding to the economy, not just siphoning it off."

We headed to my hotel together in his "rig," a blue 1989 Isuzu Trooper that had 270,000 miles on it and, when I visited, a busted front left headlight, the result of an "unfortunate" encounter with a deer (his other car, actually his wife's, was the one in the shop). As he drove, Swartzendruber mulled our plan of action for the day. Finally, he nodded, as if concluding some extended internal argument. "Today," he said, "feels like a porcini day."

We made for the mountains.

IN MANY RESPECTS, SWARTZENDRUBER'S WORK is akin to prospecting for edible gold. In 1872, Mark Twain wrote *Roughing It,* which included an account of his exploits attempting to strike it rich as a gold panner. Of people drawn west, he wrote, "Even those who came from Hannibal, Mo. left behind lives bound by old rules. They came to this strange new boom town in search of silver and gold and discovered that there were no rules."

In Nevada and California in the mid-1800s, no license was required to pan for gold and no taxes were levied on those who found it. At first, the pickings were easy; men could literally take a pocketknife and gouge out the gold from crevices in the streambed, like popping loose a chunk of cookie dough from a carton of Ben & Jerry's (or a buried mushroom from a forest floor). Of course, that didn't last long. Since there is only a finite amount of gold in the world, deposits soon turned into a game of diminishing returns. (Only 130,000 tons have been mined since the beginning of recorded history, an amount that could be placed on an acre of land and only rise to a height of six feet.)

The difference between gold and mushrooms, of course, is that the mushroom supply is not finite but rather cyclical. So every year, or every other year in the case of truffles, these fungi magically reappear. This is not to say they are an unlimited resource—fungi have a symbiotic relationship with trees, so if the trees are cut down, there go the fungi—but they are reliable enough. For men like Swartzendruber, the key is knowing when (to the day), and where (to the tree), each year's crop of mushrooms will sprout. Predicting these things correctly was, he told me, the greatest thrill of his job: every year is a gold rush.

Of course, this level of uncertainty would mentally incapacitate some people. As a trade, mushroom picking is a freewheeling, nomadic pursuit, one based almost entirely on the power of acquired knowledge. As Swartzendruber explained, anyone with a permit can pick mushrooms, and anyone can get a permit. Without ownership, it is first-come, first-serve, which means that "secret" mushroom patches, discovered and cultivated over decades, are guarded zealously (and occasionally with firearms). There is virtually no infrastructure, and Swartzendruber's overhead, so to speak, consists of two large plastic buckets, a kitchen knife duct-taped end-to-end with a paintbrush (to cut then dust the mushrooms), a pair of thick shin-high boots, and his rigs. He plants nothing, grows nothing, tends to nothing, and creates nothing, and his income is dependent on an age-old process so complex and ecosystem-reliant that scientists still do not fully understand it. Needless to say, there is no 401k package.

The same goes for job security. Even the most lucrative patch, kept under wraps for decades, can be instantly destroyed by clear-cutting. If Swartzendruber has a boss, it is that most fickle and unassailable of all employers: the weather. For without rain, there will be no mushrooms, and with too much rain the fragile fruit will drown. Like all those in the ragtag, melting-pot world of mushroom pickers—a truly motley crew if ever there was one—Swartzendruber is, to paraphrase the author and mycologist David Arora, a quintessential outsider. Figuratively, because he resides outside the mainstream, and literally, because he spends most of his waking existence outdoors.

AFTER A TWO-HOUR DRIVE, we reached our first spot of the day. I was excited, both to pick mushrooms, which I'd never done before, and to witness Swartzendruber in action, as I was still unclear on how a "professional" searched for mushrooms.

Three hours and two spots later, I was somewhat less enthusiastic, not to mention much dirtier. We'd spent the morning traipsing through, over, or under all manner of thorns, marshes, branches, and rotted logs and had but three mushrooms to show for it. This didn't seem to concern Swartzendruber, however, who was happily wedging his way through a turnstile of weeds fifteen feet ahead of me.

Like any prospector, however, when you hit it big, you hit it big. As we made our way through a patch of thickly wooded forest that looked just like all the rest of the thickly wooded forest in this part of the Willamette forest, Swartzendruber suddenly turned sharply to his left, took two hasty strides, and launched himself at the ground, as if someone had just fumbled a football out here in the middle of the Oregon high country. For someone who'd complained about his bad back all morning, it was a startlingly athletic sequence.

Bent on one knee, he rooted in the dirt with two fingers, as if sending down a divining rod, and triumphantly unearthed a baseball-size white ball with a brownish top. He caressed the earth a foot away and plunged his hand in again. And again. Three baseballs in hand, he turned to me and beamed.

"Hot damn! We got us some boletes."

By that, he meant the relatively rare *Boletus edulis*, aka porcini. At the time, they were selling for $17 a pound.

To my left, I spotted a suspicious bump in the ground and dug in. I made a small uncharacteristic yelp—who knew finding a mushroom could be this exciting?—and pulled up a bolete. I turned to see his Deeply Cynical face replaced by a Deeply Enthused one.

"Oh yeah, baby," he shouted, "the porcini's poppin' today!"

Farther ahead, we came upon a low-lying field of orange, flowering chanterelles peppered with more boletes. Swartzendruber ran over,- exulted, and—even though the mushrooms weren't about to escape— began picking as if someone had dropped a giant sack of dollar bills into the forest and he had two minutes to gather them all up. He picked until his hands were grubby and stained a Tang orange from the chanterelles, stuffing his shirt with mushrooms to carry them over to the two five-gallon buckets we'd brought. I did likewise. When the buckets were full, he sat down on a log, sweaty and grimy, and grinned like a kid on Halloween night. "In the last half hour," he said, "We've picked over one hundred and fifty dollars worth of mushrooms. Now how about that?"

Of course, he'd still have to clean them, trim them, throw out the ones with worms, find buyers, and sell them, by which point his investment of time in the endeavor would have quadrupled. At the moment, however, he looked as happy as a grimy, out-of-breath man in a camouflage T-shirt could look.

We headed back to his car and, as we approached, he slowed down. Looking up and down the dirt road suspiciously he then hurried across it as if it were the Mexican border—even though all I saw were trees and more trees. As he unloaded the mushrooms, separating them by species into baskets, he worked fast. Then, abruptly, he stopped and swiveled his head; he'd heard something. "Quick!" he shouted, "Get 'em in!"

Frantically, we shoveled the mushrooms into the back of the truck as, in the distance, the sound of a car grew closer.

Toss.

Growl of an engine.

Toss.

Sound of crunching all-terrain tires.

We made it just in time to throw a large blanket over the goods, as if hiding a dead body, before a Jeep Cherokee emerged into view. "Ah," he said, breathing a sigh of relief, "it's just a park ranger."

There is, he explained afterward, no way to know when another picker might be on to him. "The last thing I want him to see is all these boletes I've got," Swartzendruber said. "He'll know they're up and that'll ruin my picking for the next week." Hence the secrecy. So when he picks, he normally parks his Isuzu far off the road, or some distance away. He's taken to using a pseudonym on the Internet bulletin boards so that local competitors won't realize that he's found a new patch. And, ever since one of his picking peers had his hard drive stripped by an intruder, and another had $4,000 worth of truffles stolen from his backyard deck, Swartzendruber has stopped keeping records of the locations of patches on his computer. "I have what I call The Map, but I keep it inaccessible," he said cryptically. "If someone robbed my house they wouldn't find it." But how does he read it, I asked. "Oh, I don't use it," he said, tapping his head. "It's all up here. The only reason I have The Map is if something were to happen to me and my family would need it to provide for themselves."

It all sounded spy-thriller paranoid to me, but I could tell he didn't think so. We headed back home for the day, the treasure concealed in the back of the truck. As far as I could tell, we weren't followed.

IT DIDN'T REQUIRE MUCH TIME with Swartzendruber to pick up on the fact that he was happiest when dealing with mushrooms. Still, like many people, it had taken him half a lifetime to realize that he could turn his passion into his life's work. That evening, as we drove back, the autumn sun drooping toward the horizon, he told me his story.

"I first fell in love when I was sixteen," he began. His high school chemistry teacher brought in a bunch of shaggy parasol mushrooms, which look exactly like something named a "shaggy parasol" should. The class did spore prints and then looked at the mushrooms under a microscope. "And then," Swartzendruber said with awe, "she ate one and didn't die."

He paused. "It was a whole new thing to me. It was very exciting." It wasn't the contact with nature that was novel—he'd grown up on a farm, where his father bought and sold forty thousand sheep per year, and he'd driven his first sheep loader when he was fifteen (the county judge had to sign an order to allow him to drive with only a permit). It was something else—he likened it to being let in on a secret.

So he spent his weekends reading mycology guides and traipsing through the woods, tentatively trying to identify which species he could eat without dying. Then, one day in 1980, he went out picking and ran into one of his uncles, who happened to be picking as well, and learned that he could get $1.25 a pound for chanterelles. "That first day, the first patch I ever found was on Stoney Mountain," he told me, smiling at the memory. "I got sixty-five pounds that afternoon. They were big"—he took his hands off the wheel and held them apart the size of an IHOP pancake—"because nobody really picked them back then."

At the time, mushrooms were viewed by the American populace primarily as something to put on pizzas or ingest during a wild weekend at Woodstock, not food to be foraged from the forest. Not only were wild mushrooms exotic, but most people associated them with poisoning. So prevalent was the stereotype of the "killer toadstool" that in his (very thorough and very funny) 1985 book, *Mushrooms Demystified*, the author David Arora devoted a chapter to debunking "Fungophobia." In it, he describes uninformed Americans viewing mushrooms as "the vermin of the vegetable world" and "unearthly and unworthy, despicable and inexplicable," despite the fact that "there are only five or six in North America that are deadly poisonous" (which, to interject on behalf of the uninformed, is five or six too many for most people's liking).

In much of the rest of the world, however, wild mushrooms had been prized for centuries. The Chinese have long coveted a number of polypores for medicinal purposes, while the Japanese believe the shiitake mushroom strengthens the immune system. In Western Europe, mushroom hunting is popular, while in Russia, according to Arora, it is such a traditional pastime that family names are derived from mushrooms—such as Borovikov, Ryshikov, and Griboyedev (literally, "Mr. Mushroom Eater")—and Lenin was reported to have harbored a *razh* (mushroom passion).

Americans began catching on in the late eighties, when portobello caps—which were not harvested but rather grown in Pennsylvania—became popular, creating greater interest in all mushrooms. Remember *Wild About Mushrooms: The Cookbook of the Mycological Society of San Francisco*? Well, probably not, but those in the mushroom business do. Especially in the Pacific Northwest, which is fertile picking ground, a small economy began to materialize around mushrooms. Around the same time, a parallel group of hobbyists, organized in mycology clubs, began going on mushroom-hunting "field trips" in much the same way that ornithological enthusiasts go bird-watching.

By the time wild mushrooms caught on, Swartzendruber had been picking for a decade, mainly on his off days for extra money and for pleasure. The rest of the time, he was enduring an assortment of odd jobs, working as a carpenter, videographer (including weddings), and hauler of cow manure, which, he told me, was infinitely preferable to being a hauler of chicken manure. ("Cowshit's not bad," he explained. "But chickenshit smells *horrible.*") On weekends, he'd head to the woods, or go out in areas near where he drove his truck, and fill up buckets with morels. As he traveled, he compiled a map of patches, from Washington to Montana and down through California and Arizona. It would serve him well years later.

But mushrooms were just a hobby. If there were two themes to his early work life, they were that he hated toiling on the clock—the only hourly work he did was at a mobile home factory right out of high school—and he saw employment as merely a means to an end. In his case, that end was often getting hammered at a bar, going to a Grateful Dead concert, or, even if he wasn't at one, doing all those things that people at Grateful Dead concerts sometimes do (back then, as he put it, there were auxiliary reasons for knowing where certain mushrooms grew).

As an outgrowth of this, in the early nineties, he became interested in a different sort of cultivation. Not your garden variety marijuana grower, he took to the pursuit with a scientist's zeal, cross-breeding species—his most successful being an Aborigine mix with long purple and black spikes—and refining what he called a "pioneering nutrient film collector technique," whatever that is. Regardless of his horticultural sophistication, what he was doing was still very much illegal. So, after his crop was found in 1991, and he was given probation, he gave up on that endeavor. It was, he told me, his low point. "I was broke, I'd been busted, and I had no idea what I wanted to do with my life," he said. "Life was pretty shitty."

That's when he was saved. Some find Jesus; Swartzendruber found fungi.

While mucking through some low-paying jobs the following year, it occurred to him that he could probably be making just as much money by picking mushrooms. After all, he reasoned, more and more people were eating them, and the demand kept going up. He knew the patches better than anyone and he'd been picking them for years. And most important, he told me as we rumbled down the highway, "I'm willing to spend sixteen hours a day picking, cleaning, and selling mushrooms. I don't like work, but mushrooms don't seem like work."

This last sentiment was a recurring theme with the people I met while working on this book. Even if the traditional definition of work—engaging in an activity that provides a livelihood—applied to what they were doing, this was not how people like Halvorson and Nehrich and Danz perceived their livelihood. To many, including Swartzendruber, the trappings of the work, the billing and marketing, was toil. But the work itself was the reward.

To many people this concept represents an ideal; take Vocation Vacations. In 2001, a dot-commer named Brian Kurth was stuck in traffic on the Kennedy expressway in Chicago when he came up with the idea for a company that allowed people to "test" jobs. Three years later, after being laid off and driving cross-country to Portland, he opened up Vocation Vacations, which offers weekend "vacations" in which clients can try out careers such as master gardener, photographer, makeup artist, brewmaster, and fashion designer. They are expected to "work" regular hours and take on all the duties of the job. He was overwhelmed by the response. Within a year, he was offering 128 different vacations and, by 2006, he expected to have a thousand qualified "mentors" at different jobs. Many customers merely wanted the experience of trying out another job, while others actually followed up on it. Kurth told me about a thirty-five-year-old from Texas who was leaving his job at a cell phone company to go into viticulture, a librarian and an attorney who were opening doggy day-care centers, and three attorneys from D.C. who were becoming chocolatiers. There was even a reality-show pilot in the works; it would follow vacationers as they tried out a new job each episode. "What I realized is that people make apologies for what they do," said Kurth when we spoke. "They say, 'Oh well, I'm an accountant.' Our idea is to give people a taste, a teaser, let them take a baby step." He paused. "We're not changing people's lives. We're a tool for them to make the change themselves."

THAT NIGHT, I SAT DOWN to dinner with Rex and Marcy, who'd prepared pan-fried white chanterelles and fresh bread drizzled in truffle butter to go with steaks and red wine. It was delicious. As we ate, Rex launched into a gastronomic thesis of sorts on mushrooms and their preparation. Not only must they be eaten at the correct time in their maturation ("Truffles don't work on the timetable of chefs. Chefs work on the timetable of truffles!"), he explained, but with the correct handling, and physiological preparation (one has to build up to eating raw white truffles). He then rattled off some of his favorite dishes: onion and chanterelle tarts, truffle omelets, porcini risotto, dried porcini lasagna, duxelles, white truffle ice cream, and steak stuffed with black truffles. When I asked his favorite mushroom, he shook his head. "That would be like choosing a favorite child."

I asked Marcy how she felt about her husband's work. A quiet, motherly blonde, she gave me a resigned look. "We'll be driving and he'll pull over and get a weird look on his face," she said. "Normally, that means someone has to pee. But Rex will be gone fifteen minutes and come back with a handful of truffles." She paused. "I learned I could get mad or I could realize this is his passion and he's not going to change."

So she said she has learned to take the good—weekend field trips in the Cascades, a constant supply of gourmet food, "hobnobbing" with chefs—with the bad. "I'm a mushroom widow most of the time," she said. "He'll work sixteen hours a day. Then he comes home and he's doing Internet orders and processing the mushrooms."

"This might sound weird," she continued, "but I think it's a spiritual outlet for him being out there. When he's doing Web work for too long he turns into a growly bear. One day out there and he comes back renewed. He'll be like, 'Guess what I found out there today!' and his eyes will bug out."

The two met in 1999. Her car had broken down and he happened to be walking back from an arts festival and asked if she needed help. They ended up talking till two in the morning about chaos theory and other "nerdy stuff." (It was, they later determined, the second time they'd met. Eleven years earlier, she'd been working at a health food store and remembered this "geeky guy" who would come in and deliver mushrooms and disappear out the back door, too shy to talk.) As Marcy told me, laughing: "At first, I was like, 'What? Mushrooms? How much do you make per week doing that? Are you living off of this?' "

At the time, the answer was "just barely." Swartzendruber was still compiling a customer base and learning how to distribute his produce (much of which needs to be moved or dried within a day). Oftentimes, he was sending out two hundred pounds of samples a year in an effort to lure new chefs to the idea of Oregon truffles, which were seen as vastly inferior to the European kind, not so much in taste as in restaurant cred. It was a costly but ultimately effective marketing strategy. Marcy preferred to focus on the bright side of that time in their lives. "If you're going to be poor, this is the guy to be poor with," she said, looking across the table at Rex. "We'd take a two-hour hike and come out with grocery money for the week and food."

The two were married in Silver Falls State Park, a vast wooded enclave, home to magnificent waterfalls, in October of 2000. The bouquets included dried mushrooms, little plastic fungi dangled from the champagne glasses, and the ceremony was almost delayed when, on the morning of the wedding, Swartzendruber decided it would be a good idea to take all the nephews, nieces, and other children on a two-hour mushroom hunt. "I nearly went crazy," Marcy said.

Rex smiled. "I figured it would be a good way to get them out of the way."

Not long after, business got better. He began making steady deliveries to a number of chefs in Portland and his e-mail newsletter became a hit (today, it goes out to fourteen hundred subscribers). In 2000, he was approached by the Bureau of Land Management to assist in mycological land surveys—a director noted him applying for permits for odd mushrooms and figured he'd be a good choice. So, working with crews of recent grads from Evergreen State College, he surveyed habitats and mapped them out, flagging endangered species for government botanists. He also began leading private tours. Families, children, amateur truffle hunters—he took them out for $150 a day per group or, if he was leading them to truffles, $200 a head. Soon enough, he expanded to selling at farmers' markets, where not only could he move product at a higher price, but he had the opportunity to interact with people who appreciated his skills. "The European customers are the most gratifying," he told me. "They remember the boletes from their childhood and some weren't even aware they grew in the United States. Old women who used to pick as kids will come out and get very emotional. Some of them will cry."

It had been an exhausting day, at least for me. Swartzendruber, on the other hand, seemed fresh, and even called it a "light day." This made sense, considering how much he enjoyed what he did; research has shown that being engaged in one's work is actually *less* taxing, at least mentally, than not being engaged. A study sponsored by the National Institute of Mental Health and conducted by Jean A. Hamilton, a research psychiatrist in Washington, D.C., found that when two sets of people were given a simple task and electrodes were hooked up to measure their brain activity, those who said they generally became absorbed in their everyday life exerted less mental energy than those who had a hard time becoming absorbed. It's the old idea of being "lost" in one's work.

Swartzendruber clearly valued this feeling, as well as the luxury of losing track of something else: time. Marcy told me that his sense of it was infinitely variable. "I've begun telling him things start two hours before they actually do to try to get him to arrive on time," she said. And if he's late? "Then I just leave without him." She'd said this as if it was a trifling annoyance—ha, ha, that silly Rex—the equivalent of leaving the toilet seat up. This might have been restraint for my benefit, but I think it was more of a concession; she understood this was part of the package.

Certainly, Marcy cut him slack, but how free was Rex, really? As much as he talked of not being on a clock, or being able to come and go as he pleased—two themes to which he repeatedly returned during our day in the woods, saying things like "the beauty of my job is that I don't even need a watch"—his work was almost completely dependent on the market, not to mention the whims of nature and other forces out of his control. If a heavy rain fell and mushrooms were coming up, he had to go pick while the picking was good. If the price of chanterelles dropped by half—not an uncommon occurrence in the supply-driven mushroom market—he either needed to pick twice as many or switch to another species and cut his losses. If the entire market was low, he had to work crazy hours just to keep his business afloat.

A few years ago, Kevin Henson wrote a book called *Just a Temp* in which he interviewed thirty-five temporary employees and worked as one himself for a period of time. Many of them had an outlook similar to Swartzendruber's—they felt as though they enjoyed amazing freedom from the rat race. At any moment, they could bolt to Europe, or switch to another job, or just go sit in the park and look at the clouds.

But Henson came to an interesting conclusion; in reality, like Swartzen-druber, the temps had *less* freedom than those in full-time jobs because they were dependent on such a wide variety of external factors—when and where jobs were available, the need for a paycheck, no benefits—rather than a small, static set (such as is the case when depending on one employer).

There is an important difference between the two examples, how-ever. The next temp to view his work as a calling will be the first. Swartzendruber, by contrast, sacrifices freedom for something he loves. And since it's likely he'd be out picking mushrooms anyway, maybe his perceived autonomy isn't so different from the actual kind, after all.

WE MET UP AGAIN THE following morning and, after making stops to sell some of the previous day's haul with varying amounts of success—two gourmet markets bought, while two didn't need any, a frustrating process for Swartzendruber—we headed to Butte Creek, on the western slope of the Cascades, to prospect. As he drove by the crop fields and vineyards that abut the base of the mountains, Swartzendruber main-tained a running narrative that was part nature talk, part business how-to, and part philosophical musing. Mushrooming, he explained, is a mixture of science, craft, and luck. To judge when and where to pick, he spends a good deal of time tracking weather cells, as well as fire activity (morels are found in abundance in "the burn," as recovering forest fire habitats are known). He also stops in at his favorite spots on a regular ba-sis, like a conscientious parent, to check soil conditions and look for marker mushrooms—similar or related species that signal a bumper crop of his target fungi (our first day out, he'd been encouraged by an early sighting of a bleeding hydnum, a spongelike species that secretes an eerily bloodlike liquid).

As we ascended into the mountains, he pointed out local shrubs, weeds, and trees, rattling off their scientific names, history, and applica-bility. We passed a stand of Douglas firs and he exclaimed, "See those?

Those will be full of truffles in two months." The ability to discern truffle patches with the naked eye is very unusual, he explained, not to mention valuable. As the most sought after of fungi, truffles can fetch prices up to $200 an ounce for Italian whites. American varieties go for less, often in the $200 a pound range, and Swartzendruber said he reliably moved them at $110 a pound through his Web site.

Most collectors use what Swartzendruber termed the "rake and hope" method, clawing at the roots around trees. Others have tried various schemes, from spreading "slurry" (truffles run through a blender) around tree roots in hopes of coaxing up truffles the next year, to buying "inoculated trees," to bringing in pigs (which are effective but hard to transport and prone to eating the truffles once they find them, which, really, shouldn't come as a surprise).

Swartzendruber developed his truffle-finding method through years of research and trial and error. His tenaciousness has earned him a significant advantage over most pickers, who are in it primarily for the profit and couldn't care less *why* truffles grow as long as they can find out *where*. Swartzendruber made me promise not to reveal how he does it—it would be like leaking the Coca-Cola formula—but suffice to say that he uses a holistic approach that takes into consideration the life cycle of trees, their growth patterns, and the ecology and topography of different areas. To be honest, I was quite impressed. It helped to explain why he was so secretive about his whereabouts, not to mention why other pickers would follow him as if he were some sort of pied piper of fungus.

Maybe it also explained—but then again maybe it didn't—why, minutes later, when a pickup truck approached us at breakneck speed on the one-lane dirt road we were on, he didn't pull over but rather gunned the engine and veered right. For a split-second, I thought we were going to career into some oak trees, effecting an inglorious end to both of our careers. But Swartzendruber righted the Isuzu, then swore loudly.

"Probably loggers who are lit up," he said, looking in the rearview mirror and scowling. "Fuckers."

He did have the option, I noted, of slowing down. He shook his head. "I don't have a permit for this area so I don't like to stop. You never know, it could be a resource extraction manager or another picker."

Aha, I said. I checked my seatbelt.

Fifteen minutes and innumerable unmarked turns later, he slowed down, leaned his head out the window to make sure there were no other cars on the road, and then pulled over and parked discreetly off the road. Looking across the way, his face went ashen.

"Oh no, no, no," he said. Hurrying out of the car, he ran across the road to an embankment.

Cresting it, I saw what was upsetting him. His "secret spot" looked less like a forest and more like an arboreal battleground. Where there should have been shade, there was only mottled daylight. Mangled stumps jutted from the earth, tree trunks lay on the ground like severed limbs, and, all around us, everything was bathed in sawdust. Swartzendruber broke into a trot, looking behind felled logs and in clumps of weeds but there was little to be found; without the shade and roots of the trees, the mushrooms could not survive. Here and there, we found a few stunted chanterelles huddled under a crook of a log, like survivors, but that was about it.

As we picked through the wreckage, it became clear that Swartzendruber saw this not merely as the loss of an income source but as something far more profound. "The loggers just don't get it," he said, angrily tossing aside branches. "When they clear-cut they're killing so much more than trees. They're destroying an entire ecosystem!"

I asked if he had any recourse. "Oh yeah, *right,*" he said. "I've testified against the clear-cutting numerous times in hopes of stopping it in these areas. But their opinion is that I'm just a mushroom picker, so what do I know?"

This touched on something I'd been wondering about. Swartzendruber was obviously intelligent, well-versed in mycology and cared deeply about it. Why not go through the system, get a degree, and have a platform from which to speak and do research?

He frowned. "I've thought about it a lot," he said. "I could challenge out at the community college level in math and physics and then go to OSU, which has the best mycology program. It wouldn't change what I do, but it might allow me to challenge loggers in court, which might be reason enough."

What about becoming a botanist or doing research?

"For what? I'd just get caught up in the grant mill. And I'm already doing environmental survey work. Besides, what other job would allow me to work out here all the time?"

He had a point. But in exchange for being able to opt out of the world, he couldn't just opt back in when it suited him, even if he was really pissed at loggers. Every freedom has its price.

LATE IN THE AFTERNOON, WE stopped for lunch at a Mexican place. Over burritos, he explained some of the logistics, and dangers, of the job.

First off, he said, by running his own business single-handedly, he was something of an anomaly in the mushroom world. Most of the industry is partitioned into buyers, sellers, and pickers. The pickers are often Southeast Asian or Mexican "teams," run by a distributor, that descend upon an area in groups of a dozen or more. Others are families who follow a "mushroom trail" that winds up the West Coast, moving from spot to spot as the season progresses. Still others are addicts and drunks who pick bucketfuls to sell at "mushroom stations," the equivalent of low-pay mushroom clearinghouses. Some sell maps and mark areas; others bring fishing line, which they string back, tree to tree, from a patch to an access road (the line is often purposefully restrung by competitors). Many stay in impromptu pickers' camps along the trail, which are notorious for violence spurred by gambling, drinking, close quarters, and a daily influx of wages paid in cash.

Swartzendruber said he tried to steer clear of other pickers, for both business and safety reasons. Still, there are plenty of other job hazards.

In addition to ticks and bees, there are larger, furrier animals that are fond of mushrooms. One time he was picking alone in the Tillamook State Forest in the northern Coast Range, making his way down a hillside, when he came down on a branch and it made a cracking noise.

"Suddenly this head pops up from the log in front of me. It was a big black bear, maybe 250 pounds, with a chanterelle in its mouth."

Naturally, Rex did what outdoorsmen are trained to do in such situations.

"I yelled, 'FUUUUUUUUCK!' "

And?

He grinned. "It probably wasn't the best technique, but it worked. The bear ran away."

As Swartzendruber recounted the story, I got the impression that, even if he complained at times, he enjoyed the unpredictable aspects of the business—the bees and the bears and enemy loggers and patch-finding one-upmanship. It added a dash of danger and an outlaw feel to what was otherwise—let's face it—a pretty mundane practice (mushrooms, like clams, aren't especially elusive once cornered).

Late in the afternoon, we drove to the last spot of the day, Silver Falls State Park. Swartzendruber was hoping to find some lobster mushrooms, which are red and cracked and indeed crustacean-looking (visual naming is big in the mushroom world, as evidenced by specimens such as the "Bread Dough Clitopilus," the "Onion Bagel Pholiota," and the "Black Brain Jelly"). In the case of the lobsters, they start out white. It is only once they are attacked by a fungus (a fungus attacking a fungus) that they become red and, coincidentally, edible. As Swartzendruber explained: "They go from tasting like candle wax to a nice, nutty flavor if you get them at the right time."

As we walked, I thought about how the process wasn't so different from Swartzendruber's life, and the way it had taken a traumatic event—in his case, one he brought upon himself when he got busted—to spur his transformation. I asked whether he thought starting the mushroom business was following a calling, however he wanted to define that word.

"I don't know," he said. "It's rewarding to me, but in the overall scheme of things, how does it help? Maybe I've kept people from eating poisonous mushrooms by pointing them out. Maybe I've planted the idea in people's heads that it's all part of the same ecosystem. What you do to this tree"—he patted a spruce lovingly—"goes down the roots, through the mycelium and over to that tree."

He paused. "Basically, I think I'm supposed to be raising awareness of what's around us. I'm doing more than just selling mushrooms. By talking about the impact of what you buy to people at the farmers' markets, maybe they'll realize the difference of buying from someone who respects a sustainable resource and the land. If I say things and plant ideas in people's heads and it leads them to change their lifestyle or make a change, then that might be just as good as making the changes myself."

This was something many of the people I'd met hadn't mentioned when I spoke to them about their work, and it raised an interesting question: Does a calling have to help the world? There are different theories about this. When I spoke with John Krumboltz, the Stanford professor who studies careers, he argued that value is relative. "As long as you're getting paid, that means what you do is valuable," he said. "There are millions of ways to be helpful to people. If you're a caregiver, only one person might appreciate that, but they appreciate it tremendously. You might labor over a story for a week and people only read it for three minutes, but there might be a million people reading it." This theory sounds logical, but does that mean that a drug dealer is helping the world because someone values his services? Krumboltz didn't have an easy answer. What to me seemed more important was that the person doing the work realized its value, even if he or she might see it differently from others. For example, Halvorson saw herself not as engaging in a sport but as advancing women's rights, Danz believed he was making people whole again, and Spiderman believed he was bringing people together and saving buildings. Swartzendruber was still figuring it out.

He bent down to uproot a lobster and, as I squatted next to him, something whizzed by my head. I looked around but saw no one.

"Squirrels," he said, noticing my bewilderment. "They eat mushrooms too. So they get mad and throw nuts at me when I pick. I talk to them in return."

He made a weird, whistling noise and looked up at the tree, where a squirrel was indeed stuck to the side of the bark. I had no idea whether or not it had actually tossed a nut at us, but it did look a little pissed off, at least for a squirrel.

"Hey buddy," Swartzendruber said loudly to the squirrel. "You missed!"

SIX MONTHS LATER, I SPOKE to Swartzendruber on the phone. It had been a fruitful mushroom season. Too fruitful. The market was flooded and prices were down. Still, the prospecting was amazing. "The matsutakes were awesome this year," he told me. "Some years it doesn't even pay to get a permit, but this year they were really coming up. Remember the canyon you and I checked on when you were here?"

"Yeah," I said, thinking back to one of the dry spots we'd hit on our first day.

"Well," he continued. "It was *loaded*. My buddy and I filled up the Trooper to where he was holding stuff between his legs and we couldn't see out the windows."

He sounded at peace. "I've been thinking a lot more about getting that mycology degree," he told me, "and I've been doing some real cool stuff with lichens for a survey."

I asked how business was going. "It's been up and down," he said. "But that's OK. I've got it figured out by now. You're at the mercy of the weather and the international business. Basically, and this takes some people a long time to understand, you just got to figure out what works. I can stockpile during down-times and generate enough capital to pay most of my bills. Then I just put away dry stuff. It'll all sell."

"Besides," he added. "It still beats working."

EIGHT

THE NOTEBOOK

DETECTIVE

THERE IS A SCHOOL OF thought that the key to professional success is self-awareness. In 2001, coauthors Marcus Buckingham and Donald O. Clifton wrote an entire book, the bestselling *Now, Discover Your Strengths*—a modest little tome whose first sentence declares, "We wrote this book to start a revolution"—that can be summed up in one sentence: Know what you are good at and do it.

With that in mind, let me tell you what Sarah Holmes is good at. She is an intuitive thinker who is able to grasp new concepts quickly. Possessed of deep reserves of empathy, she is the type of person who, if confronted with a kitten, is likely to make a cooing noise. She loves to be around people and can connect with most anyone, though she also needs emotional reassurance on a regular basis. I know all this because her handwriting told me so.

Well, that's not entirely true. It didn't tell *me* that. To me, her handwriting looked like, well, handwriting. It was neater than most, and had some nice loopy flourishes, but I wouldn't go bragging about it to anybody. But to a handwriting analyst such as Holmes, penmanship is the equivalent of an unlocked diary or a peephole straight into the psyche. Or so she says.

Personality traits, social characteristics, weaknesses: Holmes sees them all in a page torn from a loose-leaf notebook. She can examine a fifth-grade homework assignment, a Mother's Day card, and a letter home from college and trace someone's emotional evolution. Given a one-page jury questionnaire, she can determine what type of juror someone will be and, depending on the case, whether he or she is likely to help the prosecution or the defense. No wonder that, as her mother, Ruth, told me at one point with a chuckle, "Sarah's boyfriends are always a little wary of writing anything on the first date."

Or, for that matter, of meeting her mother, because Sarah learned the trade from Ruth, who has been analyzing people's script for nearly thirty years. Together, from their home offices in Bloomfield Hills, Michigan (Ruth), and Waltham, Massachusetts (Sarah), the duo run Pentec, Inc., a two-woman company that is one of the most successful handwriting analysis services in the country. Naturally, since such businesses don't exactly dot the landscape with Starbucks-ian regularity—despite Sarah's sincere assertion that "every school in America should have a handwriting analyst"—this is a relative standard. Still, Pentec is nationally known, in part because Ruth did jury consulting for all six of the trials of Jack Kevorkian, the Michigan doctor and proponent of a patient's right to die. In fact, Kevorkian got along so well with the Holmes family that he moved in with them for six months.

While I was fascinated by the Holmeses' work, to say nothing of their houseguests, I was especially intrigued by twenty-nine-year-old Sarah's career path. Bright and personable, she attended Colby College and did her graduate work at Boston University, where she was one of four students chosen to speak at commencement. She could, quite conceivably, have done just about anything she wanted to with her life. A host of factors might have diverted her from choosing to enter her mother's career, not the least of which was the fact that many people consider it to be a big sham. I was curious about how she reconciled the public perception of her work with her own perception, and how much of an effect her mother had on that process.

After all, it is one thing to work at a job so obscure that you constantly need to explain what it is you do. It is another not only to have to explain it, but then to defend its legitimacy. Holmes's situation brought up an interesting question: How does one find meaning in a profession others dismiss as hokum? I flew to Boston to find out.

I FIRST MET SARAH ON a crisp winter morning at the spacious Victorian home she rented in Waltham with four other friends, most of them from her class (1997) at Colby.

Sarah greeted me at the door in a collared pink blouse and gray slacks. Any expectations I had of a shady, mysterious character were immediately dashed. Attractive in a perky, freckly midwestern way and sporting a short brown bob cut, she looked exceedingly normal. Tall and athletic—she rode horses competitively in college—she has the type of well-proportioned face that television news shows love when booking guest experts (a role her mom often performs and that Sarah expects to one day inherit) and is so bubbly that I initially thought it was an act. Like any trained communicator, she made a point to use my name repeatedly, even when we were the only two in the room, as in, "It's so interesting, *Chris*," and "If we were to do an experiment and I said, 'Write in your nondominant hand, *Chris*.' "

She led me through the house, which was decorated in a post-collegiate manner, as if the inhabitants couldn't quite decide if they wanted to throw ragers, have families over for dinner parties, or do both on successive nights. In the living room, a staggering assortment of shot glasses and bottles of liquor were neatly lined up next to a six-foot-high "cat tree," a sort of jungle gym for felines. Drink a shot, pet the cat.

Sarah's office was the workspace of someone who had graduated from shoebox filing to plastic containers, but had yet to make the full-on move to file cabinets. A goldfish swam aimlessly in a bowl on a shelf ("he's my best buddy—isn't he gorgeous?"), and Post-its were strewn around with various reminders (many of them words of wisdom from Kevorkian, including "be honest," "be yourself," and "sophrosone," which, Sarah explained, means "master yourself"). On her bookshelf were all manner of law books and handwriting texts, including one from 1969 with a yellowed cover that nicely summed up the timeless appeal of handwriting analysis for the opportunist. Called *What Your Handwriting Reveals: The ABC's of Handwriting Analysis,* its cover text read: "VAIN??? IMAGINATIVE??? LITERARY??? SENSUAL??? Do you really know your friends???"

"Oh that old book," Sarah said when she saw me pick it up.

"So do you really know *your* friends?" I asked.

She laughed. "I try to be discreet."

For example, in the case of her current boyfriend, she had waited "as long as possible" to check out his handwriting, which in this case meant the second date, when he graciously wrote something on a bar napkin. "I saw it and I knew he was right," she said, beaming.

She also went home and faxed a sample to her mother. Ruth's response? As Sarah recounted: "Wonderful handwriting! Spec-tac-u-lar."

Sarah waved her hand, as if to say "enough of that." She was very excited to show me how handwriting analysis worked. She pulled up a slide show entitled "Handwriting: The Landscape of the Mind" that she and her mom use for lectures. It covers the basics of the craft and is big on metaphors and similes such as "We like to think of ourselves as archaeologists on a dig," and "People are like geodes: rough on the outside and then you open it up and they're brilliant on the inside."

She pulled up some writing samples to explain the basics of the business, including a sheet that showed the "zones" that form a rough map to how personalities correlate with styles of handwriting.

I noticed that as she talked she was glancing at the notes I was taking. "See, you have very nice connections, which means you are what we call 'mentally gymnastic,'" she said, peeking at my notebook. My writing, she explained, is something called "print script"—picture someone scribbling the word "hats" and connecting the cross bar of the *t* to the top of the *s* to write more quickly. It is a sign, she explained, of simplification of thought. "It's your mind's way of shifting gears, making things faster." This doesn't necessarily mean that I am any smarter than someone who doesn't use print script; handwriting analysis is all about pointing out traits, not negatives and positives. So, for example, a slower writer would be described as "conscientious" and "thorough."

As much as Sarah said she could discern from writing, there are certain things she cannot, including the writer's sex, age, and whether he or she is left- or right-handed. In fact, she explained, no matter what part of your body you use to write with, the script will be similar. "You can write in your nondominant hand, put the pen between your toes, put it in your *mouth*, it doesn't matter," Sarah said, mimicking a horse with a bit in its maw. "All the serifs will be the same, the slant will be the same because it's coming from your brain. That's why we like to call it 'brainwriting,' not handwriting."[1]

Just then, the phone rang. It was Ruth, checking in. The two of them speak at least five times a day, and do so in a disjointed verbal shorthand that is part familiarity and part a shared personality trait. There was, Sarah told me, nothing they didn't share, including their computer files. Either woman could access the other's hard drive, something that struck me, in this age of cached Web pages, casual e-mails, and the occasional embarrassing JPEG, as the ultimate sign of trust between a parent and a child.

Though they claim to be equal partners in the business, it was clear

---

1. This idea was first posited by a psychology professor named Wilhelm Preyer around the turn of the century. Preyer ran a series of experiments on people who had lost an arm and had to write holding a pen in their mouth or between their toes. He found that, regardless of which part of the body was doing the writing, the characteristics of the penmanship remained the same. Since then, attempts to duplicate the outcome have had mixed results.

that, at the time, it was still in many ways a master-apprentice relationship. Ruth handled the largest cases, often with Sarah's assistance, and had a much-higher national profile, having been quoted or featured in *Time, Newsweek,* and *USA Today* and used for expert analysis on shows such as *Dateline* (where she was asked to examine Kurt Cobain's suicide note to determine if it was forged by someone else; Ruth decided it was indeed Cobain's handwriting). "I can only hope," Sarah told me, nodding slightly, "that I can have a career half as good as my mom's."

PEOPLE UNFAMILIAR WITH HANDWRITING ANALYSIS tend to lump its practitioners into the proverbial Crock of Shit bin alongside fortune-tellers, palm readers, and televised psychics. Not surprisingly, this really ticks off handwriting analysts. For example, when I called Renee Contento with the American Association of Handwriting Analysts (the acronym is pronounced *a-ha*), before meeting Sarah, she said: "It's not like it's the occult or something. When you get a letter, you don't even have to look at the return address to know who it's from, right? So you're already doing graphology!"

It's not quite that simple but she is right: most of the guidelines are rather intuitive. Logical, meticulous people, for example, are said to have neat, meticulous handwriting. Impulsive, creative people are said to have handwriting that looks, well, impulsive and creative (hastily written, with loops and flourishes). The basic tenets are straightforward enough to be learned by anyone willing to study (or, for that matter, read *The Complete Idiot's Guide to Handwriting Analysis*). To reach the level that Ruth and Sarah are at, however, requires years of study and practice; Sarah often spends nine or ten hours a day analyzing handwriting when doing corporate assessments.

The idea of using handwriting as a gauge of personality has been around for centuries. The Greeks, Chinese, and American Indians all used symbol recognition systems. As far back as 330 B.C., Aristotle wrote, "Handwriting is the visible form of speech. Just as speech can have inflections of emotions, somewhere in handwriting is an expression of the emotions underlying the writer's thoughts, ideas, or desires."

It wasn't until the late 1800s, however, that anyone thought to study handwriting. That's when a French monk named Jean Hippolyte Michon embarked upon the first scientific, or at least quasi-scientific, study of the craft. He compiled a rudimentary personality key, using such indicators as whether someone dots their *i*'s and how high they cross their *t*'s. He named the practice *graphologie,* from the Greek *graph,* meaning "written," and *logos,* which means "word." In 1875, Micheon founded the Société de Graphologie, which is still active.

Today, handwriting analysis is more popular in Europe than in the States. Among U.S. practitioners, Sarah and Ruth view the craft from a more scientific viewpoint than do most, some of whom are not far removed from amateur psychologists. Ruth is a Certified Document Examiner—which means that her testimony holds up in court. (Sarah is currently a candidate for certification; having passed her written exam, she now needs to testify a total of four times in court and then pass an oral exam. As of our meeting, in mid-2004, she had testified once.) Much of the Holmeses' work also falls under forensic handwriting analysis, which is recognized in court (though, not surprisingly, there is disagreement about how accurate it is).

That afternoon, when Sarah and I headed to lunch, she told me about a study she had begun while doing graduate work at Boston University. Entitled "A Neuropsychological Investigation into the Validity of Handwriting Analysis," if nothing else, it certainly *sounds* scientific. She was sending original writing samples to thirty of the top graphologists in the world, fifteen in Europe and fifteen in the States, who were examining them and reporting back to her. Her hope was that if the outcome of her study was favorable, it would bring increased respectability to the field.

As it was, she encountered a variety of reactions when she told people what she does for a living. Some were positive. Others, not so much. Unless, that is, you consider comments like "quackery" and "carnival trickster" to be backhanded compliments.

These reactions raised an interesting question, namely: Is it harder to take your career seriously if others don't? All a doctor has to do to gain insta-respect—and kick in a whole litany of associations regarding status, income, and education, not to mention mode of automotive transport—is make mention of the M.D. following his or her name. It's not so easy for people in jobs such as Sarah's that enjoy less-than-widespread acceptance. Some years ago, I interviewed John Edward, the star of the TV show *Crossing Over,* who claims he can talk to the dead, for a story in the *New York Times Magazine.* I asked him if it irked him that people thought that his life's work was a sham. He leaned forward, almost angrily. "If I really cared what people thought about me, or what I do—Oh my God I wouldn't be doing this, I wouldn't leave the house." It is a mind-set that could be summed up by the title of the late, great Richard P. Feynman's book *What Do You Care What Other People Think?,* a philosophy easier approved than applied.

Sarah had to explain and defend herself to most everyone she met. Over. And over. And over. She said she tried not to be bothered by those who scoffed at her choice of career or were dismissive, telling me that "most of our biggest clients were once skeptics" and invoking the old salesman's defense that rejection is a "treasure in disguise." If that's the case, there was plenty of booty to be had. The critics of handwriting analysis tend to focus on the personality assessment aspect of the profession, but, lately, the forensic side has also come under some scrutiny. In a 2001 case, *United States v. Saelee,* the Supreme Court wrote that the methodology of forensic handwriting analysis hadn't been thoroughly tested (a prior condition for admissibility), and that the testing that had been done "raises serious questions about the reliability of methods currently in use." Of course, the Court expressed similar qualms about fingerprinting science, and much of forensic work in general. Still, for the Holmeses, the criticism hit home, and it is one of the reasons that Sarah is pursuing her graduate study.[2]

That said, Sarah told me that most of the people she meets are in-

2. For a relatively comprehensive critique of graphology, check out the essay by Geoffrey A. Dean in *The Write Stuff: Evaluations of Graphology—The Study of Handwriting Analysis,* edited by Barry L. Beyerstein and Dale F. Beyerstein (Prometheus Books, 1992).

trigued by her work. "When I go to a party, it's like bees to honey," she told me. "My poor boyfriend is very supportive. As soon as it comes out about the handwriting—that's it—it dominates the conversation. It's almost a little embarrassing sometimes. Because people are so into it, I have to work hard to reverse the conversation. And people want to know about the handwriting, and I appreciate it and I love it, but I want to learn about what you do. But it's such an unusual calling that people are like 'whaaaat?' "

In these situations, she told me, people usually either offer up their signature immediately or tell her, unbidden, that there is *no way* they are going to show her their writing.

THREE MONTHS AFTER RETURNING FROM Waltham, I headed out to Bloomfield Hills. Sarah was visiting her mother and I wanted both to meet Ruth and to see the two of them working together. Before I flew out, I spoke with Sarah on the phone again and she told me she'd given some more thought to why she liked the job so much.

"It can be," she told me, "very important work. You have a lot of power at your fingertips. You are literally changing people's lives. There are some very serious issues we deal with."

Such as, for example, giant penises drawn on a wall.

I arrived and Sarah showed me to the living room, where she was examining two photos of crudely rendered genitalia. "See the curve here, and how it fans out at the bottom, just above the swirls?" She indicated the appropriate swirly area, which, as far as I could tell, was supposed to be pubic hair. "And here, on this one, the way there is heavy line pressure at the top."

I nodded.

"That," she concluded, "could be the work of the same person."

Just then, Ruth walked into the room. Tall and sturdy, she wore wire-rimmed glasses and her white-blond hair was cut shoulder length. Though fifty-nine and slowed by a balky ankle on this day, she still moved with a visible purpose, as if continually late for a meeting that started two minutes ago. She spoke declaratively, in a manner reminiscent of a stern grade school teacher.

"So," she said with a cursory grin, surveying the photos and the two of us. "We're going to be comparing dicks around here, are we?"

The penises in question were part of a case for a large Detroit company. A week earlier, Ruth had received a call from a manager who wanted her to take a look at some graffiti the company had found, and to determine who was behind it. So the manager sent over a sheaf of photos documenting witticisms such as "J.P. Smells," "J.P. is Gay-P," "J.P. is FAT LIKE A BIG JOLLY SANTA," and, presumably just to mix it up a bit, "I HAVE TO POOP." Also enclosed was a big black binder containing the "qualification records" of forty-six employees. These are the forms that new hires fill out by hand, providing basic information such as education, activities, and employment history.

When I arrived, Sarah was embarking on the laborious process of going through the handwriting samples and scrutinizing each one to see if she could turn up a match with the graffiti. She was looking for tiny details—a crossing of a *t* here, a curl at the bottom of a capital *R* there—in hopes of finding a telltale clue. It appeared analogous to filling in a jigsaw puzzle when a handful of pieces may or may not be missing.

As she worked, Sarah kept a running monologue going for my benefit, in the patient, instructional manner of a summer camp counselor, something she could easily pass for. What she didn't look much like, curled up on a floral print couch in sweatpants and an oversized T-shirt with a magnifying glass in her hand, was the image most often associated with handwriting analysts: a detective. Or at least not the kind you see on *CSI*. But then again, if that other (fictional) Holmes, Sherlock, were alive today and worked from home, maybe he too would do so in his boxers while listening to Power 105.

OVER THE COURSE OF THE day, Ruth and Sarah filled me in on the Holmes family business. Technically, there are three generations of handwriting analysts in the family, as Ruth's mother, Rachel, dabbled in it. Her hobby made an immediate impression on her daughter.

"I used to think my mother was nuts," explained Ruth.

But then, while Ruth was in college, she and a friend sent snippets of handwriting home—from boyfriends, girls they weren't fond of, the usual. "I was impressed," said Ruth. "She always had something to say, and often it was right."

It wasn't until much later that Ruth took up the work herself. First, she had to get married (at twenty-three to Peter Holmes, the product of an old Boston family) and, on the night of the wedding, fly from Concord, Massachusetts, to Abidjan, on the Ivory Coast, West Africa, for her husband's first job with Goodyear.

She made the best of it, learning French and, eventually, getting a job with the Africa-American Institute, where she focused on bringing French-speaking Americans to the Ivory Coast. Four years later, the couple moved to Brussels, again for Peter's job, where Sarah and her older brother, Nick, were born. In 1979, the family returned to the States.

Anxious about reacclimating to the U.S. workforce, Ruth made the heady choice of acquiring a skill few people had heard of and for which there was, at the time, virtually no market. Still, she said that something about handwriting analysis clicked with her. "I knew then: this is the epiphany," Ruth said as we sat in her living room. "This wasn't a hobby, this was a life's passion."

So she read up, learning the basics from a book. Like an aspiring hairdresser cutting relatives' hair, she began performing personality assessments on her friends, then moved to teaching others. In 1983, she founded Pentec (an acronym for Personality Evaluation Network attached to the invented suffix —*tec* to represent "the high-tech forensic part of it") and ran it out of a home office. She started a local group—the Great Lakes Association of Handwriting Examiners—and had them over for dinner regularly. Sarah was always around, always interested, so, eventually, her mother did what she felt she had to: She told her to go away. "I was in high school and she pushed me away from it," Sarah told me, looking over at her mom. "She didn't want me to do it just because she did it. She said, 'Do whatever you want, follow your heart.' "

Being fourteen at the time, Sarah had a predictable reaction: "I was like 'Oh my God, she doesn't want me to work with her.' But a few months later when I came back, I think she realized that I really wanted to do it."

Sarah went off to Colby and studied psychology, but came back in the summers to work with Ruth. By that time, Ruth was doing well; she was listed as one of Michigan's "Top 10 Women Business Owners" and placed among "Michigan's 95 Most Powerful Women" by *Corp!* magazine. Still, Pete, who'd already seen his son major in art history—"You can imagine how that makes a dad feel," he told me that afternoon, one mortgage-paying man to another—pushed her to go a more traditional route. She wanted no part of it and, not long after, joined Ruth and made her one-woman business a family one.

Despite the enduring image of the family-owned bookstore or bodega, less than a third of family businesses survive into the second generation, and only 10 percent or so make it into the third. The average life span is twenty-four years, or just about the time the SINCE 1982 sign stops looking quite so preposterous. But to call Pentec a family business isn't quite right. It seemed to me more similar to a child following a parent into the same profession, in which case it might be as much a matter of genetics as business. (Sarah's brother, Nick, for example, never showed an interest or aptitude for handwriting analysis. When I spoke with him on the phone, he said, "It's not something my dad or I could do. There's specialized training.")

The benefit of Pentec's being such an unusual business—Ruth estimated that there are only six other such firms in the country—was that they knew their competition. This allowed the Holmeses to set their fees without concern for traditional small business fears—it's unlikely they'll be undersold by the discount graphologists down the block or a competitor outsourcing to a team of highly trained Indonesian handwriting analysts in a factory. And while the forensic work (both in court cases and outside) and corporate assessments the Holmeses perform are relatively lucrative ($150 per hour for forensic work, $200 for a personality assessment), it is the jury consulting that can provide a small windfall: from $2,000 to $20,000 per trial.

IN THE UNITED STATES, BOTH sides at a civil trial may call their own expert witnesses, advocating completely different, competing positions, leaving it up to a jury of ordinary citizens to decide who is more expert or believable. The fact that many experts are paid for their analysis advances the cynical, though rather convincing, view that a wealthy litigant can get a favorable verdict by spending vast sums of money. This practice extends to everything from patent law to microscopy to fingerprinting and handwriting analysis, but the basic idea is the same: Justice may be blind, but it never hurts to take her gently by the elbow and lead her in the right direction.

On my second day in Bloomfield Hills, Ruth walked me through a liability case she and Sarah were working on involving a major U.S. manufacturer. We headed to the dimly lit downstairs basement, where she kept many of her files, a second computer, and various discarded exercise contraptions that looked like medieval torture devices. Dark and secretive, the basement had the air of a place that should be entered via a secret passageway activated by pressing a dusty old tome on a bookshelf.

Ruth pulled out a file. "We got the juror questionnaires on a Wednesday and they chose the jury the following Monday," she said, sifting through sheets of paper. "So we prepared a hundred profiles and they had them in their hands by Friday. We try to get them out in twenty-four to forty-eight hours." For each prospective juror, Ruth and Sarah work up a scouting report of sorts, providing a synopsis of that person's tendencies and categorizing him or her as a leader, a follower, or a wild card. There are also three boxes: "factual," "emotional," and "both or clueless."

I asked her if "clueless" was a technical term.

Ruth laughed. "Yeah, it means they might as well not have even been there."

What she's looking for, she explained, is any ammo she can provide the attorneys—"we like to think we empower them"—to first choose a sympathetic jury and, once that's done, appeal to their personalities. "Someone like this with big round writing"—Ruth pointed to a juror questionnaire from a woman named Cathy—"she needs to be engaged. So we recommend that the lawyer make eye contact. Whereas a guy with angular writing, we play to the facts but don't make eye contact. Let him feel he is making the decision."

"Is this ethical," I asked?

"Are we manipulating a jury, you mean?" said Ruth, looking up from the file. "The other side has the option to do the same thing."

Some attorneys want her at the counsel table; others prefer she stay out of sight, at a nearby hotel or in a hallway outside the court, the proverbial ace up the stairwell. In many of the cases, lawyers hire the Holmeses before the trial, so they can work with the focus groups doing mock trials.[3] Once the case starts, Sarah and Ruth profile not only jury members, but also witnesses, attorneys, and even judges (a fact Ruth was ambivalent about publicizing), whose writing they pull off of signed orders. "If you have the judge down, you know how to approach him," explained Ruth.

And how, I asked, is that?

She showed me a handwriting sample from a judge in a recent case. It was neat, orderly writing. Then she held up three more writing samples.

"So," Ruth said, "of these three attorneys, who are you going to send in to the judge with all these papers very well organized to make his life very easy?"

One sample looked like a doctor's—almost illegible. A second was large and fluid but all over the place, as if the author had paid no attention to where he was supposed to write. The third, the one I pointed to, showcased small, precise writing much like the judge had.

---

3. Sometimes, the people involved in the case take the stand, sometimes it is actors, which sounds like a peculiar job in itself—"I play bereaved people for a living"—but that's another story.

"Exactly. See how it makes sense. This guy"—she pointed to the sloppy writer, who happened to be the defense attorney in the case—"is going to come in with his shirt untucked, he won't be able to find the papers, he's going to make a terrible impression. We saw him during jury selection. He was pathetic. He was totally disorganized. He wasted the judge's time. So we already had brownie points."

It seemed like a small prize for so much effort: brownie points. But considering the skewed fiscal reality of the legal system, $10,000 to get on the judge's good side is not all that absurd. Factoring in the number of expert witnesses and jury consultants and the like brought in on a major case, it's probably a bargain.

The Holmeses work on all manner of cases, though a lot of them tend to be product liability—engine parts, seat belts—or forged documents (they once worked a music case that revolved around whether someone had forged funk great George Clinton's signature).

The whole process struck me as partly an intuitive venture and partly a methodical one—as anyone who has ever hurriedly scribbled a credit card receipt that resembles abstract art knows, just because someone wrote their signature a certain way once does not mean they always do. Then there was the instantaneous nature of the work. Many spouses live together for forty years and never really understand each other; in their personality assessments, the Holmeses were attempting to reduce a person to a set of characteristics in a matter of minutes, and often without the benefit of even *meeting* the person.

There were moments during my time with the Holmeses that gave me pause. When Sarah would say to me, for example, that if you have a big loop in your *p*'s then you are very active and very physical. Or, as Ruth told me, that you can tell if someone is sociopathic from their writing. Or that, purely from a double loop in a cursive *o* that someone is pretending everything is fine but is really in denial, like a mother whose husband is cheating on her and is addicted to painkillers but shows up at PTA meetings as cheery as can be (this was an actual example Ruth mentioned). Then there was the time that Ruth told me, straight-faced, "It's too bad John Gotti got into killing people. He had much purer handwriting than Ken Lay's."

THEN THERE WAS THE WHOLE Kevorkian connection. That evening, I heard the tale in detail over family dinner. In the summer of 1995, Ruth explained, she heard about his case. Sympathetic to his cause, she called his lawyer, Jeffrey Feiger, and offered her services free of charge.

Her role was to recommend which jurors to keep. In the first trial, the defense was concerned when a United Methodist bishop appeared on the jury. Worried about his religious beliefs, Feiger asked Ruth if he should boot him out of the box. After looking at his handwriting, she advised not to. "The bishop ended up backing Kevorkian," said Sarah, "and he played a crucial role in helping him win an acquittal."

Over the course of the trials, Ruth became close to Kevorkian and he began spending time with her family. This may sound like the premise for a Fox sitcom—*wacky family of handwriting analysts takes in Dr. Death*—but from what I could tell, it played out more like a heartwarming drama (think Lifetime network).

"We would go out on picnics together," Sarah said cheerfully.

"Yes, and Jack would always be messing with the jigsaw puzzles in the living room," Ruth added.

"We really got along," added Peter. "He helped out with household chores."

Kevorkian became fast friends with Sarah in particular, and the two would play flute duets (earlier that day, Sarah had scrounged up a bunch of change for snack food and visited Jack in prison). So, when, after five successful trials, Kevorkian filmed himself performing assisted suicide and gave the tape to Mike Wallace of *60 Minutes,* he knew where to go to escape the inevitable media horde. He showed up that evening on the Holmeses' doorstep, toothbrush in hand.

For the succeeding six months, he lived incognito in their upstairs bedroom, which he fondly recalled as his "haven." When he foolishly represented himself in his sixth trial and was sentenced to jail, the Holmeses stood by him. They visited often, handled his mail, and even helped him publish a book (a compendium of paintings, limericks, essays, and assorted thoughts called *GlimmerIQs,* pronounced "Glimmericks"). A good two-thirds of the Holmes basement is taken up by Kevorkian para-phernalia, including somewhere in the area of ten thousand letters in boxes, all addressed to the Thumb Correctional Facility, and a shelf of books sent from well-wishers (sample titles: *New York Times Crossword Puzzle Book* and a collection of Paul Krugman essays). It was, for the mo-ment, the unofficial (and slightly dusty) Jack Kevorkian Library.

I WAS CURIOUS HOW KEVORKIAN saw this unusual relationship and so, a few weeks later, I arranged to speak to him by phone in prison. I was told I had fifteen minutes. He was polite and laconic. At least until I asked about Sarah.

"Very loyal, very sensitive, and very confident," he said. "She's not as headstrong as her mother either."

I asked his opinion of handwriting analysis and he went silent for a moment.

"It's equally science and art," he said finally. "It may be more art than science. It depends on one's experience. There's a great subjective ele-ment to it. Just as there is in medical diagnoses. It's the same thing. That's as much art as science, in fact sometimes it's more art than science."[4]

And that is the crux of the issue when it comes to the job's re-spectability. It is not science and it is not art, but it pretends to be both. The astronomer Carl Sagan once remarked, "Skeptical scrutiny is the means, in both science and religion, by which deep thoughts can be win-

---

4. I couldn't help but ask Kevorkian about how he saw his work. He said he believed be-ing a doctor was "probably" his calling. "I am of that nature anyway," he said. "My pur-pose is probably to challenge taboos that I think are unreasonable." He paused. "And I suppose which most reasonable people think are unreasonable. A lot of taboos that exist that should not."

nowed from deep nonsense." Sagan knew of which he spoke; as a vocal proponent of the search for extraterrestrial life, he had both his admirers and his critics.

Both Ruth and Sarah professed not to be bothered by their critics, but their actions spoke otherwise. Ruth bristled at the mention of certain skeptics while Sarah had gone so far as to undertake a graduate thesis intent on debunking them. I also noticed an interesting family dynamic with Sarah's father, Peter.

A short, lithe man with thick black hair who looks younger than his sixty-four years, Peter is quiet and very serious. He had quadruple bypass surgery four years ago but is in excellent health. Only six months into retirement, he is having a hard time adjusting to his new life, or, as he puts it, "backing out of my prior career and trying to smell the roses." On the weekend I visited, he had been catching up on "deferred house maintenance" while helping Ruth with Pentec, doing, in his words, "menial errands."

It became apparent that his early skepticism about Ruth and Sarah's line of work had not been forgotten. While preparing lunch one day, Ruth not so casually mentioned that she makes twice as much as Peter does now. If Peter were given to making more than one facial expression—he seemed to be, at all times, appraising a used car for hidden defects—I imagine he might have blanched. As it was he continued sitting there.

Ruth dug back in.

"We're a long way from asking if I wanted to get a 'real job,' aren't we?" She looked at Peter.

Peter kept looking at his imaginary Buick.

Sarah chimed in. "The only thing I really remember about when Mom got into this was that you told her to get a real job."

Forced into action, Peter said: "I don't remember saying that to Mom."

And so it proceeded: Ruth and Sarah explaining their work and, whenever Peter said something, immediately correcting or critiquing his point of view in the same cheery tones with which they justified the business to me.

ME: What's the toughest thing about the job for all
three of you?

RUTH: The hours . . .

SARAH: The hours for her.

PETER: Getting the invoices out. It's the biggest
because you have so much work coming in—

SARAH (interrupting and turning to Peter): You look at
Pentec and you see dollar signs—

RUTH (setting down her spoon and jumping in): A
bank.

SARAH (gathering steam): Yeah, a bank. I understand
that, you're retired. When I see Pentec, I see lives
being changed every day by our opinions. And we
better be pretty damn sure if we go to court and
say this person wrote it, you better be sure.

Later, when I talked to Peter alone, I asked him his feelings about his
daughter joining Pentec.

"I didn't expect Sarah to pick up on it. It's certainly hard to make a
living. But if you can create a niche, it can lead to a lot of other things:
franchising, books, lectures, then higher-end stuff like jury consulting.
None of that was done ten years ago."

It was an interesting dynamic: Peter looking for financial rationali-
zations for work that Ruth and Sarah saw inherent value in. To defend
against his skepticism, mother and daughter had developed an us vs.
them mentality that applied even at home. It wasn't that they didn't love
Peter—both clearly did—but that he wasn't part of the mind-set. They'd
created a layer of mental insulation that doubters—and doubts—
couldn't penetrate.

SEVEN MONTHS AFTER MY SECOND visit, I checked in with Ruth by
phone. She'd just ushered a reporter out of her house. That Sunday, it
turned out, was National Handwriting Day, a holiday concocted by the

pen industry that is celebrated on John Hancock's birthday (of course). Work was going well, she said, and the big news was that Academy Award–winning director Barbara Koppel was making a movie about Kevorkian's life. Sarah and Ruth were to be consultants. There was also talk of a book—Ruth would analyze the handwriting of selected people who'd written Jack letters while he was in prison.

And what, I asked, ever came of the graffiti case? "We didn't have enough evidence to nail any one person but we narrowed it down to a handful," she said. "I think they reprimanded a few people. Usually if people are doing things like that they are trying to call attention to many other things. Stop something before it becomes a big issue."

The next day, I spoke with Sarah, who was upbeat as always, saying, "Business has never been better." She'd just finished working a trade show at the Javits Center in New York, doing handwriting analysis for a firm to help it draw people to its booth. "Exhausting nine-hour days but exhilarating," she said. She told me she felt as though she was starting to define herself better in the field. While her mother was more of an expert on forensics, Sarah was drawn toward the personality assessment. Her study was also nearly halfway done and she hoped to have it finished within a year. She was also moving in with her longtime boyfriend.

It sounded, I told her, like her life was about perfect. Happy home life, good relationship with her parents, a dream job.

"It is pretty close to a dream job," she said. "I'm tailoring it every day. I feel lucky that I'm only thirty and have found a niche that I love and I'm compensated for. Sometimes I can't believe that I get paid to do this."

Neither, some skeptics might say, can they. But if handwriting analysis is what you think you were meant to do, Sarah's case suggests, maybe it doesn't really matter what anyone else thinks.

NINE

THE PIGSKIN

PREACHER

S OME YEARS AGO, A HOLLYWOOD type approached Doug Blevins about making a movie of his life. It would be, the man said, an inspirational tale about a young handicapped boy overcoming the odds, the kind of heartwarming film that could dampen the eye of even the sturdiest construction worker. Blevins told me that he listened to the man's pitch and then proceeded to curse him out, "like a dog that's been mucking through the garbage. This guy told me America wants to see Doug Blevins at ten years old, crying himself to sleep," Blevins said, eyes wide with disbelief, voice rising. "But that didn't happen, not one *goddamn* time! They wanted to warp the story and I said no way."

No, what Blevins thought a movie should focus on was *football*, specifically him coaching it and others playing it. This makes sense; he is, after all, one of the top kicking coaches in the world. He has mentored NFL Pro Bowlers such as Adam Vinatieri and Olindo Mare and worked for the Miami Dolphins and the Minnesota Vikings and the New York Jets. He can watch a kicker for three minutes and deconstruct and reconstruct his form. Football, as he stressed to me repeatedly, is all he's ever cared about. The way he sees it, the fact that he has cerebral palsy and has never walked, much less kicked a ball himself, is unimportant in the bigger picture. As he said at one point, after a couple beers had loosened his already loose tongue: "Chris, buddy, the only thing I missed being handicapped was playing the game. Fuck walking. *Fuck* walking. I wish I could have played the game." Except in his Southern twang, it came out *Fuh-huck wawking.*

So while his life story certainly has its inspirational aspects (sorry, Doug) what stayed with me after visiting Blevins was how passionate— or better yet, *certain*—he was about his work. His history suggests that sometimes people follow a calling, regardless of its attainability, because it is all they have—because it is the one thing that can give their life meaning. In his case, despite the dissenting opinion of every other human being he encountered, save his mother (and even she had her doubts), it never occurred to him that he *wouldn't* be coaching football, no matter how impractical it seemed. As he might say, when it comes to finding a calling, sometimes you gotta say, Fuck impracticality. Though one has to be careful, because impracticality has a habit of fucking you back.

I FIRST MET BLEVINS DURING the summer of 2004, in his hometown of Abingdon, Virginia, where he runs kicking camps during the NFL off-season (at the time, he was a special consultant for the Minnesota Vikings). A lazy, welcoming town of 7,780, Abingdon has a quaint downtown dotted with old theaters and historic inns. It's the kind of place where people say "hi" to each other at the gas station, no one drives all that fast, and two wrong turns and you feel like you're in rural Indiana. I arrived and dropped my bags at the Quality Inn, which is grandly listed on Blevins's Web site as "The official hotel of the Doug Blevins Kicking Camp."

The camp isn't a camp in the traditional sleepaway, mess-hall style but rather intensely specialized, football-centric, and intimate. Students can come for one day, one week, or, in rare cases, for a period of months. It isn't cheap—$500 per day for two training sessions and a night conditioning session in the pool—but Blevins's track record with kickers is a strong draw. In addition to Vinatieri and Mare, he has worked with seven other kickers or punters in the NFL and helped dozens of others make it to football's minor leagues, places like the Arena Football League and NFL Europe, where the pay is minimal but the lure of getting noticed by a scout and moving up to "the league" draws hopeful players.

I arrived on a warm afternoon, in time to catch the final element of the day, the swim practice. Blevins had promised it would be "an ass-kicking for the guys." He picked me up outside the Quality Inn in his van, a silver Dodge Caravan Sport with a large sticker that read DOUG BLEVINS above his Web site address and his camp motto: THE WINNING EDGE IN FOOTBALL. To my surprise, he was in the driver's seat.

"Hawp on in!" he shouted. His wife, Nancy, was in the passenger seat, and one of his students, a twenty-two-year-old named Jonathan Feig, was in the back sitting in Doug's mechanized wheelchair, which doubles as a passenger seat. I sat in a captain's chair that was perched next to the sliding door.

Doug smiled and extended his hand. He looked like a big man squeezed into a small body. He has a wide, exuberant face that is often reddish from sun exposure and close-cropped black hair with errant strands of gray. Forty years old, he is five feet one and 145 pounds with a bit of a paunch, but his crowing voice makes him sound larger. At the waist, he tapers down—his legs are shorter than normal and thin from disuse, but he has enough muscle control to push a wheelchair (backward is faster), though not to stand. His left hand is permanently crumpled up, like a child's fist closed around a prize toy. On his right hand, his index finger crooks at the end and his third and fourth fingers splay outward, but he can type (a two-finger hunt-and-peck) and write, though he can't grip larger items such as a bottle (he brings his own plastic cup and drinks from a straw at restaurants and bars). A handshake with Doug is really a finger shake—he applies pressure from two of his fingers, which may explain why he enjoys high-fiving so much. Though, once I got to know him, I realized that he's also just a high-fiving type of guy. I imagine he'd also be the type who would love to give head noogies.

As we rumbled through Abingdon, he explained his modified driving system. To navigate, he holds a knob attached to the steering wheel, and to reach the pedals he pushes on a block of wood stacked on top of the accelerator. It was smooth riding for the most part—there was a split-second delay between when he wanted to brake and when the van began to brake—but he was a good driver.

The inside of the van resembled some sort of automotive amusement ride. Mechanized tracks ran up underneath Blevins's chair and an electric ramp lay dormant behind it. The van would have cost $60,000 converted as it was, Blevins proudly noted, but he had paid only $23,000—the Caravan base price—in exchange for doing promotional work for the conversion company, Viewpoint Mobility. That meant he appeared regularly at trade shows and on promotional videos. The same held for his (quite impressive) electric wheelchair. A custom-designed Pride Mobility Jazzy 1122 model with a joystick-control system, it had a $7,000 price tag and sported purple trim with the Vikings colors. In exchange for PR work by Blevins, Pride Mobility not only donated the chair but provided one for him at every airport on the road when the team traveled.[1]

---

1. When he was a coach in NFL Europe, he'd disembark planes in an unusual fashion; one of the team's hulking linemen would pop his suitcase under one arm and Doug under the other and walk off the plane.

"I am," Blevins told me, "the Michael Jordan of handicapped product endorsement."

When we arrived at the pool, Doug pushed what looked like a garage door opener on the driver-side visor. The van began shaking and whirring with alarming alacrity. It lowered, as if squatting, the back door opened, and the ramp deployed, like the tongue of a landing spaceship. Doug used his arms to move himself into the wheelchair with an audible grunt, then spun around and headed out of the car. After he exited, the ramp ascended and the doors swung shut with a resounding clank.

"All right," he said, grinning. "Let's go see if we can kick the tar out of these guys in the pool!" He cackled—something he does often—and motored off.

He wasn't kidding either; under the direction of Nancy—a onetime Olympian synchronized swimmer for the Colombian national team whom Doug met at a speaking engagement where she was working as a translator—the four teenage boys swam until they looked like they were going to puke. And then the high school senior did puke, repeatedly and voluminously, into a poolside trash can. Blevins's take on it? "Don't worry, this is all for your benefit," he said to the boy. "Besides, you don't look no worse than me after a night of drinking."

CURRENTLY, 764,000 ADULTS AND CHILDREN in the United States suffer from one of the symptoms of cerebral palsy. Often mistaken for a disease, cerebral palsy is a condition that is neither degenerative nor curable. Most of those who have it are born with it, though in the United States 10 percent develop CP after birth. An English surgeon named William Little first wrote of a "puzzling disorder" in the 1860s that caused stiff, spastic muscles in the legs and the arms. Named Little's disease for many years, it's now known as spastic diplegia and is one of several disorders grouped under the header of cerebral palsy.

CP is misunderstood in part because it affects people differently. Some are more able-bodied; Stephen Hopkins, one of the signers of the Declaration of Independence, had palsy and famously said, "My hand may shake but my heart does not," as he signed the document. Others, like Christie Brown, the Irish poet and playwright chronicled in *My Left Foot,* are more outwardly affected by the condition. Blevins is somewhere in the middle; stripped of the ability to walk and without the use of one hand but otherwise able to do most anything able-bodied people do.

Not that most people would know it. Blevins is often asked two questions about his condition. "People always want to know: can you go to the bathroom and can you have sex," he told me at one point. "They think I'm paralyzed or something. I say, 'No, I can't go to the bathroom. When I'm sixty-five, I'll walk into the bathroom and explode. So if you see an old guy in a wheelchair rushing into the bathroom, get the hell out of there!'" As for the sex, he was quick to state for the record that he has *lots and lots of it.* (After his divorce from his first wife, he said, his plan was "to sleep with every woman in Florida and then work my way up through Georgia.") He has one son with his first wife and, when I visited, Nancy was pregnant with their first, a girl. ("I wanted a daughter," Doug said, "because I've already got so many sons by virtue of what I do.")

After swim practice, we headed back to Blevins's house, just up the hill from downtown Abingdon. It was a small, boxy one-story structure that was outfitted to meet his needs: ramps, railings in the bathroom, no stairs. More notable, however, was the overwhelming amount of football memorabilia that filled the place. Practically every centimeter of wall space was covered. There was the Ernie Davis Courage Award that Blevins received in 2000; photos of him with Dolphins players; photos of him with his kickers. Mini-plastic NFL helmets hung from the wall and twenty-three different footballs of various sizes were displayed in the living room, including an "Outstanding Coach of the Game" ball from Miami and the ball from Adam Vinatieri's first NFL field goal. Videotapes of kickers to be evaluated lay on a table, and two satellite receivers fed signals down from the roof, allowing him to watch up to four different games simultaneously, on the big forty-five-inch TV that dominated the living room and the four smaller ones that surrounded it. It was as if the "man room," that traditional, often subterranean bastion of testosterone in many houses, had risen up, declared its independence, and taken over the entire home.

While I was examining a glass football, Blevins's mother, Linda, arrived. A pretty woman of fifty-seven with big hair and a bigger smile, she practically bloomed with Southern manners. We sat down to dinner and, in what amounted to a round-table discussion, I heard Doug's life story.

"Well, he just liked football from the start," Nancy began. "Even as a little boy, that's all he wanted to do."

On Sundays, Linda would dress Doug in a Dallas Cowboys helmet and jersey—that was his favorite team—while he watched the games. During the week, he'd play electric football, a board game, for twelve to fourteen hours at a time. Since he didn't have the dexterity to flick the ball—a necessary move to score in the game—he'd shoot Nerf hoops for field goals. He kept stats and played full seasons (he still has the notebooks).

Unable to play football in the traditional manner, he'd have Linda take him out into the backyard to "practice." She'd put pads on him and stand him up next to a big oak tree. Again and again, he'd "tackle" that tree, rolling off of it and laboriously righting himself with his arms. He'd hit it differently depending on whether he was pretending to be a linebacker or a lineman, and would stay out for three, four hours at a time. "Mom used to clean me up, put a clean T-shirt on me, put the shoulder pads back on, and send me back out," Blevins said, smiling. "I wanted to go all day."

Not strong enough to kick a real football, he'd line up a Nerf version and, using his arms to swing his body, boot through it straight-legged like a foosball figure. He even tried playing tackle football on crutches with his buddies until he broke his left kneecap.

At first, school was an issue. When Linda tried to enroll him at

Abingdon Elementary, the school district told her he would have to go into special education classes. "I said, there's nothing wrong with his *brain*," she recounted. "I mean, he was smarter than most of the able-bodied kids."

"How about we bring a teacher to your home," the district reps responded.

"No way," Linda said. *"My boy is going to regular school."* After threatening legal action, she won the battle. Doug would go to the same school as the other kids.

Linda drove him every day and every day she picked him up. Since they didn't have much money, she got an old wooden office chair with wheels on it to serve as his "wheelchair." It didn't have arms, but it would do, and as Doug said with a gleeful laugh, "It was a hell of a lot more fun." Since there were no handicapped ramps at his high school, Doug's friends carried him up and down the stairs. They also would give him a push and send him flying down the hallway, something he apparently enjoyed—"Now that was fun!" he said—despite the fact that he often tipped over and skidded part of the way on his side like a hockey puck.

From the beginning, Linda encouraged him in everything he did. She'd tape motivational signs around the house with slogans like "Reach for your Dream." "I always told Doug, 'You can do anything you want if you try hard enough.' "

Still, even Linda didn't know about football. "That's all he ever talked about," she said, looking over at him. "Never, never anything else. I'd say, 'Wouldn't you like to go into teaching, computers?' I always wanted him to be happy, but I didn't *get* football."

But Doug did. He got it in a way he didn't get anything else. So as a boy he wrote letters to all of his heroes: Tom Landry, Roger Staubach, and the other Cowboy luminaries. Amazingly, they wrote back, sending along a signed photo. But it wasn't until he wrote Ben Agajanian, the Cowboys kicking coach, asking for pointers, and received a box of pamphlets and instructional videos in return, that he determined his route

to the NFL. Nobody knew much about kicking, nobody *understood* kicking, which wasn't that surprising.

By its very nature, kicking is an auxiliary act. Even the name "point
after," the kick after a touchdown, is relegatory. It is the point "after" the
score, which is the real show. As for the field goal, it is the consolation
prize; we couldn't make it in the end zone, so we'll have to bring out the
kicker. A punt, when a team can't get a first down and is forced to kick
the ball to the other team, is even worse—an admission of defeat. The
kicker himself is rarely the hero. He's the guy who never signs at auto-
graph shows, whose face never appears on cereal boxes, who doesn't go
to the nightclubs with the stars. By the standards of pro sports, kickers
are low paid, rarely celebrated, and placed under tremendous amounts
of pressure. A kicker can make fifty kicks in a row, but if he misses one
important one, that's what he's forever remembered for (Scott Norwood
of the Buffalo Bills missed a field goal in the Super Bowl and will be
known for the rest of his life as "Wide Right").

Still, there is a democracy to the position. As Blevins proudly
pointed out, "It's the only position in the NFL where you can make the
league without going to college." Spot a kicker at a mall and—well, you
wouldn't be able to, because they'd look like any other five-foot-ten, 160-
pound guy checking out wrinkle-free khakis at the Gap. If a kicker told
you he was a pro football player, you probably wouldn't believe him, just
as most people don't believe Blevins when he tells them he's a coach in
the NFL. They are a similar breed, kickers and Blevins, both underdogs.
Which may explain why he understands them so well.

So as a high schooler, he set out to learn as much as he could about
this dark art of the NFL. He taped games, watching the best pro kickers
of the day—men like Jan Stenerud and Morten Andersen—and broke
down their technique. He applied what he learned at Abingdon High,
where he was a student assistant coach, and his senior year he won a
scholarship, the Ray Petty Memorial Award, usually given to a player.
He wore a headset to the games, lived and died with each win or loss.
Not literally, but pretty close; he'd cry, he'd be unable to sleep, and,

sometimes, he'd throw up. He still does all these things when his team loses.

During high school, people often laughed when he spoke of his aspirations. "I told people I was going to be the first handicapped coach in the NFL and they thought I was nuts," he said, taking a sip of his water. "But I knew it could happen. I knew it would happen."

It was a long road. After high school, Blevins went to the University of Tennessee, where he was an administrative assistant with the football team. Word of his skill with the kickers got around, and local parents began bringing their young boys, paying Blevins $30 or $40 to work with them. From there, he transferred to East Tennessee State in 1986 to serve as its student kicking coach and, after graduating two years later, formed his own kicking consulting company. Later he was hired as an assistant football coach at Abingdon High. The whole time, however, he had one goal in his mind: to make the NFL. So he'd stay up into the early morning reviewing tapes of kickers, grading them, and writing letters to NFL general managers. Just give me a chance, he'd write, and I can solve your kicking woes.

His break came with the New York Jets. One of the administrators at Southwest Virginia Community College, where Blevins was working a day job as director of the handicapped students services program, knew Dick Steinberg, then the Jets' general manager, and convinced him to give Blevins a call. Though skeptical, Steinberg was impressed with the depth of Blevins's knowledge. "He grilled me for two hours," says Blevins. "To my knowledge, there was not a question that he asked me that I did not have a response for."

The conversation was all the fuel Blevins needed; from that point on, he was relentless. "I'd watch every Jets game and then I'd fax them a report. I'd analyze what the kickers were doing wrong and tell them what they needed to do to give myself credibility." Before the next season, in 1994, Steinberg relented. The guy may be in a wheelchair but he obviously knew what he was talking about. The Jets hired Blevins as a kicking consultant, making him, in Blevins's words, "just about dance around the room." It was, Blevins said gravely, the best day of his life. Who cared that he was making all of $10,000?

After a regime change inside the Jets left Blevins without a job, he took a job working in NFL Europe as the league's kicking coordinator. Since the playing season ran during the summer, he was free to keep an NFL job, and in 1997, Jimmy Johnson, the coach of the Miami Dolphins, hired him sight unseen. When Blevins arrived for his first day, motoring into the office, Johnson thought someone had played a joke on him. "He didn't believe I was Doug Blevins. We went back and forth a couple of times. I'd say 'I'm Doug Blevins,' and he'd say, 'No you're not.' "

Blevins cackled as he retold the story. "Then we got to talking and he realized I was the coach he'd hired. His only concern was whether I could get around the field. I told him I had a system worked out, been doing it my whole life. My first practice was that day."

Blevins's system is all about avoidance. First and foremost, he stays behind the offense: "If the play comes your way and you're behind, no way in hell you're getting out of the way." On kicks, he positions himself in back of the kicker, around the opposite forty-yard line; that way he can see the kicker's steps approach. He times all the kicks with his stopwatch, which he bangs against his underdeveloped hand to clear. Occasionally, he'll forget where he is as he watches the ball tumbling end over end through the afternoon sky. "I get so worked up out there that I lose track of where I am," he told me. "I've been hit by balls, knocked over, but it doesn't matter. Sometimes I feel like it's *me* out there playing."

As he spoke, it was easy to understand why young men like Vinatieri and Feig were drawn to him. He had a reverence for football—the game itself, not the hypermarketed, televised, cult of personality–driven institution of the NFL—that was pure and, in many ways, innocent. To him, the "job" didn't matter, so long as it involved football, and preferably football at the highest level. He wanted to coach someplace where others cared as much as he did; the hours, the money, the duties, the location—these were all details. His passion wasn't unlike Nehrich's, born

of some inner drive, yet Blevins didn't necessarily need the world's endorsement. Though that might not be entirely fair; even if he was
coaching peewee football, Blevins was doing something considered ac-
ceptable, something worthwhile. He was coaching kids, and coaching
them in what has become—sorry baseball—the country's national past-
time, even if he was focused on the least celebrated aspect of it.

Unlike Nehrich, Blevins also expected, if not demanded, that others
share his reverence for his work. One time, his father, Willis, came to
Miami for a game (Linda and Doug's dad split when Doug was in high
school). "It was a heartwrenching loss," Doug recounted over dinner,
putting down his fork and scrunching up his face. "I can't describe to you
the depths of devastation. *I was hot,* I'm telling you. Well, I'm heading
into the postgame locker room area and this usher stops me at the door
and pats me on the head. He says, 'Look, son, you can't get an auto-
graph right now.' "

Blevins shook his head. Feig and Nancy grinned in anticipation of
what would come next.

"I said, 'Look, you son of a bitch, get out of my way,' and then I said
some other stuff that I won't repeat and grabbed the door."

"Well my dad was shocked. He says, 'It's just a game, son.' "

Here Blevins paused and turned to me, the *Sports Illustrated* writer,
and gave me a look that said, *As a kindred spirit, you understand the absurdity of such a statement.*

"So I said, 'Dad, if you're going to talk that way, you can go back
and sit in the goddam car. This is my profession and don't you ever forget it.' "

Blevins cackled. "Dad didn't talk to me until the next morning."

After dessert, I took my leave. We had a big day of kicking ahead of
us. Before I left, I noticed Blevins sizing me up. "You ever done any kicking, Chris?"

I told him I hadn't, which was essentially true. In high school, I'd
played soccer but never football—though I'd always fancied myself
something of a punter, the way that I suppose many people fancy themselves something of a singer or a comedian. But the fact that he'd in-

stinctively checked out a thirty-year-old journalist, *just in case* he might have some skill, told me a lot about how Blevins sees the game, and his work. Just like, as a writer, any interesting conversation I have or tidbit I read about is automatically processed under the heading of "might be a story" or "probably not a story," he saw humans under the heading of "kicker" or "not a kicker."

SPECIALTY COACHES IN PRO SPORTS are a relatively recent phenomenon. Whereas thirty years ago, it was common for a head coach to do his job alone, franchises now hire what amounts to an entire management team. In 2005, the Dallas Mavericks of the NBA, for example, boasted not only nine assistant coaches—whose specialties ranged from player development to player relations to translation (for foreign players)—but also strength and conditioning coaches and even lifestyle coaches (for players in need of assistance with housing or buying a suit).

In most cases, such coaches are former players, though not always good ones. In baseball, it is almost axiomatic that the best hitting coach of the day was himself an unaccomplished, if not terrible, batter. In the NFL, linebackers have their own dedicated coach, as do wide receivers and linemen and defensive backs—pretty much everyone except kickers (when I visited Blevins, he was one of only two kicking coaches in the league; Steve Hoffman with the Cowboys was the other). Even though many games are decided by a field goal or less, kickers are left to their own devices, under the direction of a "special teams coach" who spends far more time on the kick returns and punt blocks and is in charge of dozens of players.

This is in part a cultural thing. Kickers are the outcasts of the NFL, undersized specialists in a game played by giants; they're misunderstood by coaches unaccustomed to dealing with an aspect of the game not ruled by strength or speed but by technique and, more mysterious to these coaches, psyche. The following morning, I got a chance to see how Blevins tweaked and buffed the psyches of his students.

Blevins picked me up at 9 A.M. and we headed over to Emory &

Henry College, just outside Abingdon, where he used the fields in exchange for analyzing the school's kickers. It was in the high seventies and sunny, and the drive took us past a rural landscape of barns, cows, rolling green fields, and little roadside stores with names like This n' That. The sticky smell of manure rose into the air. Blevins was excited; he loved getting out and, as he put it, "getting dirty."

When he works with NFL teams, Blevins is careful not to overexert the kickers. He runs one session in the morning and one in the afternoon, and each kicker launches only twenty-five to thirty balls each session. "Matt Turk put it best," Blevins said, referring to the former NFL punter. "The human leg is like a rubber band. Only so many stretches in it before it wears out."

With younger kickers, however, Blevins works them till they drop, sometimes literally. For them the kicking practice is longer and more intense than his pro workouts and accompanied by intense conditioning, both on the field and in the pool. On this day, Blevins had some fresh meat. As we arrived at the fields we saw a shaggy-haired teenager standing with his father. His name was Kenny and he'd driven all the way from Charlottesville for a one-day lesson. Kenny was a freshman-to-be at Concord College and was hoping to kick on the football team. He'd been to a different coach the previous year but, after reading about Blevins, had saved his money. He looked nervous and his father looked skeptical, as if mentally calculating the long-term returns on all the savings bonds his son could have purchased for $500.

We headed to the field, Blevins motoring along and talking to Kenny, who gave him mainly one-word answers. On the far side, Feig was already warming up. He'd first met Blevins when he was fifteen; his mother had followed Blevins to his van and implored him to coach her son. Though his collegiate career at Washington University (St. Louis) had been marred by a hip flexor injury, Feig had talent. He could hit from fifty, fifty-one yards and his goal was to make the AFL or AFL2 that fall (the American Football League is sort of like the mini-golf of football; played on a shorter field in indoor stadiums in front of smaller crowds, for far less money).

Courteous, thoughtful, and a little shy, Feig had decided to give a kicking career a try—if it didn't work out, he told me, he'd always know he had made the effort. He'd been to all the other kicking camps, but once he met Blevins that was it. "It's a much more personal experience here," he told me between drills. "He really broke it down to a detail level where I can understand it. He'd arrived only forty-eight hours earlier, and, like me, he was staying at the Quality Inn, in his case until he found an apartment. Both he and another young kicker named Brent Barth had an unusual arrangement with Blevins, the same one Vinatieri had had: they lived in Abingdon and helped him with his camps in exchange for instruction.

Barth was the opposite of Feig in temperament. An athletic, muscled twenty-two-year-old with a buzz cut, he looked like an action hero or a homecoming king in some football-mad town. An All-American punter at Virginia Military Institute, he had expected to be drafted by the NFL but was passed over. After meeting Blevins, he'd moved to Abingdon eight months prior to my visit. To earn money, he got a job as a dishwasher at Cracker Barrel, where he worked the late shift, leaving drenched each night, his pants soaked in grime and dishwater ("a hell of a character builder," as Blevins deemed it). "I was ready to get a real job but he believed in me," Barth told me of his first meeting with Blevins. "I drove out here from Phoenix. Him saying I got a shot, that's all the fuel I needed." Since arriving, Barth told me, Blevins hadn't once brought up payment. It's understood that if Barth makes it, he'll pay back his coach. None of this—Barth being a punter, moving to Abingdon—sat well with Barth's father, who thought real men should play quarterback, as Brent had in high school.

"I asked my dad when I was young, 'What would happen if I became a kicker?' " Barth said as we sat on the grass. "He said, 'I'll fucking kill you.' So I was pissed when VMI wanted me to be a punter."

His dad's reaction?

"He didn't say nothing when I got a full scholarship." Barth paused and looked across the field. "My old man went to West Point. I know he wants me to be in the army. It's a touchy subject."

Blevins, who was within earshot, harrumphed and swiveled his chair around. "Well," he said, "I'm sure he'll be disappointed when you're in the NFL and going to the Pro Bowl and making a million dollars. *'Try to overlook my shortcomings, Dad!'* "

After stretching, the kickers split up into punters and field goal kickers. On one end of the field, Barth worked on his punts in a "punt box," which is three and a half yards long and marked off by cones. The goal is to catch the ball and have it in the air by the time you reach the front of the box. "The block point in a game would be four yards, so this gives plenty of clearance," as Blevins explained. His goal with Barth was to get his punts up, as he has no problem with distance. When he came out of VMI, he was booming sixty-yard punts, but they were flat and straight, more like a fastball than a lofted fly ball. His hang time, Blevins explained, was pitiful—in the area of 4.1 seconds. This essentially gave an NFL returner a twenty-yard head start to get going before the defense gets to him. "We call the old frozen rope punt 'Touchdown' because that's what happens," Blevins explained as Barth kicked. "You're putting a lot of pressure on your coverage."[2]

As I watched, Brent boomed a 5.16 punt that carried a good forty-five to fifty yards, rocketing upward into a cloudless blue, peaking for a moment and then spinning back to the grass.

"Now that's a Sunday punt," Blevins said approvingly.

At Barth's level, most of what Blevins was doing was fine-tuning and emphasizing consistency. So Blevins served as part cheerleader, part therapist, and part technician, honing in on details. With a newcomer like Kenny, however, Blevins was starting from scratch.

There was a lot of work to do. At first, Kenny awkwardly thwacked his punts, sending them wobbling out onto the soccer field. He looked nervous and self-conscious. Blevins's strategy was to douse him with

2. For those who care, the difference in college is that the outside "gunners," the first line of defense, can release on the snap. In the NFL, they have to wait for the ball to be punted. In the CFL, players can run on the snap, hence long kickers are coveted in Canada.

positive reinforcement when he did anything right: offering up splayed-finger high fives and saying stuff like "I'm proud of you, buddy." When Kenny actually cranked a couple good kicks, Blevins fairly fell out of his chair, yelling: "HOLY HELL, KENNY! That's better!"

Still, the boy's mechanics were a mess. Blevins decided to try a different tack.

"When you go to a strip club, how do you grab a woman's titty?" Doug barked from his wheelchair.

Kenny blushed. Unsure if he was supposed to answer, he stood there, momentarily mute. Blevins kept right on going.

"You grab it like this," Blevins said, making a palming motion. "Now you gotta grab the ball just like you would a woman's breast. Not down here—" he made a cupping motion. "You do it kind of on the side and also on top. Think Titty Principle, Ken."

Ken picked up the ball, grabbed it on top, and boomed a punt.

Blevins cackled. "It's amazing when you use the old strip club analogy how the ball gets down the field. Again Kenny. Think TITTY!"

Another nice kick.

"Now Kenny," Blevins continued. "You're holding the ball too low before you kick it. You gotta think titty again. Think two titties: yours and hers. This time, it's your titty. Hold the ball at breast level."

Kenny rocketed another fifteen kicks.

Still, the direction left something to be desired. So Blevins brought up the Peter Principle. "Whichever way your peter is pointing, that's where the ball will go," Blevins said, sparking some giggling among the other boys, who were now watching. "Dammit," Blevins barked, looking around. "It's true, no joke."

Kenny tried to focus and managed to do so. The ball went straight. Blevins was elated.

"One coachable sumbitch, I like that. Gimme five."

Kenny grinned as if told he could enter the secret treehouse club for the first time.

Afterward, as I walked alongside Blevins, I mentioned that Kenny seemed uncomfortable at first, perhaps because he didn't know how to act around someone with CP.

Blevins waved away the thought. "It's gotten to the point where they've generally read something or seen something on TV," Blevins said. "When Adam [Vinatieri] hired me, he didn't know. So I just try to start talking mechanics right away. As soon as they see that what you're teaching them works, any bias or prejudice is out the window. They only care about results."

He paused, watched the flight of a field goal attempt.

But, I asked, wasn't there a credibility gap at first because he'd never kicked himself? It was one thing to coach a sport you were mediocre at; another to coach a sport you'd never played.

"I think it works to my advantage that I've never kicked," he said, shading his face against the sun. "I've had to learn to articulate it. I've had no choice. I never did it myself, so I've had to study it. A lot of your coaches weren't good players or hardly played at all."

It occurred to me that he didn't have the luxury of any other point of view. So he rationalized his situation and tried to turn it into a positive. It was consistent with the way he treated his condition, which he called "the Cadillac of handicaps." During our time together, he complained about many things—his salary, the tactics of his competitors, the way he's been portrayed in various newspaper stories—but never once did he complain about his physical condition. In fact, he seemed to actively defy it. He didn't park in handicapped spots, hated "all the PC crap" he believed accompanied people's attitudes toward him, and detested being helped with anything.

It is a common theme among successful people with disabilities. Beethoven was deaf, Mozart had Tourette's, Emily Dickinson was bipolar. Albert Einstein was believed to have a learning disability, while Lincoln was thought to have Marfan's. Bill Cosby has ADD, same goes for Malcolm Forbes. People are remarkably resilient; a study found that of people with extreme quadriplegia, 84 percent consider their life to be average or above average. Pondering such stats and these historical examples can make one feel exceedingly inferior—*Mozart had Tourette's. I have nothing at all and can't even get a promotion*—but that is the wrong way to look at it. Maybe Mozart would have sucked at office work. Maybe he would have been unable to change the toner.

The point, Blevins would argue, is that to worry about a shortcoming is to empower it. He doesn't even like the word "handicapped," which is understandable considering its sports implications. A golfer must win despite his "handicap," a basketball team tries to prevail despite the "handicap" of playing without its best player. People overcome handicaps. No one ever says you overcome being "handicapped." And, just as Blevins hates to make excuses, he hates it even more when other, able-bodied people do. At one point during our time together, we ran into a friend of Blevins's named Lonnie, one of the guys who'd carried him up and down the steps during high school. Lonnie was now on disability—something about his back. After a brief conversation, Lonnie left and Blevins turned to me. "I find it funny when a guy like Lonnie complains to me about being on disability and not being able to work." Blevins laughed sarcastically. *"Yeah,* I feel for you, buddy."

Refusing to acknowledge a handicap in life is one thing; doing the same when it comes to work is another. There is a theory among career counselors about how to deal with people like Blevins. "We help people find what they love to do, but then we have to put it in a practical context," Mark Pope, the past president of the National Association of Career Development, told me when we spoke on the phone. "If you're forty-five and have two kids and a mortgage, you have to look at it practically." So, he continued, career counselors will suggest to an accountant who loves the outdoors, as Pope once did, that he become an accountant for the Sierra Club. By this logic, then, Blevins should be answering phones for a football team somewhere, or selling season-ticket packages, or running the stadium sound system, punching a button to summon "We Will Rock You" as the home team drives in the fourth quarter. That would be the practical thing to do.

At one point during the day, I asked Blevins whether he thought football was his calling. "I definitely feel that football was what I was meant to do," he said without hesitation. "I was blessed to be able to do this. I think God gave me the ability to do this because I could be an inspiration to a lot of people. I get letters from lots of people I've never met who say I've been their inspiration to get their degree and go to college."

He told me the story of a CP kid in Chicago who keeps a photo of Blevins on his wall. The boy wrote to Blevins telling him he was his hero. "It's a good feeling to know that you can have that effect. To be able to be a role model."

But that was a side effect, he stressed, if a wonderful one. Football was his love, and he had further aspirations. His end goal, which he mentioned at least ten times in our two days together, was to be a head coach. (On more than one occasion, he said to me, "I like you, Chris. When I become a head coach in the NFL, I'm going to give you full access.") He told me he'd traded letters with colleges about being an assistant or head coach, but he wasn't sure if their cordial responses were "just being PC." Though he didn't like to acknowledge the disadvantages of CP in his own life, he was aware of the objections his condition created in others. "I know it's not easy for someone to hire a handicapped coach, so I have to work my way up. But I know I can do it."

And, as I've mentioned before, he can't help but coach. At the end of the second practice that afternoon, I grabbed a ball and, at Blevins's urging, booted it. It was not, by any measure, a Sunday punt. I kicked a couple more but they weren't much better. Blevins watched, nodding slowly to himself.

"OK, I know what you're doing wrong," he said. "Hold the ball out even with your right shoulder. Now keep your shoulders back and drop it straight, not in."

I followed his advice and smacked the ball about thirty-five to forty yards, with a spiral. After shanking the next kick, I booted a couple more nice ones. It was remarkable what his adjustments had done.

On the drive back to his house, he gave me his critique. "I was impressed with what you did. Good leg speed. Though I'm not sure I could make you into an NFL punter. . . ."

He paused, raised his eyebrows. "But . . ." he said, mulling it over. "It *would* be interesting to mess around with it. You have to factor in that you're thirty. If you were younger it would be easier, but still. We could get you working on drops. Hmm . . ."

THAT NIGHT, AFTER PRACTICE, I headed out with Blevins, Barth, and Feig to Withers Hardware Restaurant, "the original Gathering Place" on Main Street in Abingdon. We parked in the back and, on the walk inside, a couple of off-duty busboys saw Blevins and stopped to offer impromptu homages ("Coach, I played for you in high school and you were always good people"). He is something of a celebrity in Abingdon; everywhere we went, he was recognized: at the gas station, at the restaurant, while driving. As Blevins put it, "Ain't nobody else from Abingdon ever made the NFL."

Along with his relative fame came the illusion that he was living large. The maintenance worker at Emory earlier that day had told Blevins how impressed he was with his success. Doug's response: "I wish we made as much money as people think we do." For the most part, he has scraped to get by. At Miami, he made about $25,000 a year. With the Vikings, he was essentially a freelance coach. Without the income from his camps, and speaking engagements, he'd have a hard time supporting his family.

Over burgers and beers, the trio talked football while I listened. Blevins was a fine storyteller, adept at using pauses, inflection, emphasis, and, as an exclamation point, his cackling laugh. For a while, he told me, he'd even tried stand-up comedy. He'd won a competition in Knoxville, signed with an agent, and performed at various shows around the country before deciding the travel was too much.

"I'd just get up and let it fly," he said in between bites of his chicken sandwich. "I never wrote a joke. I'd wait until someone made a comment at a table and then make fun of them. Then work around the table."

His other favorite target was the high comedy of handicapped life. Take the handicapped toilet, for example. "If you can get on it, you're so high you're looking over the stall. It's like it was made for Kareem's paraplegic brother."

After dinner, we went out drinking. Which, in this case, meant we moved to the other end of the restaurant, where the bar was. Doug was wearing his "going out" getup: a red Hawaiian shirt accented by copious amounts of cologne, which Nancy had applied earlier in the evening. He used a straw to drink his Bloody Marys and, after his third, as men three drinks into an evening are wont to do, he became philosophical.

"Chris, I gotta tell you, football is my *environment*," he said, grabbing my arm and looking me in the eye. "I'm physically handicapped and the only place I don't feel handicapped is on the football field. It's the only place I feel totally comfortable. I'm fucked up with football. I love it. I don't know what I'd do if I couldn't coach, without football."

I nodded, as if I understood, but I couldn't understand. Not really. Blevins spoke like a man who has fallen helplessly in love; the details of life recede and the goal is remarkably simple: be with the girl. Only in his case, the girl is a game, and he's willing to pack up and move on a moment's notice, if that's what it takes to be with her. Such devotion explained, in part, his ability to ignore his handicap—in his mind, it was just another insignificant detail.

A perfect example of this willed ignorance came a little later in the evening, when a young woman who'd bought a shot for Blevins and herself—Barth had made conversation—had, after drinking hers, charged both to our bar tab. Since I was paying, I was inclined to let it go, but Blevins was steaming mad about it. He turned to me and said, "Get ready to have my back, buddy, cuz there might be a fight," then rolled over and confronted the woman and her male friends. Despite a heated exchange, no punches were thrown. God only knows what he planned to do. Bump her friends with his wheelchair? Punch them with his good arm in the event that they leaned down far enough? Upon returning, he nodded sagely. "They won't mess with me again."

• • •

AFTER MY VISIT, BLEVINS AND I kept in touch. I'd often see his screen name pop up on my laptop with instant messages. After Vikings training camp, the team told him it wouldn't need him for the regular season. He was crushed, and headed back to Abingdon. "I think it came down to a money thing," he wrote me. "But I'm still watching all the games and calling the kickers anyway. I can't help it."

A few months later, the head coaching job opening came up at Emory & Henry. Blevins emailed to tell me he'd submitted his name but understood it would be tough. He wrote to me: "Obviously, it is going to be an extreme challenge and uphill battle for me to receive the appropriate consideration for the position. A lot of people on that selection committee are going to fall into the trap of thinking that Doug Blevins cannot be the Head Football Coach at Emory & Henry College because Doug Blevins is physically handicapped and has never actually played the game of football."

Despite having what he called a "good feeling," he didn't get the job, and it was seven months or so until we spoke again. He'd decided to give up on NFL teams, he told me, at least for the moment. The Cowboys kicking coach, Steve Hoffman, had also been let go, so there were no longer any kicking coaches in the league. Besides, he said, it had gotten frustrating. "I was tired of the bullshit," he said. "Of being told one thing and another thing happening. There was no respect, even though what you do is so important."

Instead, he was coaching kickers individually and branching out into player management, representing a number of players just out of college, as well as his kickers. He called it "a natural fit, and very lucrative," and saw it, and his individual instruction, as a way to effect change. "I love the game of football itself and I love the competition and the preparation. But when you really get down to it, I can make a much larger impact by developing as many guys as I can and having them have the success."

He hadn't stopped his camps. When we spoke, he was in the midst of one; he had fifteen kickers coming in that week. As for his prize students, Feig had been in the camp of an AFL team, the Rio Grande Valley

Dorados, the previous spring but had suffered a hamstring injury. Barth had had workouts with two NFL teams, the Jets and Falcons, and was aiming for NFL Europe the following spring. There were new students too, promising ones.

Things, Blevins said, were looking up. There'd even been more interest from Hollywood. The day that we spoke two producers were arriving to talk to Blevins about a movie—probably for HBO or Showtime—presumably one with a greater focus on football. He'd also been ramping up his speaking engagements; he saw it as taking advantage of what he half-jokingly called "the industry of Doug Blevins." "I think it's time I cash in on it," he said. "It would be silly not to."

It was an interesting transition. He'd spent his life with one singular goal, what is called in psychology a "path fixation": to be an NFL coach. When he'd reached that goal, he found his pinnacle wasn't quite what he'd hoped. The practicalities of his life—the low pay, the uncertainty— had overwhelmed his desire to fight the impracticality of his dream. Rather, he'd realized that what was important was the coaching itself. Certainly, he'd still jump at the chance to be a head coach, but working with the kickers at his camps was also rewarding, if in a different way. He seemed an unlikely candidate to embrace compromise, but the two of them—Doug and compromise—seemed to be getting along well.

He was still stubborn as ever, though. When I asked what career advice he'd give others, he didn't hesitate. "Don't listen to anyone else, because everyone wants to give you two-dollar advice," he said. "Fuck what other people tell you. Do what you want to do and you'll be fine."

THE BUTTERFLY

HUNTER

WITHOUT QUESTION, THERE ARE THINGS about Phil DeVries that would strike anyone as unusual. Like the fact that he will voluntarily submit to scorpion stings, and the part about eating monkey ("it tastes like primate"), and the way he will bolt from dinner to chase down some winged arthropod.

But the thing that I found most interesting about DeVries was the way he saw his work as independent from whatever job he might hold at any given time. In his mind, a job is merely a means—a vessel—to facilitate the work. Furthermore, if you require the validation, or funding, of a job title then you're missing the whole point. As he said to me more than once, "This is just *what I do*, man."

Judging by his résumé, what DeVries *does* is pretty impressive. He's the author of two books on Costa Rican butterflies, a Fulbright scholar, winner of a MacArthur Fellowship (the "genius" grants), and he has held research positions or been affiliated with names like the British Museum, Oxford, Harvard, Stanford, the University of Wisconsin, the University of Oregon, and the Smithsonian Institution. At first, I was concerned that such a weighty résumé might suggest a rather dull scholarly character, despite reports to the contrary. After a few tries, I reached him at the Milwaukee Public Museum, where he was the director of the Center for Biodiversity Studies.

"Sorry I've been hard to get a hold of," he said. "It's just that I've been busier than a three-peckered billy goat. What can I do for you?"

I told him I'd heard a rumor that he might be an Indiana Jones type, only with a net instead of a bullwhip, chasing big-game insects around the globe. He dismissed the comparison—"Who the hell carries a whip anyway?"—but then added, "Well, I *have* been to one or two remote places in search of butterflies."

Then he started listing locales. Belize, Costa Rica, Panama, Ecuador, Argentina, Brazil, Bolivia, Peru, Madagascar, Tanzania, Uganda, South Africa, Borneo, Hong Kong, Hainan Island in China, southwestern China, Germany, and England. He sounded like a grade school student rattling off the countries of the world. He paused. "Oh yeah, and a little bit in North America." In all, he estimated that over the last thirty years he'd probably spent roughly half of his waking hours in the field.

Any concerns I had about his harboring an ivory-tower mentality were quickly vanquished. Maybe it was the goat analogy, or his use of technical terms like "shitstorm," or his profession of a deep and abiding love for jazz music, but DeVries clearly drank deep from the canteen of life. For example, when I told him I lived in New York, he recounted how, when he'd lived in Manhattan, he rarely took the subway or cabs. "Everyone thought that was weird, but I found the walk from Greenwich Village to the Upper West Side to be just as interesting as anything I'd find once I got there." He paused and added somewhat nostalgically, "Yes, I know some of the seamier sides of that city."

We agreed to meet a couple months later, this being the fall of 2004, in New Orleans, where he was moving to take a new job in the biology department of the University of New Orleans.

I arrived at UNO on a warm morning at the beginning of the semester. Packs of students, the boys in cargo shorts, the girls in tight tank tops, roamed the campus laughing and giggling and posturing. I could practically see the pheromones dancing in the air. It seemed less a university and more a college with a lowercase *c*, a place for kegs and barbecues and long afternoons throwing the Frisbee, not all-nighters in musty research libraries. It struck me as an unusual place for a scientist with DeVries's credentials. There was, I would learn, a good reason for that.

DeVries's office was on the second floor of the biology building, just down the hall from the comparative vertebrate morphology lab. A small mountain range of packing boxes peaked in the middle of the room. I made my way to the back corner of the office, where DeVries sat, a pen protruding from his mouth, intently studying a sheaf of papers.

"So," he said, looking up and appraising me. "You're the guy writing a book about obsessive compulsives, are you?"

"Well," I said, "I prefer to think of them as passionate."

He smirked and paused. "Aren't they one and the same?"

He stood up. Lean, small-boned, and tanned, he looked as if at any moment he might embark on a day hike, outfitted as he was in his de facto uniform of tan North Face shirt with the sleeves rolled up, Gore-Tex pants, and laceless shoes. Though he's fifty-three, his face was remarkably unlined, and the only signs of advancing age were his mustache, which was starting to gather strands of gray, and his thinning hair. He had big, expressive eyes and one of those smiles that make its recipient an accomplice. *We are in on the joke together, me and you,* the smile said.

He offered a tour, beginning with a seven-foot-high column of packing boxes. "All these are dead bugs from a study," he said. "And," he pointed to their left, "all these boxes here are dead bugs."

He took a few steps and indicated a chest of drawers taller than his head, each one labeled with the name of a different tropical butterfly. "Dead bugs, dead bugs, dead bugs."

"And those red boxes over there," he paused, deadpan. "Yeahhh, those would be more dead bugs."

In addition, there were myriad bug-collecting apparatuses, boxes of books, papers, and, in the corner, two beat-up leather suitcases that looked as though they'd traveled across Africa by elephant, ribboned as they were with duct tape. They bore stickers from various international airlines and the words COSTA RICA etched via knife blade. "Those are my bug suitcases," he said, smiling warmly. "I've had those for, oh, thirty years. When I went to Oxford, that's how I carried everything."

He paused, running his hand over the suitcases, then looked up. "So you want to know what I do, huh?" He stroked his mustache. "Well, basically, I go up to things, poke them on the head, and ask what they do for a living. And if you make the assumption that no one has ever done that, you're bound to come up with a different perspective."

More specifically, he explained that his three main "hats," as he called them, were author (the Costa Rica books, which required ten-plus years of field work), study leader (his ongoing look at butterfly habitats in the Amazon), and scholar of all things caterpillar. He began with the latter.

"Ever heard a caterpillar sing?" he asked, then pulled up an MP3 file on his laptop and pressed Play. Out came a noise that sounded like Morse code at high speed. *Clik-a-clik-a-clik-a-clik-a.*

"That's a riodinid caterpillar," he said. "And this"—he pulled up another MP3—"is a *Chlorostrymon simaethis.*"

This time it sounded more like a chirp, or someone drumming his fingers on a plastic bucket. *Der-der-der-der-der.*

He kept going. Some sounded like jackhammers, some like nails on a chalkboard, others were softer. These were not sounds you could hear with your ear, he explained, but had been recorded using a tiny microphone he set up on the leaves—the technical term is "substrate"—where the caterpillars rested. Before DeVries, no one had ever recorded the sound, much less known it existed.

He discovered this "singing"—in some species it is the friction from tiny caterpillar organs rubbing together like sticks, in others it's unknown how the sound is made—while investigating a symbiotic relationship between caterpillars and ants. The ants were, for reasons unknown, protecting the caterpillars from wasps—which wanted nothing more than to slice the caterpillars up into little balls of flesh to bring home to a brood of hungry baby wasps. But each time the wasps tried they were foiled by a posse of ants that jumped to attention like so many "little Dobermans," as DeVries described it.

The mystery was what was in it for the ants. Ostensibly, the ants collected a "currency" of food secretions off the backs of the caterpillars, but even after doing so, they hung around. "An ant goes out of the nest to forage for food," DeVries explained. "That's what ants *do*. And yet, these ants stay on the caterpillars for a long period of time. By any ant logic, an ant should go to a caterpillar and say, 'Oh cool, food secretion!' and take it back to the nest. But it doesn't."

That's where the singing comes in. DeVries noticed that after filling up on nectar the ants would take off and then—abruptly—they'd come scurrying back. "They'd be on edge, going grrrrrr. . . ." DeVries growled and hunched forward, doing a very convincing ant imitation, swinging his head back and forth frenetically. The caterpillars, it turns out, were sending vibrations through the leaf, that is "singing," on a frequency that caused the ants to instinctively go into defense mode (a chemical secretion from the caterpillars enhanced the response). The best part for the caterpillars? The ants never wised up, no matter how many times the caterpillars made the call, sort of like a Labrador retriever who always bites on the fake throw. The result: full-time security detail.

"Figuring that out, that was pretty damn cool," DeVries said, rocking in his chair. "I mean, I'd just heard caterpillars for the first time in my life, in anyone's life, as a matter of fact." He nodded his head slowly. "You tend to work on something and it's all boring and you get pissed off and nothing's working and then you turn around and find something." He smiled. "It just goes to show, there are a whole lot more Christmas presents out there in the world."

It is a nice metaphor and an example of one of DeVries's skills: he can think like a scientist and talk like the guy next to you at the bar. There were moments during our time together when he lapsed into technical jargon, but for the most part he was able to translate complex theories and research into layman's terms. So, in pointing out the stinger on an ant at one point, he said, "Look at the 'ass end' of this thing here." Other entomological terms were reduced to "whatzits" and "that button-looking thingy." When explaining something, he often became almost cartoonishly animated, eyes bulging, face contorted into some mask of mock surprise. He would make a great animated character: Phil the Bug-Eyed Bug Guy.

Done with caterpillars, which he mimicked shoving to the side like an empty plate at dinner, he moved on to his Amazonian trap studies, which were based on the concept that you can't accurately measure any living community with only a snapshot. Take Times Square, for example. If one were to go there at 4 P.M. every Wednesday and take a survey of all the inhabitants at that moment—the tourists returning from Broadway matinees, the shoppers entranced by the flashing lights, the commuters scurrying with headphones earmuffed to their heads—one would record a markedly different count than if one were to go there every Wednesday at 11 P.M. or every Wednesday for six months, or on New Year's Eve. In DeVries's case, his Times Square is a two-kilometer patch of the Amazon, which he has rigged with a network of butterfly traps baited with a slurry of mushed bananas. For the last ten years, he has had the traps checked every three weeks, assisted by a succession of idealistic grad students. "I give them $500 and all the cockroaches they can eat to go live in an evolutionary pressure cooker," he told me, only half joking. In doing so, he has charted species diversity and fluctuation not only vertically and horizontally in space (certain butterflies live primarily only near the ground or in the canopy) but also over time. What he found was that traditional methods of measuring population in targeted areas for conservation purposes—that is, "the place with the most species wins"—are inherently flawed.

The results of the diversity study have provided fodder for further species conservation studies he has undertaken in conjunction with evolutionary geneticist (and fellow MacArthur recipient) Russ Lande, one of his best friends and the yin to DeVries's yang. ("I'm a field guy," said DeVries by way of explanation. "I know where rabbits sleep at night. I'm not really adept at being a number cruncher. That's what Russ does.") Second, and more important, the study has forced people to examine how they measure species diversity, or, as DeVries put it, "The important thing is that it made a blot on the mirror that somebody now has to say, 'Hold on, there's a blot on the mirror.' "

The studies have been something of a labor of entomological love. Aside from some initial backing, he has primarily funded them himself (hence the need for idealistic grad students). This is not as unusual as it may sound. In a 1999 paper from the National Bureau of Economic Research entitled "Do Scientists Pay to Be Scientists," a researcher named Scott Stern calculated that academic scientists sacrifice approximately 25 percent of their potential private-sector income for the freedom to study areas they are interested in at universities, in essence "paying" for the opportunity to follow their curiosity.

In DeVries's case, I got the impression that he just can't help himself. If it has to do with bugs, he doesn't just want to know, he *has* to. He is prone to stopping in mid-conversation to rush across the room, drop into a squat, and intensely scrutinize the leaves of a houseplant, a dark speck on the wall, or something crawling on the floorboards. And this is when he's inside. To dine with DeVries on a warm summer night on a back porch, when the air is thick with fireflies and moths and uncountable other flying creatures, is to dine alone. "He'll bolt, you have to figure that out about him," his friend Jennifer Clark, an illustrator for his book and his sometime travel partner, told me when I spoke to her. "Anytime you're with him, he can see something out of the corner of his eye. You could be walking with him and then suddenly—boom!—he's gone."

The morning was waning and our joints stiffening, so we walked across campus to grab coffee. Well, at least I walked; DeVries doesn't walk so much as pad, with an almost feline lightness of foot, the way a cat can navigate a dinner table without knocking over a single dish. It's a grace born of years of picking his way through thickets, down streams, and over fallen trees, as well as ascending upright ones. During the late seventies, he was among the first people to climb vertical ropes into the canopy in the rain forest, ostensibly to set butterfly traps, but also for the thrill of it. Using a wrist rocket or a crossbow, he'd shoot a filament line or a cord over a branch, pull another cord through it, and then use a mountain-climbing rope over that cord. Hooking up a harness, he could hoist himself up, then rappel down.

It was a warm day and it felt good to stroll in the sun. Meandering past sprawling lawns, discussing entomology—it felt downright collegial. Until, that is, DeVries took off, veering across the lawn, just as I'd been warned he might. He stopped at a bush with green and white flowers and squatted. I caught up to him and saw him turning his head to the side, like a dog.

"Carpenter bee," he said, pointing to a large insect that hovered over a flower. "Xylocopa. It's a tricky little devil. Look right there"—he indicated its descent onto the flower. "It's nectar robbing. Its tongue isn't very long, so it bites a hole in the base of the flower and gets the nectar from there." We watched the xylocopa for a while, going about its work, oblivious to the two humans towering over it.

As we watched, something was bothering me. "How did you see that bee from all the way over on the path?"

"I didn't," he said. "I don't look for insects, I look at plants. I've been doing it for so long, it's just natural. When I walk through a forest or a habitat, I'm automatically pulling in information. If you put me and someone else into some sort of habitat like the Serengeti, people are looking for lions and they're looking at this vast plain. I'm looking on a totally different level, much much smaller. Some people need space. As long as there are bugs, I do fine."

I stared at the bee, and the bush, and tried to envision it as a process, not a tableau. I still saw a bush, a bee, and, all around us, dozens of young students and, beyond that, a large dorm building and . . . You get the idea. I was a "vast plain" guy.

We kept walking, then he stopped again, only this time he whistled a short melody.

I looked across the quad to see a petite grinning woman waving to DeVries.

"That's my wife, Carla," he said. "She is the phylogeneticist of the family."

And the whistle?

"That's a little code we use," he explained. "It's out of a Thelonious Monk tune called 'Four in One.' The little refrain is *doo-do-deee-hoo,* and when I hear that whistle I know that Carla's looking for me or she knows I'm looking for her. Because"—he giggled at the absurdity of it— "if you're in a crowd of people and everybody's shouting 'Hey. Hey!' no-body's whistling 'Four in One.' "

We found an outdoor table across from an oak tree. It was pleasant in the shade and, if it hadn't been for the sounds of the students, we could have been on a back porch somewhere.

"So," he said, "you want some sort of natural history about me?"

IF EVER SOMEONE'S CAREER WAS telegraphed from a young age, it was DeVries's. From the beginning, he has noticed the tiny scurrying creatures of the world. As a young boy growing up in Michigan, first in Troy and later in Rochester, he took to carrying around jars of beetles and spiders and other bugs. "I actually did an experiment where I had this spider that I brought in and I was feeding it different insects and arthropods that would come through the window," he said. "Later, my mother gave me a report card she'd saved from the third grade that said something to the effect of, 'I'm really glad to see that Phil has continued his research on insects.' "

It was an independent interest. His mother, a homemaker, didn't care much for the outdoors and his father, a maintenance painter, occasionally took the family camping in the summer but never had more than a recreational interest in nature. "I'm an anomaly," DeVries said, shrugging and scanning the oak trees to our right. "I just always noticed insects. I can't explain it. And I'm sitting here now, with failing eyesight, and I'm sort of registering."

The Michigan of his youth was much different from the Michigan of today; tract houses and malls stand where once there were beech and maple forests and swamps. Back then, every walk home from school offered a world of potential adventure. His mother is fond of saying that, during grade school, he never made it off the bus to walk home without getting wet from the chest down because, in the spring and the summer, he'd always go by a series of ponds. "You know," he said, "to catch snakes and turtles."

Just wade in?

"Yeahhhhh. Well, how else you going to catch a turtle if it dives, man?"

Then there were the flying squirrels that he found in a nearby woods—"They're nocturnal so you could pound on the tree with a stick and they'd fly out like Whoooah!"—and the snakes he'd look for on the grounds of the Hunt Club, a local country club.

Wasn't that, um, illegal?

He took a swig of his coffee and smiled. "Natural historians are by and large felons," he said. "Well, not felons so much as outlaws in as much as fences with a whole lot of nature in them don't make a whole lot of sense unless you're inside of them. And certainly the people who put the fences up aren't going to look at nature anyway. Somebody has to use it."

High school was more of the same. While other kids were deep in Beatlemania, DeVries was transfixed by beetlemania. He'd be off in the woods, which he calls "a different kind of rock concert." After graduation, he became the first member of his family to go to college, at the University of Michigan. Shortly after enrolling, something happened that would shape his life. When he was nineteen, his only sister, who was three years younger, died in a car accident. Then, in a freak confluence, in the span of four months, fourteen other people close to him died. As Lande, the geneticist, wrote to me in an e-mail exchange: "I believe this profoundly influenced Phil's outlook on life, and may have been a major factor involved in the development of his complementary abilities to 'seize the moment' and also to spend most of his time in serious intellectual pursuit of intensive studies in natural history."

DeVries remembers it as a seminal moment. "It gave me pause for thought and I reasoned if I really wanted to wig out and sort of drown my sorrows or abuse alcohol or drugs, it was the perfect time and I had the perfect excuse to do it," he said, staring out across the campus lawn. He looked back toward me. "And me being me, I just said fuck that, I won't do any of that."

Instead, he immersed himself in two passions: music and entomology. The music he played on the weekends at clubs—folk at first and later jazz. The entomology led to a class with a professor who taught a course on butterfly collecting. DeVries loved the material but not the ethos. "I got around people who'd grown up collecting butterflies and it became this competitive sport, and I couldn't compete with them, because I didn't have the experience. So I just changed the rules."

Instead of looking for the butterflies, he looked for the plants where he would find caterpillars. "I was looking in very different places for butterflies—I was doing what I call predictive butterfly biology. You figure out what's going to be here in a month or so. I'll phrase it like this botany professor once did: zoology is the study of plants and their parasites."

As he spoke, a food cart wheeled by, barely audible amid the cacophony of students. DeVries halted, turned his head and moved his hand in time. "Hear that? *Dud-da-da-dut, dut-da-da-dut.'* It's got a funny wheel." He listened for a moment longer and, satisfied that he'd correctly diagnosed the cart, moved on. "Where was I? Oh yeah, next I entered the Peace Corps and headed to Costa Rica."

His mission with the Peace Corps, which he cobbled together with the director of Costa Rica's national museum, was to create its collection of butterflies. This was in the pre-ecotourism age; the national parks were just being built and the rain forests of Central America had not become, in DeVries's words "just a stop on the tourist junket."

So he shipped off to remote locations and hunted butterflies. His days were long and intense. He'd wake before 5 A.M. The jungle would already be hot, the sticky kind of heat that seeps into your skin and stays with you. Most of the time, he'd only been asleep a few hours. "I just couldn't sleep because you know, four hours, I've been asleep *four hours!*" He opened his eyes wide in mock amazement, then he laughed. "I'd be like, 'What's going on out there?' So I'd take a headlamp and find stuff. It was great. I really dug it. I really dug it a lot."

Breakfast would be rice and beans or whatever else was available. Then he'd head out, down forest trails bordered by giant ferns and along streams and through lush canyons, searching for splashes of airborne color. He got so he knew the activity peaks of each butterfly. The females might be out from 11 A.M. to 1 P.M. and they'd be touching the plants, which the males didn't do, so he could discriminate between the two. After lunch, he'd take to the forest again to hunt, a net at the ready—in his case a custom-made white silk bag, about two feet in diameter and about three feet deep, on a three-foot pole. Dinner would be fish, or cornmeal, or whatever he'd traded for with the locals (or, in the case of the monkey, and other various exotic foods he's consumed in years since then—snakes and lizards among them—whatever local delicacy he shared with natives). Then he'd sleep, or try to, and head out at night to look for caterpillars. "Those were super-intense times and real formative times. I was living on about four hours' sleep. That's what I did, I worked all the time. I defined my job as to know the butterflies of Costa Rica, but at some point the goal got raised to do a book about the butterflies of Costa Rica. I was in the forest all the time, *I mean all the time."*

He said this not in the manner of someone complaining that they're in the office all the time—a remark generally lodged either to generate sympathy ("look at me, the toiling martyr of the sixth floor") or to create feelings of inferiority ("mere humans cannot keep pace with me and neither shall you, junior administrator Sanders")—but in the manner of someone remembering how they once got to go trick-or-treating *all night long.*

Sometimes he'd head out by himself; other times he'd go along with any number of what he described as the "hard-bitten biologist types" who were in Costa Rica at the time. For a while, he shared a house near San José with Gary Stiles, a biologist who later wrote *A Guide to the Birds of Costa Rica* and now lives in Colombia. At the time, Stiles was a professor at the university but was often out on research trips. "The house was just filled with dead bugs and dead birds and books and camping equipment," DeVries said, grinning at the memory. "There were times when Gary and I wouldn't see each other for several months. I would come out of the field and he had just left that day or the day before and our schedules were completely asynchronized."

When I asked him about his favorite memories, every one of them related to his work, if you could call it that; there was no talk of the sightseeing trips he took (though he appreciated the scenery) or the beautiful native women (though he also appreciated them, from what Lande told me) or some boozy night spent at some Costa Rican bar. Rather, he recounted the thrill of ascending an alpine logging road and coming upon the *perisama barnesi* butterfly, of which there was only one known specimen in the world. Or the adrenaline jack that came after hiking down a stream checking every single palm frond, sure that he would find a close relative of the Morpho caterpillar, the *antirrhea,* and finally finding one. Christmas presents indeed.

As I had witnessed earlier, he was more adept at finding these presents than most humans. Lande described the phenomenon to me as follows: "He sees things other people don't see." Clark described him as "magic in the forest," and as "always picking up things and tasting them and smelling them." When I asked Carla, she professed to be somewhat stumped. "It's like he has a sixth sense for it," she told me. A rational thinker, she seemed not so much in awe as perturbed by the inexplicability of it. "I can find things, too, but Phil's quite amazing at it. He has an ability that's very rare in biologists."

DeVries tried to credit luck, then admitted that it was partly innate and partly learned; Clark compared him to a "caged animal" when stuck in an academic setting for too long. Spend too much time out of the forest and he could feel his senses dull. "When I come out of the field for a while, I get out of practice. I need a good steep for about six months in some habitat," he explained. "You start noticing. You walk into a forest and you're confronted by some green stuff and some brown stuff and maybe you see something flying." Then, he said, like eyes adjusting to the dark, he slowly becomes attuned to it again.

He gave an example of walking in a forest at night with a headlamp. Instead of an entire spectrum of stimuli, the whole world is boiled down to that one headlight. "It focuses you. Take eighteen different shades of brown ants and put them on twenty-five hundred shades of brown trees. What do you see? Not much. But if it's completely dark and all you can see is in this headlamp, that's all you can see."

As we sat and talked, it was almost as if I could see him shedding years, leaving the table and floating off, over the oak trees, over the campus and back to Costa Rica. It reminded me of a ballplayer talking about his glory days—the way the energy comes back, the light in the eyes. I brought up the C word.

"A calling?" He rolled the word around in his mouth, chewed on it, looked across the lawn. "I don't know if it's a calling. It's just . . . it's either a calling or just a habit. It's *what I do.*"

"What do you mean," I said, " 'what you do'?"

He started to say something then stopped and started again. "I think about butterflies every single day. Not a day has gone by in well over thirty years that I haven't thought about butterflies or some aspect about butterflies. It's just the way it is. And you have all this stuff percolating in your head and sometimes you just wake up in the middle of the night and you're like, 'Yeah! I haven't thought of that.' And you're sitting there in the dark going yeah. . . ." He looked at me. "Are you in your dreams a reporter? Do you come up with 'Yeah, that's a good angle'? Do you obsess about reporting?"

Not reporting so much, I said, but writing. Which is true. I'll often go to sleep trying to figure out how to approach a story, tearing the idea to pieces in my head and rearranging it, as if using mental Scotch tape. I can go crazy doing it and then I'll simply wake up the next morning and—poof!—the problem has solved itself. It's one of the great frustrations of my job and part of the magic of it; if I knew exactly what I was going to write each time, my work would be formulaic. It's the possibility of something unknown bubbling to the surface that is rewarding, as if I'd watered the earth of my mind and woken up to find a patch of daisies. I told him this, then described some of the other people I'd interviewed for the book and how they viewed their work. About how Swartzendruber spent sixteen hours a day with his mushrooms and Blevins dreamt about football and Danz carried around his eyeball.

"Yeahhh," DeVries said, nodding. "Those are real people. I've known a lot of people like that. People who are just doing it. It's like the jazz musicians and other MacArthur fellows I know. And though we don't all work in the same field, we're similar in that we go off and do our things. People say, 'Why would you do that?' Because that's what you do." He opened his eyes wide and said it again for emphasis, "That's *what you do*. . . ."

This all sounded well and good, I said, but what about people who don't know what it is they *do*. People who have to find that out. People who are being told by their parents or whomever else what it is they're supposed to be doing. What about them?

He seemed perplexed. "I've heard of this and the idea of what you're *supposed* to do. I still don't know what I'm supposed to do. One of these days I'll grow up and figure it out. I'm not good at doing things I don't want to. I can't. My definition of life is that life is not for doing this stupid stuff. It's too short. Yeah, I have friends who are making tons of money doing jobs. It's not me. This is what I do. I collect dead bugs. You know, I couldn't make it on the trading floor. I don't have a clue how to communicate, I really don't, with the system. It's a different world."

He thought for a moment and rattled his empty coffee cup in his hand, as if shaking dice in a cup. "You know," he concluded, "one thing I can tell you, from the bottom of my heart," he paused and looked me in the eye to let the moment sink in. "I *really* gotta take a piss now."

He laughed and headed off. The rest of his life story would have to wait while, fittingly, nature called.

IN THE MIDDLE AGES, BUTTERFLIES were thought to be fairies come to steal milk and butter. The Irish believed them to be the souls of children; they even made it illegal to kill white butterflies in the 1600s. In Mexico in the sixteenth century, the Aztecs considered the insects to be the souls of warriors.[1] In the late 1800s, butterfly collecting was seen as adventure of the highest order, and its fruits were handsomely rewarded. Collectors such as Theodore Mead, an American, and A. S. Meek, a strapping Australian, roamed the globe with nets in search of rare species. Meek traveled through Papua New Guinea and the Solomon Islands and sent back thousands of specimens to benefactors such as Lord Walter Rothschild. A wealthy banking heir, Rothschild started his own natural history museum when he was eight years old and, by the time of his death at sixty-three, had amassed a collection of 2.25 million butterflies, which he willed to the British Museum in

1. Very lucky warriors. According to popular legend, as recounted in Sharman Apt Russell's *An Obsession with Butterflies*, Xochiquetzal, the goddess of love, kept a butterfly between her pursed lips as she made love to men on the field of battle.

London. Meek and his ilk headed out with bands of assistants into the untracked wilds to bring back specimens such as the Queen Alexandra's Birdwing, the world's largest butterfly (The female grows to nearly a foot, and many collectors actually brought guns along to shoot these "bird-wings" out of the sky.) During these heady times, to hunt butterflies was to court danger.

Today, there is still a need for collectors to provide stock for museums and research, but there are also many who are in it for commerce. Butterflies such as the Birdwing can fetch up to $2,000, and collecting is big business. Even though he has, in his words, "personally whacked tens of thousands of butterflies"—DeVries disdains euphemisms as much as he disdains those who use them—he has no interest in selling them. "I don't do the dead carcass trade," he said. We were back at his office and he opened up a drawer filled with brilliant blue Morphos, each the size of a Danish and as iridescent as an oil slick. "I'm too much of a natural historian and I think conservation is important. I can't trivialize nature. I can't do it. And butterflies aren't art objects, okay? To me, each one has a story."

DeVries identified more with early scientists, men like Fritz Müller, an iconoclastic biologist with a mathematical bent who, among other things, corresponded with Darwin and hated wearing shoes. It must have been a heady time to be in the field. New discoveries were front-page news, museums were social gathering places, biologists were folk heroes, and a naturalist could walk out the door and discover a new species literally in his backyard. It's enough, I guessed, to make a scientist wish he were born at a different time.

"Of course," DeVries said, "I think that's inherent to a lot of people's thinking, although a lot of people through whatever reason or accident of history—they're in the time that they're supposed to be."

He had to attend some faculty meetings that afternoon so we made plans to meet up the next morning back at his office. In the meantime, I mulled over what he'd said.

That night, I decided to try an experiment. I left my hotel and headed out into the French Quarter to see if I could view the world from DeVries's perspective, tuning out the milling masses of humanity and searching for signs of insect life. This was easier said than done. To walk Bourbon Street at 11 P.M. is to be reminded that one should never, ever walk Bourbon Street at 11 P.M. unless already drunk. Roving packs of businessmen, with ties loosened, shirts untucked, and strings of beads around their necks, yelled at various women to take their tops off; people too old to be dancing to techno music danced spasmodically to techno music in open-front bars. The smell of vomit and spilt beer was overwhelming. I was offered things, asked for things, and propositioned to enter bars and strip clubs. One guy asked if I had rolling papers. It was all I could do to tune it out and try to focus my "headlamp," so to speak.

I did not find much. On an outlying avenue, I found—or at least I heard—crickets in a quiet parking lot. On Bourbon Street itself, I saw only ants. When I asked the young man at the "Big Beers for $3" booth if he had any bug problems, he said they sprayed heavily for fruit flies and that, while his shop *certainly* didn't have any, "There are cockroaches like this big across the street." He held his hands apart the length of a Milky Way bar. I suppose it says something about the Quarter that he didn't think to wonder why I was asking such a question.

As I walked, I tried to see the world differently, as DeVries does. See the permanence of it all, not the impermanence. Tomorrow night, these tourists and lushes and weirdos will be replaced by other, equally enthusiastic or inebriated or depressed tourists and lushes and weirdos. It was almost like a watering hole in the dry plains. All come to drink of it, some for different reasons. Some are predators of commerce, some, like the free-spending businessmen, are prey. They reminded me of DeVries's ants, called back to drink the caterpillar nectar unwittingly. Only with the college kids and the businessmen, it was the siren call of "BIG BEERS FOR $3."

Earlier in the day, I'd asked DeVries about religion. He said he practiced what he called "a spiritual philosophy that stems mainly from finding peace—briefly—when occasionally I will find my place in nature. It's a very fleeting thing, like playing music. Everyone has little epiphanies.

Every once in a while, nature knocks me down." He whistled low and long.

I asked him for an example. "It's a pretty common thing," he replied. "Seeing some aspect of light playing on the landscape that just stops me—wow—a different perspective. I'm this flyspeck in this matrix of light. Making a realization that you're one paint gob in a pointillist painting and then you kind of trundle on." He laughed. "Somebody asked [British biologist] J. B. S. Haldane what his concept of God was and he said, 'God had an inordinate fondness for beetles because there are more species of beetles than anything else.' "

As I walked back to my hotel, the clamor and odors of Bourbon Street receding behind me, I thought about what he'd said. Not about the beetles, specifically, but about those fleeting moments in life. It occurred to me that in any given week I probably missed out on one or two of those moments. It seemed so simple yet so alluring to view our surroundings as he does, with a seven-year-old's incessant curiosity. I understood why he didn't see what he did as work. But it also made me wonder how he was capable of reconciling the drudgeries of the professional world—and we all must face them—with its rewards. As I would find out the next day, the answer is that he doesn't.

WHEN I ARRIVED MIDMORNING, DEVRIES was flustered. There were office issues, Carla was closing on their new house, and, worst of all, there were more meetings. And DeVries hates meetings. "I'm really bad at them," he said, making a face as if he'd just taken a whiff of bad milk. "Intolerant, as a matter of fact. My idea of a meeting is we get together, here is the problem, here are three alternatives, let's choose between them and get the hell out of here."

There is only one small problem with this outlook and it's that the people who hold such meetings don't much appreciate it. And when one works at a university, there are lots of meetings. As Lande explained to me, "Phil does not have the usual facility of most academics at playing the political games that most people have to play. He's a very straight-forward guy. He says what he thinks and tries to cut through the bull-shit, of which there's a lot in academic circles." And, as Lande pointed out, "This is not the way to win popularity contests among your colleagues, especially when you're up for promotions."

So DeVries's academic career has consisted of a series of positions slightly lower than his talent merits—the Milwaukee Public Museum and UNO being perfect examples (his work at Harvard and Stanford was as a research associate, not a full faculty member). He got his job at the University of Oregon only after Lande, whose stature in the scientific community is considerable, campaigned for him. Said Lande of the UNO and Milwaukee hires: "He should have gotten a job at one of the really big museums associated with academic institutions, like at Berkeley, but he's not good enough at playing the games that are required."

Much of the rest of the time, it's been Carla's duty to try to keep him from being too blunt. When I asked her about his disdain for office politics, she said she understood it completely. "He's been able to combine, more so than most people, an innate ability, a passion, and a disinterest in conforming to the standards of academia. People who can't think laterally or break the rules, they don't like Phil very much. Because Phil ignores the rules, or the political handshakes, and he asks people pointed questions about science that people sometimes don't like to answer. And it's not done to irritate people. It's done because he actually does want to know."

This can lead a man to do unusual things. The scientist John C. Lilly was a pioneer in many fields, ranging from biophysics to neurophysiology, but he strongly believed that all human experiments should be first carried out on oneself. So when he worked with LSD, ketamine, and other drugs, he tested them on himself, and moreover often did so alone. This hurt not only his professional career but his personal life (not to mention his health). Regardless, he believed the potential for scientific discovery outweighed the human costs.

Of course, DeVries is not injecting his body with foreign substances (though he has submitted to various venomous stings in the name of science, as I'll come to later), but he does possess a mind-set similar to Lilly's. Because of this, he has spent much of his career scrapping for funds and refusing to compromise. In essence, DeVries won't do any work he doesn't inherently already want to do. This may sound impractical, but there is a lot to be said for the idea that the best work is done, in essence, voluntarily. In 2000, a study found that when someone believes that he is acting of his own choosing in a situation, it significantly enhances his curiosity. Likewise, there is substantial research that both internal pressures, such as guilt and fear, and external pressures such as the threat of punishment and (surprisingly) tangible external rewards, diminish curiosity.[2] This means getting paid to do something actually *decreases* one's curiosity about the task, something I can relate to. Before I worked at *Sports Illustrated,* I would have been ecstatic to learn that someone might pay me to go watch basketball games. Now, after five years on the job, I still love watching a good game, and still feel that little tick of excitement, but it's not the same. I'm working now. I don't have a choice.

DeVries has always insisted on having a choice. After returning from Costa Rica, he got his Ph.D. at the University of Texas in Austin. It was a simple time in his life: he traveled for research, he rode his motorcycle when he needed transportation, and he played his guitar. When he left to do field work, he'd store his belongings in three or four cardboard boxes and put them in his office or lab space. Sometimes they'd sit there for six months, sometimes for up to a year or two. He traveled with two suitcases that included two pairs of pants, three to four shirts, boots, butterfly nets, butterfly envelopes, notebooks, pens, flashlight, and socks. That was it. He didn't need any nice clothes ("You don't have to look nice for anything in the forest"), he didn't need money ("nothing to spend it on in the forest"), and he saw no need for anything extraneous that might weigh him down.

---

2. An interesting side note on the curiosity studies: researchers are careful to establish baseline data because, naturally, participants may be curious about curiosity studies.

DeVries's quest to reach a Zen-like level of freedom from the consumer culture of America was aided when, in 1988, he was awarded a MacArthur Fellowship. At the time, he was doing butterfly research in Panama. A man from the foundation called to tell him he was being given a MacArthur grant. DeVries's response was: "Robert MacArthur, the ecologist?"

He received $250,000 over four years to do with whatever he chose. It was a boon, allowing him to research the bulk of his second book and start his trap studies. But there was a price. As with anyone who suddenly comes into money, DeVries started hearing from people. Lots of people. Some wanted to latch on. Others, his peers, were jealous. "This is not just endemic to me, but there's a funny cost to being just given this thing," he told me, "because you don't apply for it and it has this stupid kind of 'genius grant' thing stuck on it. And it's amazing from where animosity can arise. It was a pain in the ass, basically. I mean I wasn't going to give it up but . . ."

There is a well-known study, published in 1978, that found that 22 people who won major lotteries ended up, over time, returning to the same level of happiness as 22 matched controls. It would be incorrect to compare a MacArthur grant to a lottery win for a number of reasons; for one, it is earned; for another it is a rather small amount of money by comparison. But there are some similarities in how others view the windfall and the freedom it brings. In the case of DeVries, he saw the MacArthur money as a license to bypass all that he disliked about the politics of university life. "Once Phil got his award," Lande told me, "he wasn't concerned about money. He gave it to some money manager and didn't think about it. As long as he had enough to live on, he was fine."

So he did butterfly research in Panama and Costa Rica, and all those other places he told me about when I first spoke with him. And, then, after eight years of talking bugs, he and Carla married in 1997 in what was, to say the least, an unusually relaxed and DeVries-esque ceremony. His mother was visiting him in Oregon at the time, and Phil was barbecuing on the deck in his backyard next to a forested area. A couple of older women rang the doorbell, were invited inside, and came out to join several other people in the backyard. After some conversation one of the women said, "Are we ready now?" DeVries said yes, and the woman donned a decorative shawl, pulled out a Bible, and asked DeVries to do her the honor of removing his chef's apron for the wedding ceremony. His mother nearly fainted and called out, "Surely you're joking!" to which the woman replied, "I have never been more serious in my life." Within a few minutes Carla and Phil were wed with a theoretical ring (DeVries thought it fitting, since Lande, the best man, was a theoretician). His mother cried profusely.

From my time with the two, it was clear they were a matched pair. Before Phil, Carla had seriously dated only two other men; one was a butterfly biologist and the other a fish systematist. Wiry and lively, she loved the same three things Phil did: bugs, music, and cooking. So while they cooked together at home, they talked about bugs and listened to music, or they studied bugs while talking about music, and so on. "People always think that working couples work too much and forget the couple parts—the personal stuff," Carla told me. "I don't think we ever did or ever will do that. Because number one, our attitude toward work is pretty much the same. And number two, we have so many other interests that are common to one another." She had only one requirement: "I like passionate people so it doesn't matter what kind of passion they have. If they're passionate about what they do, kudos. That's all that matters."

OUR AFTERNOON WAS DRAWING TO a close, and DeVries had meetings to go to, however unhappily, so I accompanied him across campus. We passed a group of students yelling loudly, but DeVries paid them no attention. I'd become used to this; he noticed bugs and critters far more often than he noticed other people. As we walked, he broke down his methodology.

Basically what I tell the students, you can walk out in your backyard and tap the first thing you see on the head and ask what do you do for a living and, by and large, you will find that no one's ever asked. You may get a species that's really well known because it's a crop pest and it eats crops. But you can be fairly certain that it didn't evolve in the concept of crops."

It was a simple way to look at biology. To look at something from its own perspective, not ours. It also occurred to me that, in a way, that's what I was attempting to do in this book: I was meeting people, tapping them on the head, and asking them what they do for a living. I was trying to come at it with as few preconceived notions as DeVries did in his work, and with as much of an understanding about how no one performs any job in isolation—the way Swartzendruber relies on his buyers, the way Danz would be out of a job if medical technology developed a functioning artificial eye.

"Look at it this way," he continued. "Walk into the grocery store, go to the produce section. Ask a question: What are these things that we eat every day and where do they come from? And I don't mean, oh that's a carrot. Well, was the carrot native to North America? Native to somewhere else? Here's my standard question I ask all the time. Where on the planet is the chicken from? What habitat did it live in and what did it do for a living? There's hardly any area of the world with humans in it that doesn't know what a chicken is. Where did it come from? It wasn't invented in the store."

I thought for a moment. "Ecuador?" I guessed, taking a stab at it.

He waved off my answer like a pesky fly. "We do know what it *was*. It was a bird that lived in Southeast Asia, in the understory of the rain forest. It's likely that somebody by now has studied what it did, or bits of its natural history. But you see its overall importance was that it was adapted to being stupid and living in cages and laying eggs and supplying meat. That's what's known about it. There are mega *mega* dollars being spent on how to make chickens exactly the same size. But that wild chicken is probably only living in a little flyspeck of forest now."

I had a startling thought—those chickens weren't so different from us. Here we are, adapted to "living" in cubicles or on a factory line, only instead of eggs we produce Honda Civic windshields or accounting reports or whatever else specialization demands of us. Maybe DeVries and some of the other people I'd met were like those wild chickens, still living outside the system.

It had been an illuminating two days, but in some ways I felt like it was "Tuesdays with Phil"—him talking, me listening. I wanted to see him in action. Because of his academic schedule, however, he wouldn't be headed out into the field for a while, something he was decidedly ambivalent about. The closest thing, he said, was filming a series of National Geographic videos—follow-ups to a special he'd hosted a year before called *Bug Attack!* the nature of which, much like the academic work he did, he was ambivalent about.

"I have to warn you," he said. "A lot of it is presented in a schlocky way, but the way I see it, if I don't do this stuff, who will? I just heard that Johnny Rotten is hosting a nature special. Johnny Fucking Rotten! So I feel it's my duty to do what I can, even if some of this stuff is absurd."

The next morning, flying out of New Orleans, I had one of those little epiphanies he'd spoken of. Sitting at gate C8, waiting for my flight, I was mired in the clamorous humanity of air travel: kids running, people talking on cell phones, TVs blaring, gate announcements, and, for some unknown reason, maintenance workers were vacuuming the ceiling. If I could have escaped into a nearby forest, I would have. So, sitting there, miserable, I looked out the wall of glass windows in front of me toward the tarmac and all the planes, lined up like so many giant steel ducks. And there, as incongruous as could be, I saw a large green grasshopper stuck to the window, suspended some forty feet off the asphalt. Electric green, with long antennae and what looked to be some sort of sac on its abdomen, it rested calmly, affixed to the glass as if watching all the frenetic humans inside. Outside of the potted plants in the terminal, it was probably one of the only natural things in a radius of a quarter mile. I smiled, put on my headlamp, and tuned out the rest of the world.

WHEN IT COMES TO HOSTING documentaries, DeVries is clear about one thing: nature is not to be treated in a frivolous manner. One time, many years ago, he nearly punched out a British producer who recommended that Phil "do it wacky, just make it laughable" while filming a video about caterpillars. Not surprisingly then, DeVries has had numerous run-ins with the production crews working on the films that air on National Geographic as well. He has threatened to quit a couple of times (for example, when he was asked to eat a maggot sandwich, a stunt that he deemed to be designed solely to appeal to the lowest common denominator). Viewing *Bug Attack!,* it is understandable how such situations might arise.

Bug Attack! opens with an image of a supersized hornet's mandibles clicking together like the insect Jaws of Life. "They outnumber us more than a million to one," an ominous voice-over intones. "They're organized, fearless, and sometimes . . . DEADLY. Tonight, a journey to extremes in search of the scariest bugs on earth."

Over the next hour of the video, the cameras follow DeVries as he searches out the world's most dangerous insects. He heads down the rivers of Venezuela to locate a giant centipede and a tarantula the size of a large rat (which he proceeds to roast and eat with the natives), he tracks killer bees, he dons a protective suit to chase down a hornet the size of a D battery, and he travels to the swamps of South America, where he stands patiently while waiting for a giant leech, a creature that looks like a fat black nautical necktie. When a leech finds him, he lets it feed on his leg for a while before he detaches it, its three-inch proboscis popping out like a cork from a bottle, unleashing a river of blood down his leg, which in turn pours into the actual river.

The video's peak of voyeuristic pleasure might be when DeVries visits a scientist at the Southwestern Biological Institute who has developed a pain tolerance scale of one to four to rank the effectiveness of insect stings. In the lab, DeVries proceeds stoically to surrender to the sting of a scorpion (a two on the pain scale) and a harvester ant (a three). After each takes a chunk out of his arm (in close-up, of course, with lots of gory replays of the stingers' penetration), the camera stays on him as, with remarkable scientific detachment, he explains what is happening.

On the scorpion: "Actually it hurts a little. I can feel it getting a little hot and stingy around there. You can obviously feel the penetration of the stinger. Not unlike being stabbed with a needle."

On the ant: "What I am feeling is pretty amazing. I can feel all the tissue cramping, pulling. I can feel it spreading." After twenty minutes, when the pain has gotten worse: "If my arm worked, I would throw in the towel right now."

The video is transfixing, but, watching it, I couldn't help but wonder how it fit in with his ethos about the world. Though educational, the program wasn't exactly conservation-minded, even if most of the documentaries he has narrated in the past have been. But then again, they've also been seen by far fewer people. This is the catch-22 of nature films.

So it came as little surprise that he was somewhat nonplussed about the situation in which he found himself when I arrived at his house in New Orleans one winter morning to watch as he filmed an episode of *The Nastiest Predators*. Almost immediately, he pulled me aside. "I never trivialize nature, never," he said ruefully. "But look at me now, I've got a fucking flea circus in my living room."

He was not exaggerating. He actually did have a flea circus in his living room, complete with a flea high dive, a flea cannon, a flea chariot, a flea highwire, and a flea MC—a magician named Walt Noon who looked something like Garth Brooks were Garth Brooks to wear a tuxedo stuffed with thirty minutes' worth of magic tricks ("forty-five minutes if I talk slow," Noon pointed out).

The flea circus was not all DeVries had in his living room. There was also all manner of video equipment; two 650-watt stand-up lights; a large, amiable cameraman; a somewhat flighty producer and her assistant; and DeVries's cat, Kookah, who provided fodder for a number of spontaneous jokes from Noon ("Better be careful with your cat, Phil, I'm going to lose my entire troupe!"). It would take the crew two days to film what would end up being a two-minute segment on the video.

The process was laborious. Every shot required multiple takes, from different angles. Through it all, DeVries was smooth and natural, even when repeating the same line for the sixth time—in part because he tended not to repeat a line but instead make up his own, something the producer wasn't fond of. Phil made it clear he didn't care. He had warned me the night before on the phone that this segment of the video was the "dregs of the dregs," meaning the least relevant stuff, warning me not to expect "any high-tone natural history" but rather "John Waters stuff where they try to dress nature up in pink and do silly stuff." He was right.

National Geographic had flown Noon in from Redlands, California, where he runs the nation's largest flea circus–building business out of his home. A friendly, goofy forty-year-old, Noon creates his own magic tricks and builds and sells, at $2,700 a pop, about forty flea circuses every year. These are basically big sleight-of-hand shams—the fleas don't actually do any of the tricks—but he also runs one of only two live flea circuses in the country, meaning he actually trains fleas. (As DeVries commented to Noon, "You must have had a very unusual childhood.")[3]

Noon, in tuxedo, explained the flea circus while DeVries, in his trademark bandanna and North Face shirt, provided history on fleas, proposed a name for the flea shot out of a cannon ("Pachelbel"), and, at one point, collared a flea—for a flea chariot race, of course—with beryllium wire, a process that Noon had estimated would take up to an hour. DeVries did it in five minutes, prompting the cameraman to say, "You're a Jedi, Phil!"

---

3. Not that there is that much "training" one can do, but there are a few things. For example, keep a flea in a test tube for an hour and it will stop jumping (after hitting its head repeatedly against the top); spray a ball with citronella and fleas will "kick" it to get the smell, which they hate, away from themselves.

The day ended, predictably, with DeVries holding up his right arm to the camera to display the flea that was slowly gorging on his blood, its abdomen swelling like a tiny black balloon (something flea circus trainers must do regularly to feed their "athletes"). "Once again," DeVries said to the camera, "I bleed for you."

It had been a long day—9 A.M. to 6:30 P.M.—and after the crew left, DeVries's first words to me were "Don't say a fucking thing, not a fucking thing." He uncorked a bottle of Merlot and we sat there, two guys drinking red wine and pontificating.

What I wanted to know, and it was a question DeVries would mull for the remainder of the evening, was why, if he hated the tenor of the *Bug Attack!* videos so much, he did them. Here was a man who rarely sacrificed in his life when it came to work, a man who professed to live on his terms—who was compromising for the sake of these videos. It wasn't that he was debasing himself—he managed to maintain a naturalist's air throughout—but by association, I wondered if he didn't feel as if this spectacle diminished his other work.

His first stab at an explanation ended in sarcasm. Then, after a glass of wine, he tried again. "I keep thinking about your question," he said. "And I think it's because somebody's got to do it. These days, the only nature many people come across is on television, and if you let a bunch of jokers who've never been out in nature do it, it comes across like we should be afraid of nature."

He opened his eyes wide and shook his head. *"Afraid of nature?* I'm not afraid of nature. In fact, it's actually"—and here he leaned forward and whispered—"very important."

He ran his hands over his scalp, then palmed his face. "I don't know, man. I think about getting out of it but then I think of when it works. When it works, film is *so powerful* and I recognize that. I have worked in film where it is amazingly powerful."

He looked at me. "Take you, you're a writer. To me good writers can take stupid symbolic logic, in terms of letters and phrases and all that shit, and raise up into the reader, who they almost certainly do not know, and create an entire image in their brain. That's pretty close to the definition of magic, isn't it?

"You read someone like Beryl Markham," he continued, referring to the female pilot and author of *West with the Night,* a book about her adventures in Africa at the turn of the century. "That is powerful. I mean, you are there. Isn't that magic? You never knew Beryl Markham. I never did. And so film is a very powerful medium because it has movement and light and position and, on top of that, you can put words into it and . . ." He paused. "How do you beat that. I mean, it's like an opiate."

I doubt anyone else involved in *Bug Attack!* had ever seen it quite like that. Hell, the way he described writing was enough to make me feel emboldened. Or maybe it was just the Merlot, which was awfully potent on an empty stomach. So we drove to a local barbecue place for dinner, where DeVries gave me the natural history of oysters while we looked over the menu. Clearly, this was a man who needed to be engaged at all times. In fact, it was his simple test for whether he stayed with a project or a job: was it boring.

There are many sins of work, but boredom may be the worst. The philosopher Søren Kierkegaard labeled boredom "the root of all evil—the despairing refusal to be oneself." Fourth-century Egyptian hermits characterized it as a "noonday devil" that sucked from them their energy and industriousness. Adam Smith, economist and philosopher, wrote in *The Wealth of Nations* that a person who spends his life repeating the same tasks tends to lose "the habit of exertion" and "generally becomes as stupid and ignorant as it is possible for a human creature to become." DeVries had stayed ever-vigilant of boredom, wary that it might creep up on him, wrap him in its bureaucratic embrace, and sit him down for a long, superfluous department meeting, complete with lukewarm coffee and greasy donuts. So when he sensed its presence, he fled from it like one of the winged creatures he so loves.

"If something maintains my interest and I can see possibilities and tangents and spin-offs and connections, that's what I want," he said, picking at some shrimp. "If there is one thing in my life that I've experienced that is the most debilitating, it's being bored. When you're bored, your system shuts down. Life becomes empty. If you get bored, you're dead. I guess that's the thing, when it becomes a job, then it becomes boring. It's a *job.*" He frowned and spit the word out, as if it were a bite of a maggot sandwich.

I liked the way he put it. If this concept didn't encapsulate the idea of a calling at its most pure, I didn't know what did. Such a simple test— when you get bored, get out—yet also one tricky to put into use. What if only one aspect of a job is boring, or one project within a job, or what if the kids have to be put through school—does that jump to the front of the line ahead of boredom? As we drove back to his house, I told him about Wrzesniewski and her delineation between job, career, and calling. He thought about it, then came up with his own definition.

"The difference between a profession and a calling is whether you're a jazz musician or you can *play some jazz.* You're a field biologist or "I've done field work." You're a writer or *I write for a newspaper.* Writing is like music: tone, pauses, spaces. If you don't have it, you don't have a voice. But when you read something, you read a paragraph and you go, 'I know who this is.' It's like listening to music. I used to play this game Drop the Needle with friends. We'd put on a record and say, 'Who's playing bass, who's playing drums?' and we'd go back and forth. And it was all ears. 'Ohh that's Philly Joe Jones on the drums.' And it's like a voice. Somebody calls you on the phone and you go, 'Hey how you doing.' And you know"—he snapped his fingers—"immediately who it is."

He was right. I realized that each person I'd interviewed had a unique voice in his or her work. With LaFontaine, it was literally a voice—a great, booming one—that identified him immediately. With Danz, it was the way he fashioned each prosthesis with his own signature, the six o'clock blood vessel, so that people knew it was a "Danz eye." Sometimes it was less evident; Swartzendruber's voice came through in the way that he always had the obscure mushrooms, the ones no one else had; Blevins's in the way that if someone who knew kicking watched a Blevins student, they could spot the influences of the coach. That voice signified a craftsmanship, a passion, a character in the work.

DeVries got almost as excited as I did as I talked about the people I had met and the concept of a voice. "Yeah, yeah!" he said, leaning forward, his eyes wide open. "Now that's what it is. You give me twelve notes on tenor sax and if it's John Coltrane, its instantaneous. It's not the note, it's the voice. And I can do that—bam! A lot of these musicians have it. Three notes and Dexter! Either that or it's a Dexter wannabe."

He smiled. We'd reached his house. It was now 11 P.M. Time to part ways. Before heading in, he stopped on the grass. He had one more thought. "A good friend of mine, Steve Lacy, was a jazz musician and he used to play with Thelonious Monk," DeVries said, standing outside in the cool January night. "And Monk's advice to him about music was, 'You gotta dig it if you dig it, dig it?' "

DeVries laughed his cackling laugh and repeated it, almost to himself. " 'You gotta dig it, if you dig it, dig it?' "

He turned and headed in, still laughing. I stood there alone in the moonlight, somewhere on the outskirts of New Orleans, digging it.

EPILOGUE

SIX MONTHS AFTER MY LAST trip, I met up with an old friend when I drove to Philadelphia for the weekend. My brother's wife, Angela, was having her first child and my parents were throwing a baby shower for her. I arrived the night before, in time to help them prepare.

The next morning, we began moving furniture around, clearing space for the party. It was a crisp spring morning, and light filled the room, glinting off picture frames, warming the air, and exposing every smudge of dirt and whorl of dust on the carpet.

"Somebody," my mother said, examining the floor, "needs to vacuum this thing." Then she looked at me.

So it was that I went to the closet and saw it, stationed in the back like an off-duty sentry, its upright handle at a perfect ninety-degree angle, its headlight dormant. It had been years since I'd handled the Kirby, but it all came rushing back. The click of the "Power Assist" when it kicked in, the ferocious hum of the machine when its maw made contact with the carpet, the sheer heft of all that metal. I escorted it around the room, letting its built-in transmission do the work for me, extracting all manner of dirt, sand, and loose change. And damn if, nearly a decade after my parents had bought it, that Kirby didn't suck that carpet clean. I felt a small surge of pride.

Running the Kirby could have made me nostalgic for a simpler time. My life was different now. I was married, my brother was starting a family, my friend Eric was in the Foreign Service and his second child was due. It had been six years since I'd lived in Philadelphia and much longer since I'd thought of those days, just out of college, when I had no idea what to do with my life. I'd been to graduate school, written a book, and spent five years at *Sports Illustrated*. I'd learned the finer points of IRAs and 401(k)s and HMOs and all the other uppercase necessities of a real job. The post-collegiate days when I slept until noon if I wanted to and the future stretched out like I-80 does through Nevada, flat and straight and seemingly endless, were far behind me. The same way that certain songs and movies take you back to a night or a girl or a summer, ripening with time, the Kirby could have been my portal.

But it wasn't. My exact thought as I wielded the machine was: *I am so glad I don't have to try to sell this damn thing anymore.* I had no buyer's remorse about becoming a writer, just the same complaints and doubts and concerns as anyone in a job that challenges him. If working on this book had taught me anything, it was that it is important to value, and ferociously protect, what it is you are interested in. Otherwise it is too easy to listen to others as they tell you what they think you should be doing.

The people I met, almost to the man and woman, weren't the type to listen to the clamor of life's "should's." Certainly, they worried about money, or about the market, or about their social life, or, like Nehrich and LaFontaine, about whether they were appreciated for what it was they did. But rarely, if ever, did they worry about what it was they did. It was, as DeVries said, just *what they do.* I don't know if that's a calling in the traditional sense of the word, but it certainly is something else: a blessing.

I found myself drawn back to their lives, interested to see how their stories continued. The next summer, I spoke with LaFontaine and learned that he'd been honored with a lifetime achievement award at the Key Art Awards, the movie industry's version of a technical Oscars. He'd been called up onstage, after a montage of some of his finest moments, and two thousand people had risen out of their chairs and applauded. Afterward, there'd been a party in his honor. For once, it was him in the spotlight, not just his disembodied voice. "It was profoundly moving," he told me. "One of the best nights of my life. It is nice to be validated, especially by your peers, because those are really the only people who count."

Others had setbacks. Penny Halvorson learned she'd need another knee surgery, but it wasn't stopping her. She planned on spending the summer doing Jack-and-Jill cuts with her son and Jill-and-Jill cuts with her daughter, both of whom were entering the sport. She wouldn't compete in the open events but was excited about her family carrying on the tradition, and she had another grandchild on the way to boot.

Elsewhere, Wrzesniewski's latest paper was on track for publication, Swartzendruber was thinking of expanding his Web presence, Spider-man was off on one project or another, near impossible to track down, the Holmeses were considering hiring an assistant—the first full-time, nonfamily employee of Pentec—and Doug Blevins was making his way as an agent.

In San Francisco, Danz had finally found an apprentice, though it wasn't his son Dave but rather Rachael, the assistant who'd enjoyed painting irises; interestingly enough, he said it was my interview, when I'd asked her about her career ambitions, that had sparked her to make the decision. In New York, John Nehrich checked in to say he'd moved to a new apartment, only a thirty-second walking "commute" from campus, and had a roommate, which meant he didn't have to come home to an empty apartment. As part of the rent agreement, he had to take care of the lawn. So, ever antitechnology, he went out and bought a manual lawn mower. "I like the soft clatter it makes instead of the roar of a gas engine, and it is good exercise," he wrote in an e-mail. "I also got a broom to sweep the driveway instead of using their (noisy) leaf blower."

As for DeVries, he had, in his words, "survived" a year teaching in the classroom and was excited about a summer trip. He and Carla were leaving to collect caterpillars in Malaysia for a month. There was, he said, the possibility that the old-world butterflies of Southeast Asia were relatives of the Morphos in the new world. If so, it was important stuff. "Maybe not in the big scheme of things," he told me. "But certainly in my world."

And that, I suppose, is all that matters.

Notes

INTRODUCTION

6 *"active in his calling, he shall stand before Kings"*: Proverbs, chapter 22, verse 29. Also translated as "active in his business." Cited in Max Weber, *"The Protestant Ethic and the 'Spirit' of Capitalism" and Other Writings* (New York: Penguin Books, 2002), p. 12.

7 *the search phrase "How to Find a Job" on Amazon.com*: the number is as of September 13, 2005. No doubt it's grown since then.

7 *$400 million-a-year industry*: "Inside the Head of an Applicant," *Newsweek*, February 21, 2005, p. 32.

7 *"Everything interesting happens at the margins"*: Richard Florida, *The Rise of the Creative Class* (New York: Perseus Books, 2002), p. 184.

7–8 *a pair of Harvard Business School professors*: G. W. Dalton and P. H.

Thompson, *Novations: Strategies for Career Management* (Glenview, Ill.: Scott Foreman, 1986). As cited in Arthur P. Brief and Walter R. Nord, eds., *Meanings of Occupational Work: A Collection of Essays* (Lexington, Mass.: Lexington Books, 1990), p. 137.

8 ponos, *which also meant "pain"*: Joanne B. Ciulla, *The Working Life: The Promise and Betrayal of Modern Work* (New York: Three Rivers Press, 2000), p. 31.

8 *craft guilds sprang up in Europe around* A.D. *1100*: Ibid., p. 67.

9 *"Luther placed a crown on the sweaty forehead"*: Adriano Tilgher, *Work: What It Has Meant to Men Through the Ages*, translated by Dorothy Canfield Fisher (George G. Harrap and Co., 1931). As cited in Richard Donkin, *Blood, Sweat & Tears: The Evolution of Work* (New York: Texere, 2001), p. 39.

9 *in 1648, Massachusetts passed legislation*: Juliet B. Schor, *The Overworked American: The Unexpected Decline of Leisure* (New York: Basic Books, 1992), p. 70.

9 *second most popular book*: Donkin, p. 108.

10 *1836 bestseller entitled* The Book of Wealth: Alain de Botton, "Workers of the World, Relax," *New York Times*, September 6, 2004, p. A17.

10 *"a philosophy of avarice"*: Weber, p. 11.

10 *"specialists without spirit, hedonists"*: Weber, p. 121.

10 *"Political economy knows the worker"*: *New York Times*, September 6, 2004, p. A17.

10 *in 1908 founded* and other background on Frank Parsons: Mark Pope, "A Brief History of Career Counseling in the United States," *The Career Development Quarterly*, March 2000, vol. 48. Also, Edwin L. Herr and Michael Shahnasarian, "Selected Milestones in the Evolution of Career Development Practices in the Twentieth Century," *Career Development Quarterly*, March 2001.

11 *Parsons believed there were three factors*: F. Parsons, *Choosing a Vocation* (Boston: Houghton-Mifflin, 1909). As cited in Pope, p. 196.

11 *by the end of the war* and Western Electric background: Donkin, p. 187.

11 *a U.S. chart of real income per capita*: Gallup polls and World Value Surveys, as cited by Richard Layard, *Happiness: Lessons from a New Science* (London: Penguin Press, 2005), p. 30.

11 *overarching and quite depressing study*: Work in America: Report of a Special Task Force to the Secretary of Health, Education, and Welfare (Cambridge, Mass.: MIT Press, 1973).

12 *"blue collar blues"*: Ciulla, p. 117.

12 *"workaholics are surprisingly happy"*: Marilyn Machlowitz, *Workaholics: Living with Them, Working with Them* (Reading, Mass.: Addison-Wesley, 1978).

13 *in the 1890s, the poorest 10 percent*: Dora L. Costa, National Economic Research Working Paper No. 6504 (1999), as cited in Ciulla, p. 172.

13 *"leisure snacks"*: Donkin, p. xxi, xxii.

13 *Columbia economist Eli Ginzberg:* Ginzberg, Ginsburg, Axelrad, and Herma (1951), as cited in Walter S. Neff, *Work and Human Behavior* (Chicago: Aldine Publishing, 1977), p. 133.

14 *changing jobs an average of every 1.1 years:* Bureau of Labor Statistics, 2001, as cited in Florida, p. 104.

14 *2004 Gallup poll found that only 50 percent of American workers:* Gallup Poll News Service, August 24, 2004. In the poll, 50 percent said they were "completely satisfied," 39 percent were "somewhat satisfied," and 11 percent were "dissatisfied." I chose this poll because it is one of the more optimistic of the ones I saw. For example, *Business 2.0* (November 2004) wrote that "surveys report that up to 80 percent of American workers aren't satisfied with their jobs." The discrepancy, I believe, is a matter of polling semantics.

14 *As the author and scholar Alain de Botton wrote: New York Times*, September 6, 2004, p. A17.

18 *Anxiety fuels passion:* an idea first presented in Mihaly Csikszentmihalyi, *Flow: The Psychology of Optimal Experience* (New York: Harper, 1990), pp. 52, 74.

ONE: THE SKYWALKER

22 *an account of how he taught a Florida SWAT team:* "Spiderman Shows Deputies the Ropes," *Pensacola News Journal*, February 12, 2002, p. 1C.

22 *his Web site:* it's www.spidermans.com.

24 *did a story on risk taking:* Paul Roberts, "Risk," *Psychology Today*, Nov./Dec. 1994.

24 *a pioneering psychologist in the field*: Marvin Zuckerman, ed., *Biological Bases of Sensation Seeking, Impulsivity, and Anxiety* (London: Lawrence Erlbaum Associates Publishers, 1983).

24 *23 percent of Americans described themselves as:* Harris Poll, 1999, cited in Jim Rasenberger, *High Steel: The Daring Men Who Built the World's Greatest Skyline* (New York: HarperCollins, 2004), p. 13.

31 *twelve to fifteen window cleaners:* according to a spokesman at the IWCA for the years up to 2001. More recent stats weren't available.

32 *According to Plato, Socrates once said:* Christopher Peterson and Martin E. P. Seligman, *Character Strengths and Virtues: A Handbook and Classification* (New York: Oxford University Press, 2004), p. 215.

41 Background on the ironworkers and Mohawks from Rasenberger; and from Peterson & Seligman, p. 227.

47 *provide restitution:* legal information from Assistant State Attorney Gerry Champagne, who presides over Escambia County, in a phone interview, September 9, 2005.

TWO: THE EYEBALL ARTISAN

61 *idea of "flow" . . . perfectly balanced on an axis:* Csikszentmihalyi, pp. 52, 74.

62 Background on the history of the field in part from Wolfgang Trester, "The History of Artificial Eyes and the Evolution of the Ocularistic Profession," *The Journal of the American Society of Ocularists,* August 2, 1981.

64 *Jack Nicklaus . . . almost became a registered pharmacist:* "The Road Not Taken," *Sport Illustrated,* December 27, 2004, p. Z20.

65 *sons who follow their fathers into careers are 5 to 8 percent:* Arnold Chevalier, as reported in *New Scientist,* March 25, 2002.

65 *In the controversial book:* Frank Sulloway, *Born to Rebel: Birth Order, Family Dynamics, & Creative Lives* (New York: Random House, 1997).

66–67 *The top five most-respected fields:* 2003 poll conducted by CNN, *USA Today,* and Gallup.

67 *people who have a strong sense of identity tend to:* B. Goldman, S. Masterson, E. Locke, M. Groth, and D. Jensen, "Goal-Directedness and Personal Identity as Correlates of Life Outcomes," *Psychological Reports,* 91, 2002, pp. 153–66.

THREE: THE LADY LUMBERJACK

76 History of work-sports and numerous examples from Frank Zarnowski, "Working at Play: The Phenomenon of 19th Century Worker-Competitions," *Journal of Leisure Research,* vol. 36, no. 2, March 22, 2004, p. 257.

76 *"in his glory at a fire":* New York Clipper *National Police Gazette,* as cited in Zarnowski.

77 *"cussingest, rottenest bunch":* "A Family Tree in the Forest: Generations of Loggers Celebrate Lumberjack Heritage in Oregon," *Dallas Morning News,* July 19, 1998, p. 20B.

78 *"The more a job inherently resembles a game":* Csikszentmihalyi, p. 152.

78 *"The example of the typesetting 'Swifts' ":* Zarnowski.

88 *1.7 million people in 101 companies:* Marcus Buckingham and Donald Clifton, *Now, Discover Your Strengths* (New York: The Free Press, 2001), pp. 5, 6.

88 *"Reflected Best Self":* "How to Play to Your Strengths," *Harvard Business Review* (Laura Morgan Roberts, Gretchen Spreitzer, Jane Dutton, Robert Quinn, Emily Heaphy, Brianna Barker,), January 2005, p. 74.

FOUR: THE RAIL-AHOLIC

94 NMRA numbers are from the NMRA librarian as of late 2005. The NMRA's makeup is 98 percent male (of 20,000 members); 97 percent of hobbyists are male.

95 *a "living legend":* "A Model Society Built Around the Railroad Series," *Los Angeles Times,* November 12, 1989.

102 Background on railroad publications from: John Stilgoe, *Metropolitan Corridor: Railroads and the American Scene* (New Haven: Yale University Press, 1985).

106 *workaholic pro football coach:* "OD'ing on OT; The Men Who Run NFL Teams Often Work to the Point of Exhaustion and Illness," *Sports Illustrated,* January 17, 2005, p. 18.

107 *2004 report by the International Labor Organization:* for more info, visit www.ilo.org.

107 *the argument that there is a "time famine":* Florida, p. 151.

107 *long hours by the need for money or by the need to escape a bad home life:* Arlie Russell Hochschild, *The Time Bind: When Work Becomes Home and Home Becomes Work* (New York: Henry Holt & Co., 2000).

108 Background on the city of Troy from Troy Visitor's Center and its ever-helpful staff (aka Will Gill).

117 *His response: So what do I search for now?:* from "The Search" by Shel Silverstein, *Where the Sidewalk Ends* (New York: HarperCollins, 1974), p. 166.

FIVE: THE TIME-CLOCK PHILOSOPHER AMID AN INDUSTRY OF ANSWERS

119 Information on all conference scenes from 2004 International Career Development Conference, held in Sacramento, October 27–31, 2004.

121 *endlessly conflicting concepts:* John Micklethwait, and Adrian Wooldridge, *The Witch Doctors: Making Sense of Management Gurus* (New York: Times Business Books, 1996), p. 15. As cited in Ciulla, p. 137.

124 *a prime example of a phenomenon she calls "job crafting":* Amy Wrzesniewski, Jane E. Dutton, "Crafting a Job: Revisioning Employees as Active Crafters of Their Work," *Academy of Management Review,* vol. 26, no. 2, 2001, pp. 179–201.

126 *paper that first drew my interest:* Amy Wrzesniewski, C. R. McCauley, P. Rozin, B. Schwartz, "Jobs, Careers, and Callings: People's Relations to Their Work," *Journal of Research in Personality,* 31, 1997, pp. 21–33.

SIX: THE SIXTY-SECOND SALESMAN

143 *wrote a 1991 book studying six child prodigies:* David Henry Feldman, *Nature's Gambit: Child Prodigies and the Development of Human Potential* (New York: Teachers College Press, 1991).

143 Background on Lewis Terman from Joanna Schaffhausen's fascinating article "Child Prodigies" on brainconnection.com.

147 *Trailers were overridden with exclamation points* and other trailer background from "Pic Biz's Promo Sapiens," *Variety,* February 23, 2004, p. 52; and *Weekly Standard* (online edition), May 25, 2004.

148 *As a boy growing up in Chicago, Kuehn used to edit tape using an ice pick:* "Trailer Pioneer Kuehn Dies," *Daily Variety,* February 2, 2004, p. 23.

148 *"A trailer has but one goal":* *Daily Variety,* February 2, 2004, p. 23.

151 *Many of the great advertising men of history* and other background on advertising pioneers and Rosser Reeves from "You Are What You Buy," from *Smithsonian,* vol. 31, no. 7, October 1, 2000.

153 A note on *Bergerac:* LaFontaine's rendition is not word-for-word accurate, but pretty close. He leaves out a section at the end, but closes in the same manner as Hooker's translation.

156 *A survey of children ages ten to thirteen:* Juliet Schor, *Born to Buy: The Commercialized Child and the New Consumer Culture* (New York: Scribner, 2004) p. 149.

156–57 *A recent Associated Press poll showed that people who make more than $75,000 a year are far more likely than those:* "Science Discovers the Rat Race: Money Really Doesn't Buy Happiness," *Associated Press,* October 12, 2004.

157 (footnote) Information on the National Bureau of Economic Research sex frequency study, is from "Study Finds No Link Between Money, Sex," *USA Today,* June 9, 2004, p. 1B.

157 *Harvard students were asked to choose:* Sarah Solnick and David Hemenway, "Is More Always Better? A Survey on Positional Concerns," *Journal of Economic Behavior and Organization,* 37, 1998, pp. 373–83. As cited in Layard, p. 41.

SEVEN: THE FUNGUS PROSPECTOR

166 Roughing It, *which included an account of his exploits attempting* and background on the book from Michael Lewis, "The Mark Twain Trail," Slate.com, posted Thursday, April 24, 2003.

166 Background on gold panning from "Authors, Geologists and Historians Discuss the Gold Rush of California and Its Lasting Impact on the State and Country," Talk of the Nation/Science, National Public Radio (NPR), January 22, 1999.

168 *Figuratively, because he resides outside the mainstream:* "Tales of Adventure, Nature Love, and Money on the Globalocal Mushroom Trail," *Mother Earth,* March 22, 2000, p. 60.

171 *devoted a chapter to debunking "Fungophobia":* David Arora, *Mushrooms Demystified: A Comprehensive Guide to the Fleshy Fungi* (Berkeley: Ten Speed Press, 1986), chapter 1.

171 Background on international tastes for mushrooms from Arora, *Mushrooms,* p. 3.

177 *A study sponsored by the National Institute of Mental Health:* "The Power of Concentration," *New York Times Magazine,* October 8, 1989, p. 26.

177 *A few years ago:* Kevin Daniel Henson, *Just a Temp* (Philadelphia: Temple University Press, 1996).

EIGHT: THE NOTEBOOK DETECTIVE

185 *In 2001:* Marcus Buckingham and Donald Clifton, *Now, Discover Your Strengths* (New York: The Free Press, 2001), pp. 5, 6.

192 *tend to focus on the personality assessment aspect* and other background on critiques from "Is Handwriting Analysis Legit Science?" from *The Straight Dope,* April 18, 2003.

NINE: THE PIGSKIN PREACHER

209 Statistics and background on CP from United Cerebral Palsy. For more information, go to www.ucp.org.

222 *of people with extreme quadriplegia:* "Optimism Often Survives Spinal Cord Injuries," *USA Today,* June 9, 1995, p. D4. As cited in Seligman, p. 48.

TEN: THE BUTTERFLY HUNTER

230 One of the DeVries books is still in print: Philip J. DeVries, *The Butterflies of Costa Rica and Their Natural History: Volume II* (New Jersey: Princeton University Press, 1997). His thoughts on species extinction: "I write epitaphs for a living."

235 *academic scientists sacrifice approximately 25 percent of their potential private-sector income:* Scott Stern, "Do Scientists Pay to Be Scientists," National Bureau of Economic Research, Working Paper 7410. As cited in Florida, p. 93.

244 *In Mexico in the sixteenth century, the Aztecs considered the insects to be the souls of warriors* and other historical background from Sharman Apt Russell, *An Obsession with Butterflies: Our Long Love Affair with a Singular Insect* (Cambridge, Mass.: Perseus Publishing, 2003).

248 *[Lilly] tested them on himself:* Peterson and Seligman, p. 125.

249 *found that when someone believes that he is acting of his own choosing:* E. L. Deci and R. M. Ryan, "The 'What' and 'Why' of Goal Pursuits: Human Needs and the Self-Determination of Behavior," *Psychological Inquiry,* 4, 2000, pp. 227–68. As cited in Peterson and Seligman, p. 139.

250 *22 people who won major lotteries:* P. Brickman, D. Coates, and R. Janoff-Bulman, "Lottery Winners and Accident Victims: Is Happiness Relative?," *Journal of Personality and Social Psychology,* 36, 1978, pp. 917–27. As cited in Seligman, p. 48.

258 *Fourth-century Egyptian hermits* and other boredom background from "We Try Our Best to Avoid It, But Boredom Has Its Benefits. Today, It's a Lost Art Form," *San Francisco Chronicle,* April 2, 2004.

After a string of his own oddball jobs, including working as a cafeteria cook in Yellowstone National Park, a Ping-Pong instructor, door-to-door vacuum cleaner salesman, and toll booth counter on the Golden Gate Bridge, Chris Ballard landed at *Sports Illustrated* as a staff writer covering the NBA and writing profiles and features. He has appeared on CNN, *The Charlie Rose Show*, *All Things Considered*, and *ABC World News* and has written a number of profiles for the *New York Times Magazine*. He is the author of *Hoops Nation*, which was named one of *Booklist's* Top Ten Sport Books in 1998. Ballard recently moved from New York to Berkeley, California.